Rescue Squad

Rescue Squad

The Origins of Rescue Co. 1
Fire Department of the City of New York
1915–1925

Paul Hashagen

Fire Books New York 2024
Massapequa, New York

Published by Fire Books New York
70 Division Ave.
Massapequa, NY 11758

First Edition

Softcover ISBN: 978-1-938394-88-1

Library of Congress Control Number: 2024922699

Printed in the United States of America

Front cover photo: Staged photo of Rescue 1 member "rescuing" a brother fireman during training at FDNY Fire College on East 68th Street in 1915. The photo from author's collection, was made by Honorary Battalion Chief Albert Dreyfous.

Back cover photo credit: Glenn Usdin

Dedicated to the captains of Rescue 1
during my years of service:

Capt. Brian O'Flaherty
Capt. John Cerato
Capt. Charles Kasper
Capt. James Rogers
Capt. John Norman
Capt. Terence Hatton
Capt. Fred LaFemina
Capt. Robert Morris

Also by Paul Hashagen

Historical Fiction

The Twelfth Hour
2008

The Fire of God
2010

Young Heroes
2020

Non-Fiction

100 Years of Valor Rescue Company 1 NYC Fire Dept.
MT Publishing Company 2015

A Distant Fire
DMC Associates 1995

Stories of Fire
Fire Books New York 2017

Fire Stories
Fire Books New York 2024

Fire Rescue—The History of Rescue 1 FDNY
Fire Apparatus Journal 1989

The Firehouses of the Fire Department of the City of New York
MT Publishing Company 2014 (with Larry Woodcock)

The Bravest—The Official History of the FDNY
Turner Publishing 2000 & 2002

Cartoon Books

Hot Flashes
Firehouse Books 1987

Rescue Crew
Fire Books New York 2018

The Big Book of Firefighting Dinosaurs
Fire Books New York 2020

More Hot Flashes Vol. 1 & 2
Fire Books New York 2021

Contents

Foreword

When I was a child, my grandfather gave me a fleet of toy fire apparatus. He showed me how the hoses attached from the hydrant to the pumper and then from the pumper to a hose line to fight a fire. When I came home after my tonsils were removed, I found a new truck waiting for me. On the side it said, "Rescue Squad."

Being familiar with the responsibilities of both engine and ladder companies, I asked in a quiet ice cream-coated voice, "What do they do at a fire?"

Papa Paul answered simply, "They rescue firemen."

I kind of knew right then what I wanted to be when I grew up.

Later, when I was grown and married, a chance meeting brought me to the volunteer fire service. Now a member of the Freeport Fire Department, I put the basic training I'd received from my grandfather to work. While reading various fire service magazines and books, the work of the FDNY Rescue Companies, especially Rescue 1, caught my eye.

Realizing I could make firefighting a career, I worked out, studied hard and was able to pass the exam. I became a member of the FDNY in October of 1978. My childhood dream was coming true. While learning the job from the great firemen around me, I kept a quiet eye on Rescue 1.

Finally, after turning first grade, I followed my friend Chris Glianna's advice and visited the Captain of Rescue 1, Brian O'Flaherty. (Chris was a member of both the Baldwin

Fire Department, where we worked many fires together, and a member of Rescue 1.) This interview led to my detail to Rescue 1 on February 3, 1983.

My dream had come full circle. I was now responding to fires in a huge red truck with Rescue Company 1 emblazoned on the sides in gold leaf. On my first day we responded to a fire downtown. As we headed south, Richie Cody was sitting next to me and said, "I like your new flashlight."

I replied, "Thank you."

He paused a moment and added, "If anything happens to you, can I have it?"

I chuckled and replied, "Sure!" I knew I was where I was supposed to be.

That was the start of a 20-year assignment that sent me to: the roofs of burning tenements, subcellars of downtown loft buildings, inside burning ships, the tops of skyscrapers, into darkened subway tunnels, and the bottom of murky rivers. I received specialized training in building collapse, high-angle rope rescue, confined space rescue, hazardous material operations, motor vehicle crash entrapment and extrication, and underwater search and rescue.

Working in Rescue 1 was everything I dreamed it would be and more. During those years I responded to thousands of alarms, worked fires and emergencies in every borough, and even responded on mutual aide to New Jersey for in-water firefighting at a major pier fire in Hoboken, and a major building collapse in Jersey City. I also worked tours in every FDNY Rescue Company.

Several friends I made when I first became a member of Rescue 1, would also change my life. The first was Herb Eysser, FDNY Manhattan Dispatcher 124. Herb was a wealth of FDNY history and operational knowledge. After a footnote in a building construction book caught my eye, I wanted to know more about the early FDNY. Herb got me started, showing me where and how to research the information I wanted. My first article was published in *WNYF*, the official FDNY magazine in 1988.

The following year, Captain O'Flaherty began planning for the company's 75th Anniversary and asked me to write a small pamphlet about the company's history. This project turned into *Fire Rescue—The History of FDNY Rescue Company 1*. This 88-page book was published by Jack Calderone's *Fire Apparatus Journal*, a fellow FDNY historian and member in the department. (Jack would become a battalion chief and always remained be a great friend and amazing resource for photos and information.)

The second man who set me on my writing course was the late-great Harvey Eisner, who became the editor of *Firehouse Magazine*. Harvey gave me the idea to write a monthly historical column called *Rekindles*. He also encouraged me to write feature articles for the magazine.

Because of these two men, I would be asked by Fire Commissioner Thomas Von Essen to write the official FDNY history called, *The Bravest*, published in 2000. I later wrote *One Hundred Years of Valor—Rescue Company 1 1915-2015*, in time for the company's 100th anniversary.

Even after all this writing, the earliest years of Rescue 1 still intrigued me. How did those men, do what they did? What was it like? So, my research continued and eventually became this book, *Rescue Squad*.

I reserve special thanks to the officers and members of Rescue 1 who were serving in the company when I was assigned in 1983. Officers like John Cerato, Tony Limberg and Jimmy Curran made learning easy. But most importantly were the senior men, quiet men who led by example. Bill "Dutch" Bessman, William Riley known to all as "Mister Riley," Jack "Spanky" McAllister, John Driscoll and George Kreuscher. They set the bar very high for those who followed.

I was honored to become a member of Rescue 1 and to work there for 20 years. It is also my honor to continue to tell their story. In this book are stories of the original members and those that followed, as they set the standard for modern rescue work. A direct line can be drawn from these ten men, their smoke helmets and a small cache of tools back in 1915, to the present day technical and heavy rescue companies. Theirs is quite a tale to tell. I hope I do them justice.

Paul Hashagen
Massapequa, NY, 2024

Author's Note

Ammonia was among the early refrigerants used in large commercial mechanical systems and continued to be used for many years. These refrigeration machines, used in breweries, ice plants, large hotels, and cold storage warehouses, used ammonia within a closed cycle of evaporation, compression, condensation and expansion. The size of the machine and the amount of ammonia being used depended on the size of the area being cooled. Problems arose when piping or valves used in ammonia refrigeration systems leaked or burst.

Ammonia, NH3, is a colorless gas with a pungent odor. It is potentially toxic, but its average odor threshold is 5ppm (parts per million), well below any danger level. This means the smell and the effects it has on human eyes and sinuses drive a person away before any permanent damage can be done. Therefore, even the toughest fireman without breathing protection would be forced from an area with a significant ammonia leak. This would then require a special-call for Rescue 1 and their Draeger smoke helmets. These leaks did not only occur in Manhattan, but all over the city.

Illuminating gas, also known as manufactured gas, was made by the gasification of combustible materials, usually bituminous coal. Illuminating gas was a mixture of many chemical substances, including hydrogen, methane, carbon monoxide and ethylene. The percentage of carbon monoxide varied from 6 to 35 percent, according to the proportions of coal gas and water gas that were put into the illuminating gas by the manufacturer.

This additional carbon monoxide added to the smoke and made breathing extremely dangerous for firemen. The use of ordinary Army gas masks, and ordinary commercial smoke masks were inadequate protection in many illuminating gas leak situations. The carbon monoxide penetrated the masks and rendered the wearer unconscious. It was therefore necessary to utilize a closed-circuit oxygen breathing system like the Draeger smoke helmets to operate safely in these situations.

Chapter 1: The Origins of Rescue Company 1 FDNY

In January of 1912 the New York City Fire Department faced a major fire in the huge Equitable Building in lower Manhattan. That fire posed unique problems the department was not equipped to handle. The most striking of these were the bars imprisoning several men in a basement vault. The windows of the vault overlooked the sidewalk on the Broadway side of the building and were protected by two-inch-thick iron bars placed close to each other. Trapped behind these bars were three men; two alive, pinned down by broken floor joists, and one dead, killed by a fallen beam. There were also flames raging behind and above them.

As hose lines were pulled into position to protect the imprisoned men the first attempts to free them were by members of two ladder companies. Armed with mauls and other heavy hand tools, they tried to wrench the bars free. This effort proved futile. Hacksaws were procured from nearby buildings (the FDNY did not carry any on their apparatus at this time.) For more than an hour Engineer of Steamer Seneca Larke, aided by Engineer of Steamer Charles Rankin, Fireman Luke Henry and others, sawed until the bars were finally cut and the men were removed to safety. The rescue work was both time-consuming and extremely dangerous but had been successful. The lack of special tools and equipment was obvious. The department would have to fill this gap in their arsenal of firefighting and rescue gear.

In the FDNY Annual Report for the Year 1912, Fire Commissioner Joseph Johnson reported to Mayor William Gaynor, in the section titled Bureau of Repairs and Supplies:

Two pieces of apparatus for melting steel bars with a mixture of oxygen and acetylene gas were purchased and placed in service early in the year. The need for such equipment was emphasized by the Equitable Building fire. On that occasion it required one hour and a half arduous labor to sever two steel bars so that a rescue could be made. With the new type of cutting apparatus, a steel bar, such as encountered at the Equitable Building, could be severed in a few seconds.

The February 3, 1913, issue of *The New York Times* covered the FDNY Annual Report and mentioned the purchase of a new cutting torch, but there was no mention of where the torches were assigned, or if they were ever used.

So apparently, the department felt it had solved its problem by purchasing the cutting sets. To be fair, the FDNY was amid a major wave of expansion and improvements. In 1912, 46 new fire department buildings were being constructed, the new Fire Prevention Bureau had made over 130,000 building inspections, an exhaustive investigation into arson-for-profit was underway, and by the end of the year 78 motor-driven vehicles and apparatus had been added to the fleet. By 1913 the high-pressure hydrant system had expanded into the Red Hook and Gowanus sections of Brooklyn. Thirty new fire companies were organized, 755 new firemen were appointed, and 311 promotions were made. In 1914, 77 pieces of new apparatus were added to the firefighting fleet.

The department continued responding to challenging fires and was successful in saving lives and property with relative ease until the morning of January 6, 1915, when a fire situation occurred that again tested the department to its very limits.

At 8:10 a.m. there was an electrical fire downtown at the Spring Street Station of the Interborough Subway in lower Manhattan. (This disruption would cause the subway line to run sporadically that morning.) A few minutes later, another short circuit, this time in an electrical splicing chamber beneath Broadway near 53rd Street, also affected the system. This short circuit sparked a fire within bundles of wires and their insulation. The burning insulation created a potentially deadly and debilitating smoke condition. These electrical power cables were coated with a combination of cotton, tar, and other combustible materials. These burning materials gave off a thick, biting smoke while the short-circuiting condition continued heating wires and further fueling the fire.

As the flames grew and began spreading along the cables and their flammable insulation, the dense smoke slowly filled the subway tunnel. The cable splicing chamber held all the main power, signaling systems and lighting system wiring in the same place. The expanding flames burned through all the wiring until there was a complete power failure that plunged the tunnel into total darkness and stranded several subway trains filled with passengers. Near the burning cables were three crowded trains that stalled between Columbus Circle and 50th Street. A six-car local train bound for City Hall and a ten-car express train heading to Brooklyn were stopped next to each other and nearest to the fire, and opposite a subway ventilation grating at Broadway and 55th Street.

Inside the trains were hundreds of people travelling to their workplaces. All the cars were uncomfortably full, as they always were during rush hour. Crowded into seats, hanging on hand straps or standing on platforms, they had no warning and little idea of just how bad things would soon become.

As the tunnel became dark, the meager light given off by the two emergency lamps in each car gave some consolation. Stoppages were all part of the subway experience, and everything seemed normal until the clouds of noxious smoke began filling the passenger cars.

For almost 20 minutes the passengers were held in place even as the toxic smoke began to seep into the crowded subway cars. Train personnel were reluctant to open doors and allow passengers to climb down onto the tracks due to the dangers of electrocution from the third rail and the dangers of moving trains. They held the passengers inside the cars as the smoke condition worsened. Finally, when breathing became difficult panic swept the passengers. Windows were broken, and frantic fists pounded on closed doors. Blinded by the smoke, the passengers moved from car to car seeking fresh air or an escape.

Conditions inside the trains became worse as the broken windows allowed more smoke to enter. Train crews eventually relented and opened the doors allowing the panicking passengers to exit onto the track bed. Visibility was zero, but the passengers knew the stations were near—if they could only reach them.

Above the unfolding emergency, the temperature in midtown Manhattan was about 39 degrees with intermittent light rain. The damp streets and sidewalks shone with moisture as the high humidity stopped the smoke from escaping.

At about 9:14 an NYPD patrolman in civilian clothes noticed the smoke and walked to the quarters of Engine Company 23 on 58th Street just off Broadway. He recommended that a couple of firemen should go check things out. Working that morning as the engine officer was Lieutenant Edwin Hotchkiss who was detailed from his normal assignment at Hook & Ladder 21. Hotchkiss turned out the entire company and quickly rolled to the scene. They found smoke pouring from the sidewalk subway gratings at the northwest corner of 55th Street and Broadway. They also found numerous passengers struggling to escape the fumes and smoke.

Hotchkiss and his men—Firemen Grant, Walsh, Reardon, Connolly, O'Reilly, Branfuehr, Gillon, Wanner, and Belfield—opened a sidewalk subway grating and placed a portable ladder down into the smoke-filled darkness. They brought a hose line with them as they descended. Acting Battalion Chief Moran arrived and immediately transmitted a second alarm. Moments later Hook & Ladder 4 arrived with Lt. Mortimer Walsh in command. He and his men, Firemen Cody, Carmody, Ryan, Ness, Large, Gorman, and Gesswein (detailed from Engine 23), pried open 60-feet of sidewalk grating, placing a half dozen ladders before descending into the base of the sidewalk opening.

This was a ventilation opening and emergency exit from the subway tunnel below. The gratings were 5 X 60-feet long and ran along the sidewalk at the curb line. They connected through to the tracks at the south end by a narrow steel ladder.

Along the route evacuees had to also pass through a narrow 3-foot-wide door between the subway tunnel and the ventilation point above.

Chief Kenlon arrived and saw the first alarm units taking a beating as they worked in the smoke-filled tunnel with no breathing protection. Fireman after fireman carried up an unconscious victim, placed them gently down and then returned to the suffocating smoke of the tunnel. Members of Engines 40, 54, and 65 worked with Hook & Ladders 4 and 35 rescuing dozens of unconscious passengers. With three alarms already transmitted, at 9:35 a.m. Chief Kenlon took unique action by transmitting a signal that had never been used before. Signal 3-3-3-3. This brought 200 extra firemen without apparatus to the scene. (Kenlon needed men to search, not water or ladders.)

As the passengers reached the street, they resembled victims of a mining explosion: their clothes were dirty, and in tatters, and their faces, especially around their noses and mouths, were blackened. The unconscious victims were carried by firemen as the other passengers, in varying states of consciousness, staggered out onto the street.

The owner of the Buick dealership, Mr. A.G. Southworth, one of the first to call about the fire, opened his showroom, located on the same corner as the sidewalk gratings, and helped set up a first aid station. Southworth had all the autos on display removed so Dr. Harry Archer and other medical professionals had room to work, out of the elements, on the growing number of patients arriving by the minute. Southworth then ordered his new car inventory to transport the seriously overcome victims to nearby hospitals.

Arriving ambulance surgeons, members of Con Edison's pulmotor squad, and civilian volunteers took places in the Buick dealership as nearly every pulmotor in Manhattan was pressed into service. Newspapers reported that 29 pulmotors were in operation at the height of the rescue and resuscitation efforts.

As the last of the victims were treated or removed to hospitals, the media descended upon the firemen. Lt. Edwin Hotchkiss was quoted saying, "When we got there, we put a line of hose down, but we did not use it." At that point Hotchkiss reeled and had to be steadied by his men. He'd been the first fireman to enter the tunnel and had been down there for more than two hours.

It was estimated that between 200 and 250 passengers had been taken up through the sidewalk grates to safety. When the smoke cleared the totals were staggering. One woman had died, and more than 700 men and women were injured by the fire and smoke. The shutdown of the subway system also affected riders across the entire system, with more than 100,000 other passengers stranded in Brooklyn alone. Trains across the city were stopped and their passengers left to find other ways home or to work.

Lt. Hotchkiss center, flanked by members of Engine 23 on sidewalk after the fire.

Almost immediately investigations were initiated as to the cause of the overloaded electrical wires, the fire and smoke, and the difficulty faced with evacuating the tracks. The firemen received high praise for their, "matter-of-fact gallantry," but questions about smoke helmets and better equipment for the brave firemen were also raised.

The New York City newspapers ran editorials citing the bravery of the firemen and calling for better safety measures in the subway system. In the January 16, 1915, issue of *Scientific American,* a major story explained how the FDNY should be utilizing smoke helmets as used in Europe fire departments and by the United States Bureau of Mines for rescue work.

They stated that FDNY was supposed to be one of the best equipped in the world, but that not a single smoke helmet was available for use.

That the New York Fire Department should take such an apathetic attitude in this matter is the more surprising as the reports of almost every big fire in the city contain mention of firemen being overcome by smoke while engaged in the performance of their duties, and in some cases we read of firemen being laid out in rows on the sidewalk, where remedial treatment was applied. As long as this indifference to human safety was confined to members of the paid department the public has assumed that such things were unavoidable, or at any rate all a part of the day's work of a fireman; but since the dramatic incident in the subway people are realizing that it is a subject that is of vital interest to them, and undoubtedly movements will result that will compel the New York Fire Department to properly equip itself for the saving of life as well as saving property.

Scientific American also ran a technical article about the subway fire and the various safety issues involved. It explained the subway's power system, cable insulation, the nature of the short circuit, the subway's lighting system, fire escapes, and emergency exits. It also listed several safety remedies that should be taken.

These articles coupled with some newspaper editorials, apparently hit the mark, because both the subway system and the fire department immediately began to act.

Chief Kenlon must have gathered his closest confidants and trusted allies within the department—even civilians closely associated with the department—commonly known as "buffs." The term "buffs" could be used in a derogatory way, especially by the members of the department, then and now, who believe civilians have no business interfering in department business. Back in 1915 there were some very influential civilians—buffs that greatly contributed to the growth of the FDNY—its apparatus, tools, and the health and wellness of firemen and their families, and those of deceased members.

Top of the list was Harry Archer, M.D., a Columbia University and Bellevue Medical College graduate, who began treating injured fireman while serving as an ambulance surgeon. He began responding to fires and treating the injured in the 1890s and by 1907 was made an honorary medical officer with the rank of Battalion Chief and served with no compensation.

Another important civilian was the wealthy Wall Street banker Robert Mainzer. Also drawn to fires and firefighters, he became friends with Archer and would aid the doctor at large fires. Mainzer was also a world traveler, and at the time of the subway fire had just returned from Europe where he was making a study of firefighting there, specifically the breathing apparatus being used.

The department also reached out to the Safety Division of the U.S. Bureau of Mines, gathering information on the latest breathing apparatus being used in this country. Together with the oxyacetylene torches already purchased by the department, the FDNY began gathering specialized rescue gear.

A call was sent across the department stating that a new company was being formed and requested volunteers to submit their names. Hundreds answered the call, and Chief Kenlon and his team began the process of choosing the men. Kenlon's choice to command the new unit was John J. McElligott the 31-year-old captain of Hook & Ladder 1. The man chosen to be McElligott's lieutenant was one of the heroes of the recent subway fire—Edwin A. Hotchkiss of Hook & Ladder 21. Hotchkiss was 40 years old and a 15-year veteran of the FDNY when he was assigned to Rescue 1.

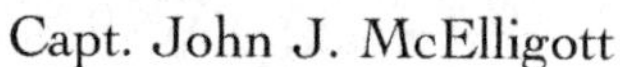

Capt. John J. McElligott

Lt. Edwin A. Hotchkiss

The first fireman chosen was Thomas Kilbride of Hook & Ladder 1. The 39-year-old former driver joined the FDNY in 1905. He left the department for two years in the NYPD before returning in 1907. He was assigned to Hook & Ladder 1 and within a year was on the Roll of Merit for heroic actions. Kilbride was cited for bravery four times including being awarded the Mayor Strong and Department Medals in 1913, before being assigned to Rescue 1.

The next fireman mentioned on the transfer order was

Walter A. O'Leary of Engine Company 33. O'Leary joined the FDNY on December 22, 1909, and was assigned to Hook & Ladder 104 in Brooklyn. He later transferred to Engine 21 in Manhattan before moving to Engine 33 on Great Jones Street.

Fireman John F. Mooney from Hook & Ladder 4 was also chosen. The 33-year-old Mooney's name appeared on the Roll of Merit four times prior to his transfer to Rescue 1 including a Class I with the Werthheim and Department Medals for a rescue in 1912, another Class I in 1914 with the Bennett and Department Medals.

Another member of Engine 33 that was also chosen for Rescue 1 was Fireman John P. Ryan. The former driver began his career in 1906 and was assigned to Engine Company 13 on Wooster Street in Manhattan. He transferred to Engine 33 in 1911. The 33-year-old had more than eight years on the job when he went to Rescue 1.

Fireman Frank C. Clark of Hook & Ladder 24 was another medal man when he was chosen for Rescue 1. He was awarded the Bonner and Department Medals for his outstanding rescue on March 3, 1909. The former motorman was also 33 years old, with more than eight years on the job when he was assigned to Rescue 1.

Fireman Alfred Kinsella joined the FDNY on May 6, 1905, and was assigned to Engine Company 74. Born in Ireland in 1881, he became a U.S. citizen in 1904 and was a bartender in his brother's saloon before joining the FDNY.

Fireman Alfred V. Henretty was a member of the FDNY since 1906 when he volunteered to become a member of Rescue 1. He worked in Hook & Ladder 20 before transferring to Hook & Ladder 15. He was 26 years old when he joined Rescue 1.

Fireman James Shaw joined the FDNY on May 17, 1905, and worked at Engine 9, Hook & Ladders 21, 33 before he became an original member of Hook & Ladder 43 when it was organized on November 27, 1913. In January of 1915 Shaw volunteered for Rescue 1 and was among the chosen. He joined the other new members as training began.

The original members of Rescue Company 1. In service March 8, 1915. Front (left to right): Fireman Thomas Kilbride, Capt. John McElligott, Lt. Edwin Hotchkiss. Rear: Firemen Frank Clark, James Shaw, John Ryan, Walter O'Leary, Alfred Henretty, Alfred Kinsella, and John Mooney

One interesting note was the apparent addition of Francis Blessing to the new company. The former machinist joined the FDNY on May 15, 1907, and by August had been transferred to Engine 33. He later transferred to the Bronx and worked in Hook & Ladder 17, until he was detailed to drive the Chief of the 7th Division, Thomas Ahearn. Shortly after Ahearn retired, Blessing was detailed to drive Acting Chief of Department John Kenlon.

When Kenlon's position became official on August 2, 1911, Blessing was transferred back to Engine 33 and continued his detail driving the chief. In 1913 he was detailed as a chauffeur to Engine 79 in the Bronx for a month and to Hook & Ladder 23. These companies were being motorized for the first time. Hook & Ladder 23's 1906 American LaFrance hook & ladder now featured a Christie tractor. Blessing would be the primary driver as the other members of the company gained experience with the new apparatus. On March 20, 1913, Blessing was then transferred and assigned as chauffer to the new company, Engine 93, being organized on West 181st Street in Manhattan.

Despite the fact he'd been assigned to Engine 93 for two years, as Rescue 1 became a reality Frank Blessing was apparently detailed on an onion skin. (FDNY slang for a detail not published on department orders but rather just handled by a paper report, the copy of which was as thin as an onion skin.) It is not clear exactly when he started with Rescue 1, but he is visible in photographs taken during the first days of the company's organization. He is shown at the wheel of the company's 1914 customized Cadillac. FDNY Special Order No. 82 dated May 3, 1916, published the Roll of Merit for 1915. Paragraph II, named the members of Rescue 1 being awarded Class As, which included Francis Blessing. It is mentioned he was in Engine 93 but detailed to Rescue 1. Six specific operations, "of exceptionally hazardous nature," were cited with the earliest date of July 24, 1915.

So, it appears Frank Blessing was there from the start.

Chapter 2:
Training

The January 18th order directed the newly chosen members to report to the Old Headquarters, 157-159 East 67th Street, beginning Tuesday, January 19th at 10 a.m. for a period of instruction. One of the centerpieces of the new company would be the Draeger smoke helmet. This new tool would allow the members of Rescue 1 to venture into areas filled with smoke and gases that would otherwise be debilitating or deadly.

According to a report from Captain John J. McElligott dated October 7, 1915, the Draeger helmets were not the only breathing apparatus field tested by the new rescue members. The report follows:

FIRE DEPARTMENT
OF THE CITY OF NEW YORK

RESCUE COMPANY NO. 1

New York, October 7th, 1915.

John Kenlon
Chief of Department,
S I R:-

In compliance with orders hereto attached relative to the "Draeger Oxygen Helmets", used by this company, I have the honor to report as follows:

Since the organization of the company on March 8th.1915, these helmets have been very successfully used by the members of this company under almost every condition met with in Fire Department operations, where the work and efforts of men operating without smoke helmets were greatly hampered if not entirely futile, as for instance, in shutting off valves on burst ammonia pipes; in removing from buildings carboys and drums of acids which have broken or leaked, throwing off deadly fumes; in ventilating and in using hose lines in smoky ship holds, cellars and sub-cellars.

Before these helmets were accepted by this Department, a test, under the following conditions was made at the smoke house at 68th.Street drill yard: a smudge was made by starting a fire in a pile of material consisting of excelsior, oakum, sulphur, rags, paper etc.; this combination emitted a dense, noxious smoke and shortly after closing the door, heat up to 280 degrees Fahr. was generated: this of course was a dry heat, but notwithstanding this, at no time during the test were any ill effects experienced as regards breathing, the air supply up to the last being quite cool: the heat however, had a very uncomfortable effect on the body, and the exposed parts, such as the hands and neck were so discolored from the smoke that about five weeks elapsed before it finally wore off: the duration of this test was 75 minutes.

The selection was made only after a series of most exhaustive and severe tests of a number of makes and types of breathing apparatus and the confidence of the members of this company has been strengthened each time the helmets have been used since organization.

This brief synopsis covers in a general way our experiences with Draeger helmets, but their successful operation depends, in no small degree, upon the care they receive after each time they are used: being mechanical and the result of human endeavor, they are not, of course, infallible or absolutely safe, and are liable to show poor results and ever prove to be a menance, if neglected; this of course applies to anything mechanical, and for this reason our helmets are tested for air tightness, daily; they are thoroughly cleaned after use; once each week every machine is taken apart, cleaned, re-assembled, then tested out on the Water Gauge and Measuring Bag, and the ones that had been on the car during the previous week are placed in reserve and those which had been in reserve during that time are placed in service thus giving all machines about an equal amount of service, and four always ready for service, in reserve.

FIRE DEPARTMENT
OF THE CITY OF NEW YORK

RESCUE COMPANY NO. 1.

New York, October 7th. 1915.

2---
John Kenlon
Chief of Department,

Another very important requisite in connection with the use of rescue apparatus is that every man using them to thoroughly understand every part of their mechanism, to have implicit confidence in their machines, and also in their own ability to use them; over-confidence however, must be avoided as it tends to lead to carelessness, the one thing above all others to be avoided.

Very respectfully,

Captain.

The fourth paragraph mentions the selection of the smoke helmets was made after a series of exhaustive and severe tests of several makes and types of breathing apparatus. Photos show members wearing unusual breathing apparatus prototypes. Newspaper articles and fire reports mention the FDNY had "smoke helmets" as early as 1908 but they were not in regular use.

A photo from 1908 shows members of Hook & Ladder 20 surrounding a fireman who's entering a cellar wearing a Vajen-Bader smoke helmet. The earliest mention of a smoke helmet in the FDNY was 1897 when it was worn in a rescue attempt of a trapped fireman.

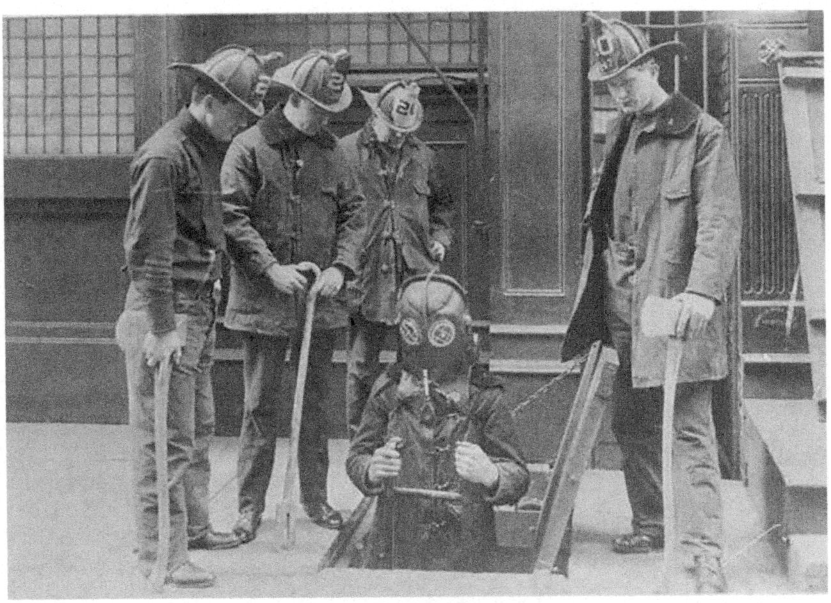

The 1908 photo of H&L 20 members with Vajen-Bader smoke helmet.

Chapter VI in a publication known as *The Book of Progress*, a 1915 publication of *Scientific American*, stated that the New York Fire Department tested six or seven varieties of smoke helmets and finally adopted the rather formidable Draeger smoke helmet. Fire Commissioner Robert Adamson stated in a newspaper interview in January of 1915, as the training was being conducted, "We tested every make of smoke helmet that is made."

One type of the smoke helmets tested by Rescue 1 in 1915.

As stated in his report to Chief John Kenlon, Captain McElligott, the commander of the new Rescue Company, gave the ultimate test of the Draeger smoke helmet under extreme conditions. At the former headquarters building and site of the FDNY Fire College at 157-159 East 67th Street in Manhattan, there was a concrete room, 20 feet square, used primarily for testing sprinklers. Into this room they piled excelsior, straw, oakum, rubbish, wood scraps, and Sulphur. This was ignited and quickly began producing thick smoke and high heat. Captain McElligott donned his rubber boots, rubber fire coat, and a telephone equipped smoke helmet and prepared to enter the room.

Dragging the telephone wire behind him the captain stepped into the blinding smoke. The rescue men found it difficult to close the door due to the building pressure of the expanding heat being generated in the enclosed space. Armed with only a thermometer that could register up to 500-degrees, a watch, and the smoke helmet, he settled in. As the heat built around him,

McElligott periodically checked the increasing temperature. He was not surprised when the thermometer quickly reached 280-degrees.

Despite the intense heat, the captain remained in the room, glancing at the index pointer of the smoke helmet's finimeter (oxygen gauge) until it read zero. His wristwatch verified he'd been inside the smoke house for an hour. He told the team waiting outside that he decided to push the test to the limits and stayed an additional 15 minutes.

At the end of the test, McElligott emerged from the smoke house thoroughly exhausted, sweat streaming inside the helmet, his clothing and boots. His clothing was rotten from the smoke and the skin on his hands was so blackened it was impossible to wash them clean. It took weeks for the discoloration to wear off.

The captain had set the bar high for his men. For the next several days they would each don a smoke helmet and duplicate his test. They also used axes to chop wood for 10-minute stretches while wearing the helmets to learn how to work within the limits of the available oxygen provided. Members also worked on the rope signals they would use during real fires and gas leaks. Finger pressure rope tug signals were developed to allow communications with the outside. Two of the helmets featured hard wire telephone systems, but the rope signals allowed communications to continue while using the other helmets or in case the telephones failed. (One newspaper quoted a member of Rescue 1 saying, "The telephone worked great, but the wire caught on everything.")

In a 1918 article about Rescue 1 and their smoke helmets, the NFPA *Fire Journal* magazine stated the company's policy. "Men should always operate in pairs in charge of an officer. In dense smoke always use a guideline, which is also used as a signal line. A simple code of signals should be made up and practiced, such as:

1 pull on rope—Send in more hose and signal line.
2 pulls—I am going up or down stairs (this will be known by existing conditions).
3 pulls—I am backing out (which when received by men outside will cause them to pull out hose and signal line).
4 pulls—Stop pulling hose and signal line.
5 pulls from men outside—Back Out.
2-3 pulls—I understand.
3-2 pulls—Repeat signal.
1-3 pulls given from either inside or outside—Distress.

Lt. Hotchkiss holding tending line as members in smoke helmets enter cellar at FDNY Headquarters drill yard.

Always leave at least one man with a helmet outside who will take and give signals, watch outside conditions, report same to crew operating in the building, and act in an emergency which requires a helmet, such as an accident, to men inside, etc.

Each helmet is equipped with a telephone receiver and transmitter, and there is carried as part of the outfit a reel of

400-feet of telephone cable, also a set of dry-cell batteries, and a receiving and transmitting outfit used by the man or officer in charge on the street; but the rope signal has proven so efficient that it has been rarely necessary to resort to the telephone equipment of the helmets.

The new company also focused on the oxyacetylene cutting torch. Hours were spent cutting metals of various thicknesses and a record of the number of cuts, thickness of the metal, and the time required for each was compiled. Interesting to note in the many photos and films made of the new rescue company by Al Dreyfous and Dr. Ernest Stillman, the firemen wore no protective eye gear when using the cutting torch. These early photographs also show a lack of hand protection. Rescue 1 firemen, like all the other firemen in the FDNY, rarely wore gloves in this era. They worked at fires and emergencies in uniform coats or rubber fire coats wearing the smoke helmets, fire helmets, or even uniform caps with bare hands. They did however wear rubber gloves when handling acids.

Fireman John Ryan cutting window bars at FDNY Drill Yard

The Draeger helmets were without a doubt the tool that separated the rescue firemen from everyone else. They could work in dense smoke, ammonia fumes, and other toxic or poisonous gases, while the firemen without the helmets were knocked unconscious. This allowed them to approach and control ammonia leaks, one of the most common and debilitating problems firemen of this era faced. Ammonia was the major refrigerant in use at the time and leaks occurred often.

Leaking ammonia has a pungent smell that is detectable in concentrations as low as 5ppm (parts per million.) When concentrations reach 1700ppm, humans begin coughing, and laryngospasm and edema of the glottic region begin. (Laryngospasm is when the vocal cords suddenly spasm, blocking the airway. Edema is when too much fluid is trapped in body tissue; this swelling in the glottic region of the airway near the vocal cords blocks the airway.)

Another deadly problem that was commonly faced by firemen was leaking illuminating gas. This natural gas, used for lighting and cooking, was odorless and when flames reached gas meters the heat often melted pipe fixtures, allowing the gas to escape and mix unnoticed in the smoke. The first signs of this new danger were when firemen began to fall unconscious. (A major gas leak in a Texas school building in 1937 went undetected until a spark ignited an explosion that collapsed the building and left more than 295 dead. This prompted the eventual nation-wide addition of odorizers like mercaptan to natural gas to allow leaks to be smelled.)

There is no mention in either the 1915 or 1916 annual reports of the purchase of the Draeger smoke helmets by the department. There are however some strong clues as to how this equipment was obtained. Newspaper articles chronicled Mainzer's trip to Europe in the summer of 1914, and while in London it was reported he was investigating the breathing apparatus used by European fire departments. His interest was so strong he donned a smoke helmet and went into an oakum fire. (Oakum is tarred fiber used to seal gaps in wooden ships and in plumbing. It was also used to produce very thick smoke for training with breathing apparatus.)

Honorary Fire Officer Robert H. Mainzer

In a story in *Commerce and Finance* Magazine, on February 2, 1916, Richard Spillane wrote of the testimonial dinner given on January 18, 1916. He described Mainzer's various titles beyond that of banker:

He is a private aide to Fire Chief Kenlon. Officially he is an honorary officer of the Fire Department of New York and as such has a gold badge much like that of the chief himself. . . . Two years ago Mr. Mainzer was in Europe. He was the only American member of the International Fire Service Council and as such represented the New York Fire Department at the conference in London in June 1914. While there he saw the excellent work done by the Smoke Helmet Squad of London. He formed the idea this would be of great value to the New York Department. He is thorough and painstaking. He gathered a mass of information which he submitted to the Fire Commissioner of New York, with the idea of forming rescue squads with oxygen, smoke helmets, acetylene gas cutters, pulmotors and all kinds of rescue paraphernalia. We now have one of these rescue companies which responds to all second alarm fires in the district between the Battery and 125th Street and to all third alarms in Greater New York.

Other newspaper articles mentioned his generosity, especially to the fire department. It would be a fair assumption to conclude that Robert Mainzer purchased a good portion of the specialized equipment Rescue 1 carried that first year.

The intense training continued as each man was shown how to disassemble and maintain the smoke helmets. After each use they were taken apart, cleaned, and inspected for wear. They were reassembled and tested for possible use. The torches were tested, cleaned, and stored. The portable oxygen tanks were then filled by members from a bank of large cylinders set up in quarters. This cascade filling system is a high-pressure gas cylinder storage system that is used for the refilling of smaller compressed gas cylinders.

The new rescue men also trained with the Lyle gun. This rope rifle was designed to shoot a brass projectile with a strong cord attached. The cord was then used to pull a larger rope up to a location. This rope was then tied off and could be used to escape danger.

They also worked with hydraulic jacks for lifting heavy objects or forcing open doors. As the company went into service, they would carry five jacks: 15-10-5 tons on the new rig.

Another tool the company would become famous for was the pulmotor. This resuscitator, manufactured by Draeger, was just gaining in popularity in hospitals. Rescue 1 undoubtedly worked with Doctor Harry Archer, as they refined their life-saving procedures.

As their training continued, Battalion Chief Charles Demarest and his crew at the department shops were working on a 1914 Cadillac touring car that was being transformed into the first specialized rescue rig. This gleaming red, high-powered vehicle featured a four-cylinder 32.4 horsepower engine. Originally designed to carry five passengers, the shops widened and extended the rear section to allow room for two bench seats (with storage beneath) on either side. There was also a center storage compartment.

1914 Cadillac Rescue Rig at Great Jones Street firehouse

Frank Blessing at the wheel, Capt. McElligott in front. Firemen Frank Clark (left) and Walter O'Leary in rear.

The right-hand drive rig also featured a large bell and a hand-cranked siren located in front of the driver and officer's seats. Gold leaf lettering on the sides of the rear crew compartment proclaimed "Rescue Co. 1 FDNY" on both sides.

The new truck was presented to the department several days before the company was placed in service. On the afternoon of March 2, 1915, Chief Demarest brought the new truck to the Municipal Building in lower Manhattan and presented it to Fire Commissioner Robert Adamson and Chief of Department John Kenlon. The new apparatus attracted a large crowd of interested citizens, FDNY officials and the news media. The company took charge of the new rig and began the task of placing the tools and equipment in the best locations.

On board the rig the morning of March 8, 1915, were:

- 4 Draeger smoke helmets (1 with telephone, transmitting set for street, battery equipment, and 300 feet of telephone wire.)

- 6 oxygen cylinders at 2,500-pounds pressure used in conjunction with the smoke helmets and capable of 80 minutes duration.
- 16 regenerating cartridges for use on masks to remove carbon dioxide when exhaling (Carbonic acid gas is given off by the lungs, and the potash in these cartridges neutralizes the poison.)
- 1 Blau gas cutting torch, capable of making 26 1-inch cuts in iron or steel.
- 1 cylinder of oxygen at 2,250 pounds pressure for cutting torch.
- 1 cylinder of Blau gas at 700 pounds pressure for cutting torch.
- 2 Pulmotors (40-minute capacity, 4 extra oxygen cylinders at 2,500 psi.)
- 2-cylinder pillows (used with Pulmotor to position patient.)
- 4 pairs of rubber wader trousers (protection from ammonia fumes.)
- 4-120-foot-long Manila ropes (used as helmet signal line.)
- 2-4-pound axes
- 2 small jimmy bars (prying tools.)
- 1 life gun (Lyle gun) with canister and line.
- 2 pairs of rubber gloves
- 2 stretchers
- 2 Pyrene extinguishers
- 1 Ever Ready hand electric searchlight & 2 Dietz hand lanterns

A 1915 Ever Ready hand electric searchlight like the type used by Rescue 1.

Dietz hand lanterns on Rescue 1's back step.

1908 photo of Capt. Jennings H&L 20 and his lieutenant with Dietz lanterns.

Chapter 3:
Going Into Service

At 8:00 a.m. on the morning of March 8, 1915, Rescue Company 1 was ready to be placed in service. A telephone call was made to the fire dispatcher's office to make it official. The company then assembled on the apparatus floor of the Great Jones Street firehouse and gave a demonstration of their new equipment and training to Mayor Mitchel, Fire Commissioner Adamson and Chief Kenlon.

A mock-up of iron bars appeared to "trap" a beautiful lady. The bars were quickly cut away with the torch, freeing the damsel. Then a helmeted fireman holding the electric torch (flashlight) disappeared into a smoke-filled room and returned after "rescuing" an imaginary million dollars that was about to be consumed by the flames. The rope rifle then shot a line to another "trapped damsel" who called for help from a window above.

The pulmotors were then demonstrated as the rescued smoke "victims" were administered oxygen by the rescue men. Various first aid equipment and procedures were also displayed for the invited guests.

The firemen then gathered their major tools and posed for a company photograph on the apron in front of quarters.

Rescue Company 1 was now ready to respond to fires and emergencies across the city. A new chapter of firefighting, hazardous materials mitigation, and rescue work was about to be written.

Great Jones Street, Capt. McElligott, Firemen Clark, Kinsella, O'Leary, Kilbride, Henretty, Shaw, Ryan, Mooney and Lt. Hotchkiss pose with some of their special tools: smoke helmet, pulmotor, cutting torch and rope rifle. Frank Blessing is behind the wheel.

The firehouse at 42 Great Jones Street, a beautiful red brick trimmed with limestone, is a Beaux-Arts structure designed by Ernest Flagg and W.B. Chambers. Engine 33 moved to this brand-new trim firehouse on June 1, 1899, from their old quarters at 15 Great Jones Street. Engine Company 33, a double company since 1883, was originally organized on November 1, 1865, and is one of 34 original engine companies in the FDNY. In 1915 it was a busy company that responded to 371 alarms and worked at 126 fires.

The two-bay Great Jones Street firehouse usually held a motorized steam pumper, its accompanying motorized hose wagon, and a motorized high-pressure hose wagon. This firehouse served as the night quarters of the chief of department, so it also housed the chief's automobile. Rescue 1 added their customized rig on March 8, 1915.

42 Great Jones Street the original home of Rescue Co. 1

Great Jones Street is a two-block portion of 3rd Street between Broadway and Bowery. This location was ideal for the new rescue company. Sitting just above the area of the city now known as Soho (South of Houston Street) this section of Manhattan became known to firefighters as "Hell's Hundred Acres." The area boundaries were Chambers Street to the south, Bowery on the east, West Broadway on the west and West 8th Street to the north.

In the early 1900s the area above Chambers Street to just below Canal Street, from Broadway to West Broadway was known as the Dry Goods District. This area was not as busy for the FDNY as above Canal Street, but it was the site of many of the most stubborn cellar and subcellar fires ever fought. In the area between Canal and 8th streets stood many loft buildings with high ceilings and equally high fire loads. Many were old, converted tenement buildings never designed for the heavy machinery and stock that was jammed inside. Other buildings had suffered numerous fires over the years and were shoddily repaired. Firemen routinely faced dangers in this area rarely seen in other sections of the city.

The Great Jones Street location provided several important things for the new company. First, by using either the Bowery or Broadway (two-way until the 1960s) it was an easy and quick response downtown. A quick trip south to Delancey Street allowed easy access to the Williamsburg Bridge and the Borough of Brooklyn.

In accordance with FDNY Special Order No. 10, Rescue 1 would respond to all second alarms in Manhattan below 59th Street, and all third alarms below 125th Street. They could also be special-called to any alarm in the city with the transmission of signal 2-2-2-[Box number]-1. So, if signal 2-2-2-459-1 was received it meant Rescue 1 was to respond to Manhattan Box 459, Broadway and 34th Street.

So, it appears the first "jobs" Rescue 1 responded to were on March 11, 1915. A second alarm was transmitted at 12:33 a.m., for Box 10 at 24 Bridge Street. Burning herbs and cheese caused a noxious smoke condition within the iron shuttered commercial building. Lt. Hotchkiss and his men entered the structure wearing their smoke helmets and worked their way down from the top floor, searching and venting as they descended. It was reported the dense smoke had no effect on the helmeted rescue men.

Later that morning at 2:21 a.m., a second alarm was transmitted for a fire in a rear tenement at Box 12, 15 West Street.

However, on March 12, 1915 at 3:20 a.m., Rescue 1 was

special-called to a fire at 231-233 Green Street, and they would have a major impact on operations. The responding units were faced with a basement fire in a large commercial building that ran all the way through to Mercer Street. Heavy smoke was hampering the firemen as they attempted to press into the basement.

Chief Kenlon had a choice; either transmit a second alarm and subject his men to a traditional pounding into unconsciousness or do it a new way. Kenlon had his aide special-call the new company. A few minutes later the rescue rig arrived again under the command of Lt. Edwin Hotchkiss. Advised of the conditions, Hotchkiss and his men prepared to don their smoke helmets. Hotchkiss tied a rope around his waist and entered the basement while the other men clung to the same rope and followed him in.

In total darkness, they located the seat of the fire and reported back to the chief. They were given two hose lines and stretched them deep into the basement. After 15 minutes of work the fire was declared out. There must have been smiles all around. A deep-seated basement fire was extinguished, and no firemen were left unconscious or gasping for air.

Newspaper articles stated, "Twice in the first four days of its existence the Fire Department's new Rescue Company No. 1 demonstrated its efficiency in tackling fires too smoky to be fought effectively by firemen unequipped with special apparatus."

"Even so old and experienced firefighter as Chief Kenlon," the *New York Evening Sun* commented, "is said to have been amazed at the speed with which the smoke-eaters worked through the fumes to the source of one of the fires and extinguish it."

Then on March 29th at 12:25 a.m., Rescue 1 responded to the second alarm at Box 227, a fire in a six-story loft building at 237 Rivington Street, Manhattan. At the start of the fire, Isaac, the building's watchman, decided not to leave the burning building until he warned his friend of the danger. Isaac made his way to a top-floor room and woke Borah Ruch, the clothing company's other watchman. As it turned out, Ruch was able to make it to the fire escape, but Isaac never appeared.

The men of Rescue 1 donned their smoke helmets, plunged into the furnace-like atmosphere and began a grueling search. They found the watchman, Isaac, dead in the rear of the top floor. He apparently wandered, lost in the smoke, until he was overcome and fell unconscious, each subsequent breath leading to his death. The unfortunate man had immigrated from Russia three years earlier.

On April 1, 1915, FDNY units responded to a fire at 637 East 17th Street, a five-story cigar box manufacturing company. Manhattan Box 367 was transmitted at 2:37 p.m.

A fire started in a ground floor sawmill. An explosion then blew out a section of the rear wall allowing flames to auto-expose to the floors above. People working in the occupancies above scrambled to find their way to safety as the flames extended and the smoke thickened.

Arriving companies went to work rescuing those trapped, while attacking flames. A second and third alarms were quickly transmitted, when reports indicated the expanding flames were also threatening nearby buildings. Dense smoke shrouded the entire neighborhood, making it dangerous even outside the fire building. When Battalion Chief McGuire and some firemen were overcome on the roof of an adjoining building, Rescue 1 sprang into action.

Hearing of the plight of their comrades, the rescue men

grabbed scaling ladders, climbed to the roof, and were able to move the unconscious men into a safe space within the building. There, in the clear air they were able to revive the overcome men. With assistance the battered McGuire and his firemen returned to the street.

The dangers being faced by the members of Rescue 1 became all too clear just after 6 p.m. on April 16th. The company responded to a very dangerous situation at 353 East 58th Street in Manhattan, the location of Rose & Company's cleaning and dye establishment. The FDNY was called earlier when a small fire broke out in the basement of the three-story building. Acting Chief James Sherlock, Capt. Seymour Guy and the members of Engine 39 entered the basement with a hose. They were accompanied by several members of Hook & Ladder 2. Seven firemen from Engine 8, under the command of Lt. Gustave Moje, also stretched a hose line into the smoke-filled basement with the intention of protecting stored drycleaning chemicals.

As both groups moved deeper into the basement a backdraft knocked them to the floor as a sheet of flames roared overhead. Ordered to withdraw, four of the firemen fell to the floor unconscious as they attempted to leave the cellar. They were quickly located and carried to safety by their comrades.

Arriving on the second alarm, the members of Rescue 1 prepared to deploy with their smoke helmets as Capt. McElligott conferred with the chiefs. McElligott, Lt. Hotchkiss, Fireman Alfred Kinsella and two other rescue men donned the smoke helmets and pulled a hose line down into the basement. Their advance halted as they reached a wall of heat. Hunkering down they prepared to renew their attack on the flames, when a second backdraft toppled the rescue men.

In the tangle of smoke, heat, hoses, bodies and stock, Al Kinsella's smoke helmet became dislodged. Almost instantly he fell to the floor unconscious. The rescue men scrambled to control the fire and remove Kinsella to the fresh air. By the time they reached the street, Kinsella was awake and after a few moments to catch his breath, he re-donned the smoke helmet and joined the company in the final extinguishment.

Several of the firemen caught in the first backdraft were seriously burned about the head and face and were taken to a nearby hospital.

It was 7:20 p.m. April 22, 1915, when Manhattan fire companies were summoned to 206-208 Canal Street, the Sheffield Plating Works. Arriving at the scene Deputy Chief Langford took one whiff of the potentially poisonous fumes pouring from the building, and immediately ordered all the firemen outside. Battalion Chief Crowley and members of Engine 31 and Hook & Ladder 6 were already working deep inside when Langford arrived. Upon leaving the building the crew reported there was no fire inside the building but that smoke-like vapors were present.

Langford special-called Rescue 1 to the scene. With Acting Lt. Ryan in command, Rescue 1 arrived, and ventured into the building wearing their smoke helmets. Inside they found a 30-gallon tank of nitric acid had cracked or overflowed, and that the fluid was pouring out onto the floor and vaporizing. (Nitric acid is an inorganic compound and is a highly corrosive mineral acid. It can be used to convert metals to oxidized forms.)

When attempts to carry the tank outside proved futile, the rescue men began to bail out the acid into buckets, before pouring it down the sewer. (Sadly, a common practice in those days. You must also remember there were no established hazardous material response protocols yet. Rescue 1 was the de facto hazardous materials team with oxygen helmets, waders and rubber gloves. A pioneering team that had only started a month and a half earlier. Rescue 1 was writing the book as they went.)

When the tank was finally emptied, the area was ventilated, and the remaining FDNY units and the members of Rescue 1 were released from the scene and returned to quarters.

It was after the alarm that the effects of the poison started being noticed. While operating at a small fire on John Street, Fireman John Spineer, Chief Crowley's aide, and Chief Crowley both collapsed. Back in their quarters after the earlier Canal Street response members of Hook & Ladder 6 began dropping to the firehouse floor unconscious. In all, 17 were rendered unconscious, after the fact, by the fumes.

Chief Kenlon praised the work of Rescue Company 1 removing the deadly hazard. "If the call had come during the day when the people were at work in the factory, the fumes would have caused a condition that I dare not anticipate. None of the men of the Rescue Company were affected by the fumes because of the oxygen helmets they wore."

The Sun newspaper reported in a 1921 story about Rescue 1, that at this Canal Street acid leak emergency: "A number of other firemen had breathed the fumes from the acid and were seriously affected. One captain lost all his teeth from the effects of the fumes, and two other men later developed pneumonia."

It was just after 7 p.m. April 26th when workers in the Manhattan Refrigeration Company, located on the corner of West and Horatio streets, realized a leaking pipe joint between two ammonia tanks in the cold storage plant was posing a great danger. They turned off the supply leading into the tanks, then switched on ventilation fans, and opened doors leading into a 40-foot ventilation shaft that extended up to the roof. The workers hurried to where oxygen helmets were stored for emergencies. As they were strapping the helmets on, the ammonia exploded.

Seven plate glass windows, with wire woven into the glass for protection during fires, instantly became shrapnel that tore into the crowded street and sidewalks. It was lunchtime, and workers from various businesses were enjoying the fresh air on the Horatio Street sidewalks. The pulverized glass, metal wire bits, chunks of splintered window frames, and chunks of brick blasted outwards, some finding human flesh. Fifteen people were sprawled across the pavement, all seriously injured.

The street scene turned to panic as the shrapnel-like projectiles tore through people and embedded itself in brick walls across the street. The strong odor of ammonia fumes filled the streets, further complicating the chaos.

Police Officer Doyle of the Charles Street station saw the injured and bleeding men run out into Horatio Street and sent in calls for the police reserves, the fire department, ambulances and specifically requested the new FDNY Rescue Squad. Doyle then dashed into the building, despite the ammonia fumes, and found a worker unconscious and seriously injured on the floor.

Doyle lifted the man into his arms and started for the exit, before he, too, was overcome by the ammonia fumes. The brave officer and the injured man both fell to the floor. Moments later members of Rescue 1, under the command of Capt. McElligott and wearing their protective smoke helmets, found both men and brought them out to safety.

The explosion had also torn away insulation from a cluster of electrical wires. The wires short-circuited and ignited a fire in a nearby switchboard. The flames were spreading as Rescue 1 members tore away at the burning insulation and piled heaps of burning material in the street where it could be wet down.

Fire Engineering Magazine reported:

> Rescue Company 1 bore the brunt of the task of removing the injured from the wreckage, and it is likely that without their aid some of the victims might have died from the deadly fumes. Equipped with oxygen helmets, the

rescuers entered the building and carried out those unable to stand.

On the following day, April 27th, Rescue 1 was special-called to 442 Pearl Street for a fire in Toriano & Defino Company, dealers in paper stock and rags. A score of women were working in the shop at the time of the late afternoon fire, and escaped injury by fleeing to the roof of the building and crossing to the adjoining structure.

A rubbish fire in the cellar was producing thick smoke. Several pipe connections also melted adding illuminating gas to the smoke. This rendered unconscious Acting Battalion Chief John Donohue (captain of Hook & Ladder 15); Firemen John Mahoney of Engine 9, and Frank Wintrick and John Dillon, both of Hook & Ladder 6. They were carried out to the sidewalk where Rescue 1 members began resuscitation efforts with their pulmotors.

Working with hospital surgeons, who'd responded from Hudson Street Hospital, the unconscious men were given oxygen with manual resuscitators, and pulmotors carried on the ambulances and Rescue 1. They also treated a civilian and the police officer who'd rescued him from the dense smoke. Also suffering from the smoke were the firemen who'd pulled out their unconscious comrades earlier.

Everyone made a full recovery.

It was 3 o'clock on the afternoon of May 2nd when companies responded to Box 146 for a fire at 3 Howard Street, a four-story loft building being used as a rag and paper company. The upper floors of the building housed several large machines that greatly added to the already dangerous weight of the stored rags and paper.

As the firefighting progressed Deputy Chief Langford had an uneasy feeling and pulled all the firemen from the blazing structure. Just as the crew from Engine 31, the last men inside were leaving, three floors of the building collapsed. Langford immediately transmitted a second alarm and ordered a roll call.

Rescue 1 and Assistant Chief Smoky Joe Martin responded on the additional alarm. Rescue 1 was quickly put to work searching for any possible firemen caught in the collapse. Everyone was relieved when this search proved negative, and companies reported back that all members were accounted for.

The operation continued from the outside as a massive amount of water was needed to extinguish the deep-seated flames.

On the morning of May 15th employees were busy working in the five-story building at 206 East 19th Street, near Third Avenue. The basement, first and second floors were occupied by the J.E. Rodgers Company, manufacturers of printing inks and varnish. On the second floor were large vats of resin, varnish and oils. On the third floor, flash powder supplies were being made for the Prosch Manufacturing Company, a photographic supply firm. (Flash powder was used to create a flash effect for photographers and consisted of a mixture of magnesium powder and potassium chlorate.) The fourth floor was a supply storage area for a nearby drug company. This building was literally loaded with explosives.

On the second floor in the ink and varnish company's laboratory, chemist Nicholas Doody was mixing colors when a violent explosion shook the structure. Doody was knocked to the floor. Regaining his feet, he started to leave the building, until he remembered the others working above. As he dashed up the stairs, another explosion toppled a wall partition, again knocking him to the floor.

As he heard Ruth Scott calling for help from the third floor, Doody saw the stairs were now gone and flames were rapidly extending to the floor above, where the flash powder was stored. He told the trapped 20-year-old woman, whose dress was catching fire, to slide down the elevator chain. Doody caught her as she descended and carried her to the street. Both were badly burned. A third worker, Morris Nyborn, was carried out by civilians. All three would be transported to the hospital.

At 8:43 a.m. on May 15th, Box 363 was pulled and FDNY units were quickly on the scene as repeated explosions from the third floor rocked the building at 206 East 19th Street. Flames raced upward through the building setting off more explosions. Arriving units were faced with a rapidly extending fire that threatened the surrounding structures. Rescue 1 arrived and was assigned to remove barrels of oils and varnishes from the second floor of the blazing building. Once those hazards were cleared, they were assigned firefighting duties.

This fire went to a third alarm.

In mid-May of 1915 Rescue 1 responded to several multiple alarm fires and emergencies. On the evening of May15th they worked a 3-alarm fire at 424 East 18th Street. The following evening May 16th they worked a 2-alarm fire at Manhattan Box 556, then a fire at 317 West 59th Street. On May 19th Rescue 1 responded to 95 First Street and shut off broken ammonia valves in the basement. On May 22nd they worked another 2-alarm fire, this time at 240 West 23rd Street.

June 5th at 5:47 p.m., Manhattan Box 262 was transmitted for a fire at 567 West Broadway an eight-story structure known as the Livingston Building. Erected 21 years earlier, it was known to the members of the FDNY as a bad luck building. The term "HOODOO" became attached to the building after more than 20 men were killed during its construction. Subsequently, the building had also suffered numerous fires. Today's fire began in the paper box company of Albert & Son on the ground floor and spread quickly, filling the floors above with heavy smoke.

On the fourth floor, three young women and two men were cut off from using the stairs to the street and fled to the fifth floor, from there they made their way to the rear fire escape. Captain Kelly and the crew of Hook & Ladder 20 were checking the rear of the building when they heard shouts from the trapped workers above.

A portable ladder was rushed into position in the rear. Unable to position the ladder directly below the trapped people, they placed it against the building as near as they could and quickly climbed up. With the ladder too short by at least five-feet, Captain Kelly climbed onto a fifth-floor window ledge that was less than two-feet wide. While his men held his legs for stability Kelly reached across through a cloud of hot pumping smoke and lifted a young woman from the fire escape. One by one the people, several of whom had become unconscious, were removed from danger and delivered to Doctor Archer for treatment.

Conditions had become so extreme, that members of

Rescue 1 donned smoke helmets, and helped push the attack lines into the raging flames. At the height of the fire, voices from a crowd estimated at 10,000 people, advised firemen that another fire was burning across the street in 64 Washington Square South. This fire too, was quickly brought under control. This fire required a third alarm.

On June 12, 1915, members of Rescue 1 took part in the FDNY Fiftieth Anniversary Celebration. A large, celebratory parade, medal presentation and firefighting demonstration was planned. The parade started at Fifth Avenue and 45th Street, went up to 57th Street, over to Broadway, up to 86th Street, then over to Riverside Drive. Continuing up Riverside Drive, past the reviewing stand at 100th Street, then continued to 106th Street.

The reviewing stand, located directly in front of the Fireman's Monument, was decorated in red, white and blue bunting. A new pedestal fire alarm box, wired to the FDNY dispatcher's office was featured on stage. (This was used after the review of the parade, speeches, the medal presentation ceremony.)

The line of march featured firemen and equipment from the city's historic past. Capt. James F. Wenman, 92 years old, a volunteer from 1843 and president of the Volunteer Firemen's Association, led a contingent of redshirted former volunteers. The original hand-pumper purchased by the city back in 1725 was carried on a department flatbed truck. Various old-style hand-drawn apparatus, horse-drawn rigs, and finally the newest motorized fire apparatus being used by the paid department followed. This included the new 1914 Cadillac rescue rig. Members of the new rescue company marched wearing smoke helmets.

Members of Rescue 1 on parade wearing smoke helmets.

Veterans of the paid force that went into service in 1865 also marched proudly. They were followed by the Chief of Department John Kenlon, who wore a red sash across his uniform and led the current membership of the department. He was closely followed by his deputies, Thomas Lally, Joseph Crawley, Joseph B. "Smoky Joe" Martin, Thomas J. Hayes and Thomas Langford. Next were the chaplains and honorary officers.

The next division included the honor men of 1914, who would be decorated with medals after the parade. They were led by Deputy Chief John Binns, and honor companies of previous medal recipients. Half of the current members of the department followed, now numbering 5,000 uniformed officers and firemen. Also honored were several long-serving fire horses and a dozen dogs, mascots of various firehouses.

At the conclusion of the parade, Mayor John Purroy Mitchel stepped down from the reviewing stand and prepared to award the medals. After this, the calisthenics squad marched into position and performed a vigorous workout. Then the crowd turned its attention to a four-story temporary structure built across from the reviewing stand and designed to simulate a tenement building.

When smoke and flames were seen inside the structure, the on-stage fire alarm box was transmitted by Chief Kenlon. Two minutes later Hook and Ladder 22 arrived from their quarters at 97th Street and Amsterdam Avenue. They raised their ladder and were able to rescue a life-size rag doll known as "Susie." Thus began a series of demonstrations. Susie was again rescued, this time by the scaling ladder squad who swarmed the front of the smoking structure. Then they dropped the doll into a life-net.

The ground floor of the structure featured iron bars and the department's newest unit, Rescue Company 1, quickly cut through the bars with an oxyacetylene torch. Then, again wearing smoke helmets, they dashed into the black smoke and dragged out an "overcome victim." The company then revived the victim using their resuscitator.

Members of Rescue 1 using cutting torch at anniversary/medal day demonstration.

Members of the demonstration squad then slid ropes from the roof, shot a line up by a life gun and several other rope evolutions. Down in the river, four fireboats made a brilliant water display.

The mayor turned to Chief Kenlon, "This has been a good show. The men all did well. This demonstration shows how well trained these men are. The thing that struck me, just as it struck me at the police parade, was what young, vigorous, clean-cut, well set up men they all are."

A letter from John Purroy Mitchel, Mayor of the City of New York to Fire Commissioner Robert Adamson, was also published in the newspapers. "Sir: I wish to congratulate you most heartily upon the impressive showing."

The relaxed feelings of the parade, medal presentation and demonstrations were short lived for downtown fire companies including Rescue 1, when Box 68 was transmitted at 5:06 that afternoon for a fire at 382 Pearl Street, down near the Brooklyn Bridge.

A few minutes after 5 p.m., Patrolman O'Connor saw smoke coming from the fourth-floor windows of the five-story Johnston & Oswald paint factory. He transmitted the alarm, and in the three minutes it took for the fire department to respond, the flames had taken control of the top floors of the building.

Faced with a serious fire condition, Deputy Chief Thomas F. Dougherty transmitted a second alarm upon arrival. As the first due units were raising ladders and stretching lines into position, Dougherty transmitted a third alarm.

Inside the building a muffled explosion could be heard as firefighters began their attack. Lines were stretched up ladders and up the front fire escape. From there the hoses were advanced from the front, unburned section of the building and directed at the deep-seated flames. While they were working these lines, the first major explosion rocked the building.

Twenty firemen working on the fourth floor were toppled by the blast, including Captain Thomas Walsh, who was thrown through a window and out onto the fire escape. Fireman Vanderventer of Hook & Ladder 1 was overcome by the smoke before he could reach the fire escape and was carried to safety by his comrades.

Chief Dougherty also telephoned the elevated railway officials ordering a power shut off so they could relocate hose lines and use the elevated railroad platform as a vantage point.

The first explosion was a warning sign that Chief Dougherty heeded. He withdrew the companies from the fire building and redirected their attack from the elevated train structure and from the roofs of the adjoining buildings. So, when the second, and more devastating explosion occurred, all the firemen were already out of harm's way. Said to be one of the most violent concussions and backdrafts ever to occur at a fire in New York City, the blast sent a huge white-hot ball of fire through the roof of the burning building. The members of Rescue 1 and three-alarms worth of companies continued pressing the attack until the fire was finally brought under control at about 6 p.m.

On July 15, 1915, Fireman Second Grade William A. Dorritie of Hook & Ladder 16 was transferred to Rescue Company 1. The 30-year-old Dorritie, a former stagehand, joined the FDNY on May 1, 1913. He was assigned to Engine Company 39, before transferring to Hook & Ladder 16 on November 27, 1913. Dorritie was the first fireman officially transferred to Rescue 1 since it was organized in March.

On July 24, 1915 at 2:45 p.m., the FDNY was called to the pier at the foot of West 23rd Street in Manhattan for a fire onboard the British steamship *Cragside*. The ship was being loaded with sugar from lighters owned by the National Sugar Company.

A fire broke out in Hold No. 2, forward of the bridge. When flames were seen the crew began firefighting efforts. In the blazing compartment were 24,000 bags of sugar each weighing 100 pounds. In the hold the sugar was burning, melting and boiling. Worried the flames would extend to other holds, the fire department was called.

Rescue 1 member enters the ship's hold wearing smoke helmet.

Assistant Chief Smoky Joe Martin watched the companies battling the flames and noted the exhaustion the hot, smoky fire was causing. He special-called Rescue 1 to the scene. Donning their smoke helmets the rescue men advanced a hose line into the hold. After an hour the fire was declared under control. Noted as working this fire were: Firemen Blessing, Dorritie, Kilbride, Ryan, and Shaw.

It was speculated that this fire may have been an act of sabotage. A series of suspicious fires had occurred on Allied shipping for the past several months and several arrests had been made. It was believed German agents, and their accomplices were responsible for placing firebombs among the cargo. This was a problem that plagued the Port of New York all during World War I.

In the early morning hours of August 15, 1915, an explosion rocked the Jacob Ruppert Brewery at 205 East 98th Street. John Schuler, the engineer, J.E. Kennedy, the dynamo tender, and Fred Peterson and Valentine Spindler were all in the engine room when the explosion occurred. Schuler shouted to the others to run, but they were overcome by the expanding cloud of ammonia fumes and dropped where they stood. Instead of trying to save himself, Schuler dashed to the engines, shutting off six of them. He started for the ammonia tanks but was forced to the floor by the building ammonia gas and rolled toward the door. The night watchman, Ernest Plate, a former fireman in Engine 31 who'd retired in 1910, was able to drag all the overcome men to the street.

As this was happening inside the brewery, the 16 families in the neighboring tenements were forced from their homes by the toxic clouds rolling into the building through the open windows. The brewery was said to be the largest ammonia installation in the country. A patrolling policeman raised the alarm and the FDNY was quickly on scene. Deputy Chief Thomas J. Hayes of the Fifth Division arrived and special-called Rescue 1.

Captain McElligott conferred with D.C. Hayes and a plan was devised. Ernest Plate and Assistant Chief Engineer Charles Gunther were given a quick lesson as the smoke helmets were fitted to their heads. They guided McElligott and two rescue men to the engine room. Within moments the two civilians were overcome and had to be removed. When Gunther was revived, he again donned a helmet and led the Rescue back into the building.

Ammonia valves were shut down on the first and fifth floors of the huge brewery. The main break Rescue 1 had to deal with was in a two-inch supply pipe on top of some condensers on the first floor. A similar accident had occurred at the plant before and took eight hours to control. The actual shut off and control took Rescue 1 members only 10 minutes this time. But ventilation of the plant took an hour and a half. Firemen Kilbride, O'Leary, Ryan, Mooney and Shaw worked this job.

Newspaper clipping of ammonia valve being shut down.

It was shortly after midnight August 16, 1915, when workers were busy in the Hotel Biltmore's third-level subcellar. They were trying to repair a defective ammonia pipe that was part of the hotel's ice plant. (The two-towered, 26-story luxury hotel opened in 1913 at 335 Madison Avenue near 43rd Street.) Leo Regnert, the night electrician, was on a ladder inspecting the pipe while building engineer R.A. Broadford and the assistant night electrician Charles Gillick stood nearby.

Suddenly, an explosion hurled Regnert from the ladder and across the room. The blast threw Broadford and Gillick through a nearby doorway. The blast also damaged water pipes and electrical wiring and plunged the cellars into darkness. The dazed duo attempted to reach their injured friend but were driven back by the powerful ammonia fumes. Gillick staggered a few feet before he fell to the floor overcome by the dense fumes. Blinded, gagging and choking, Broadford stumbled from the subcellar and grabbed a telephone to report the accident to the night manager. A call was then sent to the FDNY.

The first-due companies arrived and Acting Battalion Chief George Fox immediately special-called Rescue 1. Members of Hook & Ladder 2 arrived and attempted to penetrate the wall of ammonia fumes but were driven back. Outside, Rescue 1 arrived with extra smoke helmets. Conferring briefly with Chief Fox, Captain McElligott and his men, Firemen Blessing, Kilbride, O'Leary, Mooney and Shaw donned their smoke helmets and using their new Edison pocket lamps (early version of a flashlight) moved into the subcellars. (As always, the rescue men worked in pairs and had a safety man in a clear, safe area ready to come to the aid of the helmeted members.) A team quickly returned carrying the badly injured assistant electrician up to medical attention.

Inspecting the blast area, they saw Leo Regnert pinned behind pipes and a large hole was torn through the concrete ceiling up into the barber shop in the second subcellar above. Walls were toppled and damaged. Torn electrical wiring hung from the ceiling and walls as twisted and broken pipes poured water onto the floor.

First, the leaking ammonia system had to be controlled and made safe. The refrigeration equipment included three 40-ton and one 10-ton machine. The rescue men inspected the system and closed valves to stop the escaping ammonia. Then, several men began efforts to free Regnert, as a second team moved to the second subcellar and began to use axes and drills to loosen pipes to help free the trapped body below.

Under the direction of Assistant Chief Smoky Joe Martin, the hotel's huge air handling equipment was used to help ventilate the dense clouds of ammonia fumes trapped below. After three hours of intense work while wearing the smoke helmets, the members of Rescue 1 were able to completely control the ammonia leak and recover the electrician's body.

The response to hazardous materials problems was becoming almost routine to the members of Rescue 1. Ammonia leaks were a constant challenge and were now being handled with relative ease. The helmets were working as designed, despite the one incident back in April that left Fireman Al Kinsella unconscious briefly. The most critical part of the helmet's construction was the rubber seal around the face. When properly inflated it effectively sealed off the face, preventing leakage of the toxic atmosphere. (This author was told by a fireman who had experience using smoke helmets, that the seal at times squeezed the neck and left the user with a throbbing headache. Learning to control your breathing while working was an important lifesaving lesson.)

As stated in John McElligott's paper to the Annual Convention of the International Association of Fire Chiefs in 1932: "There is, of course, danger of over-confidence; untrained men may go too far, as breathing is unimpaired." This was recognized in Special Order No. 41, issued March 6, 1915, shortly after the formation of Rescue Company No. 1, for therein appears the following caution:

> Chief officers are hereby notified that sound judgement and discretion must at all times be used in directing the operation of this company; they will consult with and furnish all possible information, with regard to the location of the fire, and such other conditions and circumstances as may come to their knowledge, to the officer in charge of the

rescue company, and if after the examination of the premises on fire, or the conditions and surroundings of such fire, the officer of the rescue company is of the opinion that it is unsafe for him and his men to attempt entrance, the chief officer in charge will be guided by such opinion and shall not insist on forcing the company to go into places where, in the judgement of the officer in command of the company, it is extra hazardous or impossible to make headway.

Members of Rescue 1 in front of quarters testing smoke helmets and pulmotor.

Such was the case when just before noon, September 7, 1915, 60 employees working in the general laboratory of the United States Rubber Company at 561 West 58th Street, were driven from the building by leaking toxic gas. The leak was discovered by Dr. Whittleson, chief chemist, when several of the employees began coughing violently. When greenish yellow fumes were seen seeping up from the cellar, Whittleson immediately thought of the 100-gallon steel tank of Sulphur chloride stored in a vault under the sidewalk in front of the building. The building was quickly evacuated, and the fire department was called.

Owen McKernan, chief of the ninth battalion, arrived on scene along with Hook & Ladder 35. They attempted to enter the cellar vault and were driven back by the fumes. *The New York Times* reported:

> A fireman from Hook & Ladder 35 said the gas seemed to grip the lungs with paralyzing force. "In the case of smoke we don't mind, for we can always get fresh air by putting our mouths close to the ground, but that stuff lay like a carpet, and the only way to breathe was to go up near the ceiling, and you know we can't work up there."
>
> Faced with this dangerous situation McKernan special-called Rescue 1. Upon their arrival Lt. Hotchkiss and his men huddled with the chief and the company's chemists. As the plan of operation was drawn up the chemists advised the members of Rescue 1 that the gas was like that being used in the trench war in Europe. They were further warned that the slightest defect in their oxygen supplying system might result in death.
>
> Lt. Hotchkiss requested the street be cleared in the direction the wind was blowing. This order was enforced by police reserves as the members of Rescue 1 donned their helmets, attached themselves to a rope, and entered the gas cloud. With great difficulty the tank was located and moved to a position where it could be raised to the street.
>
> Both vehicular and pedestrian traffic on the street and sidewalks were halted. Under the direction of the chemists, the members of Rescue 1 transferred the deadly gas to another tank and sealed it. It took more than an hour to ventilate the building and allow the workers to return for their belongings.

The old Ninth Mounted Cavalry Building stood at 213-227 West 26th Street, between Seventh and Eighth avenues. The cavernous brick building was purchased in 1914 by the Famous Players Film Company, one of the nation's top silent movie producers, and renovated into a film studio. Other sections of the building were being used by the Corrugated Paper Products Company (basement and first floor), and JW Schuer women's dress company on the second floor. The Independent Braid Company was on the third floor. (The film company also used a portion of the third floor for celluloid film storage.) On the top floor was a film laboratory and theatre, and another film laboratory was located on the second floor. Both labs were stocked with large quantities of chemicals and film stock.

At 7:59 p.m. September 11th, 1915, the night watchman noticed a fire on the third floor and turned in the alarm. FDNY Box 375 was transmitted sending companies under the command of Acting Battalion Chief Lawrence McGuire to the scene. The building was 150-feet wide and ran back 75-feet deep. Heavy smoke and flames were pouring from third-floor windows as firemen began stretching hose and raising ladders.

Sizing up the fire, ABC McGuire saw flames now at the roof level and sent in a second alarm, followed quickly by a third. Rescue 1 arrived and were requested to vent the roof. The smoke condition was so severe they took their axes and smoke helmets and climbed the stairs of the adjoining building, 211 West 26th Street. Ladders were then placed from this roof to the roof of the blazing film studio. They donned their helmets and climbed onto the roof of the fire building and began venting.

Meanwhile, inside the fire building nozzle teams were battling the flames and the dense smoke. The burning celluloid was producing a noxious mixture that was difficult to breathe. Teams were being rotated as the smoke began to take its toll on the men inside. Members of Engine 19 fell unconscious and were dragged outside and revived with pulmotors.

Assistant Chief Joseph B. Martin arrived and transmitted 4th- and 5th-alarms. Smoky Joe then special-called two water towers before venturing inside to get a better look at things.

On the roof conditions were becoming extreme. Members of Rescue 1 broke all the skylight windows. (Huge windows covered sections of the roof allowing natural sunlight into the top floor for filming.) They also opened bulkhead doors and scuttle covers. Suddenly an explosion rocked the building, sending the helmeted rescue men scrambling to escape the sagging roof as flames shot up through the clouds of thick smoke.

All the members of Rescue 1 reached the edge of the roof and their ladders safely when it was believed two men were missing. A team returned to the blazing, sagging roof and searched for the missing men until they were called back as a new head count proved everyone safe. They returned to the street for further assignments. (This was probably the first time in the history of the fire service that roof ventilation was accomplished by firefighters wearing breathing apparatus.)

Operating on the third floor, Lt. Gibney of Hook & Ladder 24 became separated from his men when the explosion occurred. When the members of Hook & Ladder 24 realized their officer was missing Fireman George Hauser directed the other men to move to safety while he returned into the fire area in search of his boss. Hauser was able to locate Gibney who was overcome by the smoke. He dragged him clear just as the roof began collapsing into the fire building. Exhausted, Hauser was able to carry his officer outside where he was resuscitated in the street.

Smoky Joe Martin and a crew of men were working in a separate third floor area when the explosion occurred. Three of the men were overcome but were carried out by the chief and other men.

With flames now shooting more than 100 feet into the air Chief Martin pulled all companies from the blazing structure and set up an exterior attack in hopes of preventing the huge body of fire from spreading to exposed buildings nearby. Twenty-five streams of water were directed into the fire from 26th Street. Two water towers were directed into the blazing top floor, as 25 additional lines were utilized from the adjoining roofs.

The flames and smoke attracted huge crowds that filled the streets and sidewalks nearby. It was estimated as many as 30,000 people watched the blaze. On the corner of 28th Street and Eighth Avenue, companies were utilizing a high-pressure fire hydrant. Standing nearby and watching the action was a 15-year-old boy named Frank Gardener. Suddenly, a high-pressure hose burst and struck the boy, catapulting him through the air and directly into a brick wall.

Two women doctors from Bellevue Hospital, Dr. Geraldine Watson and Dr. Annie Thomsen, who were also watching the fire, saw the accident occur, and immediately began rendering first aid to the injured youngster.

Meanwhile, two blocks away on 26th Street and Eighth Avenue, Engineer of Steamer William Fredericks of Engine 21, was struck by another high-pressure hose burst. Struck in the abdomen, and hurled through an iron railing, Fredericks suffered several injuries including a fractured skull. He too was quickly tended to. Both were rushed to the hospital. The two lady doctors then joined with Dr. Harry Archer and members of Rescue 1, reviving unconscious firemen with the pulmotors.

This five-alarm fire stopped street cars and other traffic for more than four hours.

The City of New York was growing in leaps and bounds in 1915, as skyscrapers continued to soar above, and subways were being extended below. As part of the extension of the IRT Broadway–Seventh Avenue Line, a subway line was being constructed on the west side of Manhattan that would run between South Ferry in lower Manhattan and run north to Van Cortland Park–242nd Street in the Riverdale section of the Bronx. This construction was being accomplished in two portions. The first part was the completion of the line that ran north from 42nd Street, up 7th Avenue and Broadway. This part then split into the Broadway Branch and the Lenox Avenue Line. This section was opened to the riding public in 1904 and 1908.

The second part of the line running south from 42nd Street was part of what was known as the "Dual Contracts," which were signed between the IRT (Interborough Rapid Transit Company,) the New York Municipal Railway (a subsidiary of the Brooklyn Rapid Transit Company,) and the City of New York. This new service would extend down Manhattan's west side into lower Manhattan and on into Brooklyn.

The method of construction being used on this portion of the subway was known as "Cut and Cover." This oldest method of tunneling involved digging a trench, constructing a tunnel, and then returning the surface to its original state. This was obviously disruptive to the street traffic, businesses, and tenants living along the work zone, but was economical and relatively quick.

After the street was opened and work began, a temporary cover was constructed using heavy wooden planks on top of wooden beams. This allowed the street and sidewalk traffic to resume. Even temporary trolley car rails were installed as the tunnel was completed below.

Sadly, this was also a time of bombs in New York City. Anarchists, the organized crime group known as the Black Hand, and others were using bombs to send messages and to intimidate the public. The Black Hand were immigrant Italian gangsters, that used bombs to extort money. The anarchists were using bombs to initiate political change that would abolish the government, which they felt was both harmful and unnecessary.

In July of 1914, an explosion occurred in a brownstone building on the upper east side where bombs were being built. This blast killed several members of a group intent on bombing the wealthy businessman J.D. Rockefeller. Bombs were also detonated in Saint Patrick's Cathedral on Fifth Avenue and Saint Alphonso's Church on West Broadway, on October 13, 1914. These actions of course were addressed by the NYPD. But, the FDNY also had a serious interest in these bombings since they responded to the damage and chaos that was left.

It was 8:31 a.m. on September 22nd when a dynamite explosion tore through the subway construction site at Seventh Avenue and 25th Street. The blast caused nearly two blocks of the temporary wooden roadway to drop 35-feet into the long trench below. The construction at the point of the accident was being done by the United States Realty and Improvement Company. The excavation work was almost completed in this area and much of the timber shoring had been removed to allow the placement of iron work.

During the night two holes were bored and the explosives placed ready for the following workday. Signal men with red flags were in place on 21st Street as the 8 o'clock hour approached. After the first blast, the traffic was allowed to flow. It was unclear if the flagmen knew there were to be two blasts.

The second blast rocked the entire neighborhood causing the nearby shoring to collapse. This placed strain on other sections and allowed the planking and supports to sink into the excavation. Pedestrians on the sidewalk, trucks and other vehicles dropped into the huge hole. A northbound streetcar with eight passengers aboard was approaching the intersection when the blast occurred. The temporary wooden roadway sank along with the tracks, creating a chute that increased the car's speed. The plummeting vehicle gained momentum until it crashed into the tangled debris below.

Stunned onlookers immediately pulled the fire alarm box and telephoned nearby hospitals requesting ambulances. Arriving with the first due units was Acting Battalion Chief Lawrence McGuire (the first due chief at the huge Famous Players Film Studio fire 11 days earlier). Before him was a giant open pit filled with mangled vehicles, and twisted debris. Water from broken mains poured into the 35-foot-deep fissure as the cries of the injured drifted up from the dust-covered wreckage below. McGuire immediately transmitted a second alarm.

The first reports from workers who'd escaped the collapse, indicated there were as many as 85 workers pinned in the wreckage. Without waiting for ladders many firemen climbed down into the trench following the cries for help. The bottom of the trench was now a huge mass of heavy splintered and broken timbers and twisted steel girders. Long ladders were rushed into position and lowered down into the hole. As soon as the ladders were stabilized, firemen began carrying the injured up. Others were brought to an impromptu aid station set up at the bottom of the excavation, on the West 25th Street side, near the spot firemen were digging out trapped victims.

Within two minutes of the initial collapse a Consolidated Gas Company emergency crew had shut off the broken 8-inch gas main. Water from the high-pressure fire mains was also quickly controlled.

Rescue 1 arrived, carried their torch and special tools down into the trench and began cutting away twisted metal. Victim after victim was freed and carefully carried to safe locations, before being brought to street level.

In the street above, Chief Kenlon arrived and was immediately surrounded by businessmen from the neighborhood. The chief summoned the construction foreman Thomas Marshall. At first, Marshall denied there had even been a blast. Then he said there were no sticks of loose dynamite, and that all the explosives were in a powder box further up the street.

Chief McGuire stepped forward, "That's not so!" he said extending his hand, "Here are twelve sticks of dynamite found down there by one of my men."

Marshall refused to say another word. Kenlon now realized his men were swinging picks and cutting with torches near loose sticks of dynamite. The rescue work continued despite the multiple dangers around them.

Firemen clearing debris on the west side of the trench near 25th Street, heard a voice under their feet, at around 9:30. Tearing away timbers and stones they located the head of a man pinned down by a great mass of debris. The trapped man was conscious, but unable to speak English. Chief Kenlon was called over and took personal charge of this rescue. For nearly a half hour, firemen worked by hand to uncover him. The man was suffering serious crush injuries to his left arm and leg. A temporary stretcher was rigged, and the man was carefully carried up one of the long ladders.

As each recued person reached the street, a doctor directed them toward additional medical help, a trip to the hospital or to a temporary morgue on the 24th Street sidewalk, where a line of sheet-covered bodies was growing. In all seven persons lost their lives and dozens were seriously injured in this accident.

On October 5, 1915, Rescue 1 was special-called to 119 Mercer Street, where companies were battling a particularly smoky cellar fire in the Universal Folding Box Company. Capt. McElligott, Lt. Hotchkiss, Firemen Blessing, Dorritie, Kinsella, O'Leary and Ryan operated a line in the cellar and vented cellar windows.

December 8, 1915, saw Rescue 1 respond to a most unusual and potentially deadly fire at the Manhattan Refrigerating Company at 100 Gansevoort Street also known as 527 West Street. It was 1:20 a.m. when FDNY companies arrived at the cold storage facility and were faced with a thick smoke condition that proved to be impenetrable. Barrels of spinach and garlic were burning in the cellar of the cold storage compartments. Firemen arrived, but could not breathe the smoke and their extinguishing efforts came to a standstill. Faced with the fire possibly extending to nearby ammonia refrigeration units, Rescue 1 was special-called. Capt. McElligott, Lt. Hotchkiss and their crew of firemen including Frank Blessing, William Dorritie, Al Kinsella, Walter O'Leary, John Ryan, and James Shaw went to work at the scene.

Several members donned smoke helmets and moved in to operate. In keeping with the company's policy of using a signal rope on helmeted firemen, Jim Shaw, without breathing protection, was holding the signal rope a distance away from the smoke-filled compartment. As the helmeted rescue men chopped a vent hole in the top of the compartment, the cold smoke rolled out and began filling the surrounding area. In a matter of seconds Shaw dropped to the floor unconscious, as his body went into spasms.

Helmeted rescue men grabbed him and rushed into clear air where a pulmotor was used to resuscitate him. Shaw was taken back to quarters by automobile, still suffering from his close call.

The remainder of the company extinguished the small fire and vented the building all while wearing smoke helmets. Once again, the dangers of the places the Rescue company was now routinely working in were shown. They were learning this new craft as they worked.

What was described as "the smokiest fire in several months," happened on December 27, 1915, when fire companies responded to a cellar fire under a saloon at 67 West 23rd Street. First due units found it impossible to operate in the dense smoke in a cellar filled with boxes of liquor and tightly packed excelsior. Special-called for their smoke helmets Rescue 1 arrived quickly.

Chief John Kenlon, Assistant Chief Smoky Joe Martin, and Fire Commissioner Robert Adamson met with Captain John McElligott and his men—Firemen Frank Blessing, Al Kinsella, Walter O'Leary, Frank Clark and John Ryan—outside the chimney-like bar. They agreed the smoke condition was so dangerous that each rescue man entering the building would be wearing a smoke helmet and would be attached to a rope before entering the cellar. With zero visibility the team was able locate and extinguish the fire in only a few minutes. Ventilation and overhaul would take a bit longer.

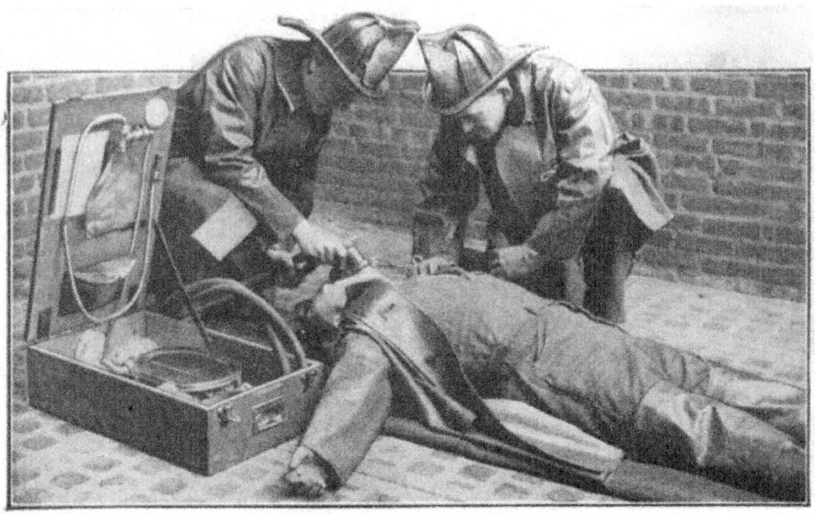

Rescue 1 members utilizing a pulmotor demonstrate reviving an unconscious fireman.

As Rescue Company 1's first calendar year ended, their record of service was impressive. They'd responded to 86 alarms and worked at fires, explosions, ammonia and gas leaks, a ship fire, and a major construction accident. The new Rescue company had captured the imagination of the newspapers of New York City. They were often referred to as the "Smoke Squad" or "Smoke Eaters." But mostly they were referred to as the Rescue Squad, and their exploits were becoming legendary. In truth, they were working in uncharted territory when it came to rescue work and hazardous material incidents. They were now routinely venturing into and working in deadly environments, including scalding atmospheres filled with toxic, poisonous and even explosive vapors. They were writing and then rewriting the book with each response.

SEVENTY-FIRST YEAR

SCIENTIFIC AMERICAN

THE WEEKLY JOURNAL OF PRACTICAL INFORMATION

VOLUME CXII. NUMBER 13. NEW YORK, MARCH 27, 1915 10 CENTS A COPY $3.00 A YEAR

Rescue Company No. 1 of the New York Fire Department

THERE is nothing a fireman dreads so much as a smoky fire, and when that smoke contains choking fumes and poisonous gases his task is hazardous in the extreme. Nevertheless he must penetrate that smoke to its source, regardless of personal danger. Time and time again have the firemen of New York city risked their lives in fires of this kind, bravely rushing into veritable death traps, struggling until overcome, then being dragged out in the nick of time by their companions; and sometimes they have not been dragged out in time.

Although such conditions have existed for a long time, and the work of mine rescue squads has pointed out the value of smoke helmets in just such conditions, it was not until after the subway fire last January that any definite action was taken. At that time, it will be recalled, hundreds of passengers stalled in the subway were overcome by the fumes of burning insulation, and the firemen had no end of difficulty in dragging them out. The SCIENTIFIC AMERICAN then pointed out the urgency of having a rescue squad of firemen equipped with smoke helmets. Immediately after the fire, with commendable promptness, such a company was organized.

The air regenerating apparatus.

Tests were made of six or seven varieties of smoke helmets in order to determine the best for firemen's use. Finally the one shown in the accompanying illustrations was adopted with a slight modification at a point which was thought to show a slight weakness, and ten helmets of this type were bought. The manufacturers claimed that this helmet with its oxygen tank and regenerator would keep a man supplied with fresh oxygen at the rate of two liters (about two quarts) per minute for an hour. At the end of that time a gage, known as the "finimeter," would register zero, but there would be still enough oxygen in the tank to keep a man supplied at the same rate for twenty minutes more. In order to make sure of this, Capt. John J. McElligott, in charge of the rescue company, decided to try out the helmet under extreme conditions. At the Firemen's College there is a concrete room, twenty feet square, where sprinklers are tested. Into this room a quantity of smoke-making fuel was put, consisting of excelsior, straw, oakum, rubbish of all kinds, and sulphur. This was set afire and it produced dense volumes of smoke and intense heat. Into this inferno Capt. McElligott went equipped with his smoke helmet, and the door was closed behind him. The firemen found it difficult to close the door at first because of the outflow produced by expansion of the air in the room. The helmet was equipped with a telephone, by which Capt. McElligott could communicate with the outside. He had with him a thermometer registering up to 300 degrees, and he found that the temperature rose quickly to 280 deg. Fahr. Despite this intense heat, he remained in the room watching the index pointer of the finimeter gradually swing down to zero, when his watch showed him that he had been in an hour, and then he remained fifteen minutes more—seventy-five minutes altogether in a temperature which, for at least three quarters of an hour, was up to 280 deg. Fahr. At the end of that time he emerged thoroughly exhausted, streaming perspiration, with the sweat slushing in his shoes at every step. His clothes were rotted by the action of the fumes, and his hands were so blackened that it was impossible to wash them white again. The discoloration did not wear off for weeks.

It is astonishing what an intense heat one is able to stand in dry air. Water at a temperature of 130 degrees would scald a person. In a Turkish bath the temperature may go up to 200 degrees. But 80 degrees above that is decidedly uncomfortable, to say the least, and it is really remarkable that anyone should have been able to stand it for an hour and a quarter. Capt. McElligott states that it was very distressing, but that he experienced no scalding effect except at one time when a drop of water, which evidently had condensed upon the ceiling, splashed down on the leather flap of his helmet and burned right through to his neck.

This kind of helmet apparatus has been described in the SCIENTIFIC AMERICAN before, but a brief explanation of its operation may not be amiss. From the helmet there are two tubes leading down to a pair of "breathing bags" that rest on the breast of the wearer. One of these bags takes the surplus inspiratory air and the other the surplus expiratory air. The air that is exhaled passes from the breathing bag to the back of the wearer, where it is forced through a regenerator consisting of a receptacle containing caustic potash. The caustic potash removes the carbon dioxide. The regenerator is shown at the left in the rear view of the apparatus. At the right is the tank in which oxygen is kept at a pressure of about 1,800 pounds per square inch. This passes through a reducing valve so that it will flow out at the rate of two liters per minute, and passing through an injector serves to force the exhaled air through the regenerator. As some heat is produced in the regenerator, the air mixed with fresh oxygen passes through a cooler before making its way to the inspiratory breathing bag. Thence it is inhaled through the tube shown at the left hand in the front view of the helmets. In order to make an effective seal of the helmet, it is provided with a soft rubber tube which is inflated to fit snugly around the face, and this is pumped up by means of the small bulb pump which may be seen hanging from the face plate of the helmet. On the opposite side of the face plate is a small projection, which is the handle of a sponge mop with which the fireman may wipe the perspiration out of his eyes or brush away any irritation. This is a feature that is very much appreciated. Divers who have no such means of relieving itching or irritations of the face, frequently suffer untold agony.

For nearly two months eight men besides Capt. McElligott and his lieutenant have been practising with this apparatus and also with pulmotors and a Blaugas-oxygen torch, and on March 8th they were established as Rescue Company No. 1. They have a motorcar fitted with the Blaugas torch apparatus, two pulmotors, stretchers, smoke helmets, and additional cylinders of oxygen for the pulmotors and the helmets, besides the customary life-gun, fire-extinguishers, axes, etc. They respond to every two-alarm fire south of Fifty-ninth Street and to three-alarm fires as far as 125th Street. Already they have shown themselves invaluable. At a recent fire in a building extending from Greene to Mercer streets, the fire was at one end of the building and the entrance at the other. This meant that the firemen would have to grope through two hundred feet of black smoke before reaching the fire. Ordinarily this would have meant the suffocation of many of the men, but the helmeted men went to the front without the slightest difficulty and located the blaze.

As yet the torch has not been put to any service, but it is provided for occasions where armored doors are encountered which resist the battering of axes. With the torch the locks can be cut out with practically no delay. In a test of this apparatus a bar of steel four inches square, in cross-section, was cut through in 67 seconds. The apparatus carried by the company has a capacity of fifty-six 1-inch cuts. It will be recalled that when the Equitable Building burned down a number of men were trapped in the basement behind windows guarded by thick iron bars. The firemen exerted almost superhuman efforts in endeavoring to cut through these bars. Had the Rescue Company been in existence then, the bars could have been burned through in a couple of minutes and the lives [illegible] saved.

Members of the first rescue company of the New York Fire Department.

Chapter 4:
1916

With 1915 under their belts, the members of Rescue 1 were encouraged with the addition of 33 first alarm response assignments. This would mean more fire duty and their quicker response to some of the city's most difficult fires. Rescue 1 was now routinely assigned to fire duty in the most hazardous area of the city, the manufacturing center and dry goods district of lower Manhattan. The new response area was within the area between Fifth Avenue and Broadway, from 17th Street to Canal Street, taking in also the district bounded by West Broadway, Lafayette Street, 8th Street, and Canal Street. This basically was the section of the city that became known in the FDNY as Hell's Hundred Acres.

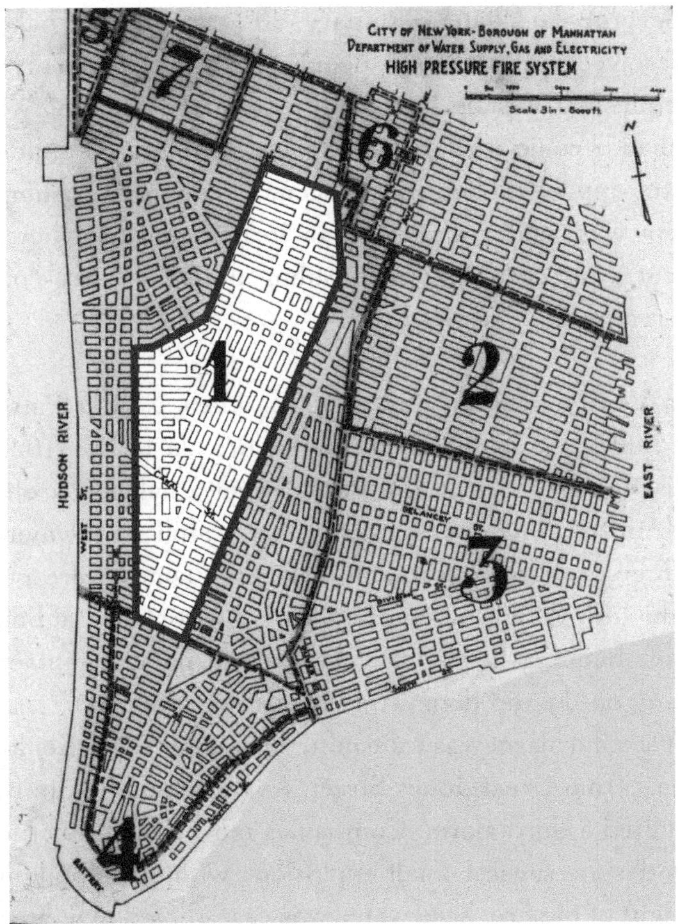

Area of additional first alarm assignments for Rescue 1

The new year started off in unusual fashion as a citizen ran up to the Great Jones Street firehouse on January 12th and requested Rescue 1 respond to a tenement building two doors away, where a man had attempted suicide using a gas stove. The lifeless body was on the floor as the members of Rescue 1 rushed into the apartment. They were told an ambulance had been called but had yet to arrive. The crew immediately began using the pulmotor to resuscitate the man. Their efforts paid off, as the man began breathing again.

Several days later, January 20th, another verbal alarm was received when excited people arrived at company quarters requesting Rescue 1 respond to a nearby building where a horse had become stuck between a wall and an iron railing. The company quickly rolled to the scene. Calming the animal, the problem was sized up and a plan formulated. Members carefully cut away sections of the railing until the horse could be safely removed.

It was 12:12 a.m. February 6, 1916, when NYPD Patrolman Cahill pulled the handle of the street fire alarm Box 102. He'd just discovered a fire at 438 Pearl Street a half block off Park Row. Approaching the scene Officer Cahill was waving the firefighters toward a spectacular sight; Flames were pouring from the fifth-floor windows of a six-story commercial building. This loft building housed a chemical and paint manufacturing company on the top floor—the floor above the fire.

A second alarm was transmitted bringing Chief Kenlon and Rescue 1 from Great Jones Street. As the attack began, Kenlon transmitted a third alarm. Companies moved in and battled the flames despite several small explosions within the building. At the height of the fire, hose water was cascading down into lower floor occupancies, members of the Fire Patrol were busy throwing tarps over valuables.

In the cellar, Fire Patrol Engineer Barney Miles was trying to relieve the buildup of water. After a few minutes Miles began to feel he was being overcome by the dense smoke. Unable to fight his way back through the thick clouds of smoke he retreated to the rear of the building in search of a window. Unfortunately, the window was covered with 14-inch steel bars. Miles was trapped and began calling for help.

Members drilling with cutting torch.

Members of Rescue 1 became aware of Miles' plight and under the command of Captain McElligott, moved into position with their torch. The blue flame of the torch began cutting through the thick bars as Engineer Miles sunk to the floor unconscious. In just a few moments, the last piece of steel was cleared, allowing members of Rescue 1 to enter the cellar and pull Miles to safety.

Resuscitation efforts began immediately. Rescue men worked their pulmotor until the unconscious man began to stir. Their efforts were successful and Miles made a complete recovery. The members working this job were: Capt. McElligott, Firemen Walter O'Leary, John P. Ryan, James Shaw, Al Kinsella, Frank Blessing, and William Dorritie. This rescue operation was the exact thing the department was unable to complete only a few years earlier at the Equitable fire. Rescue 1's extensive training and hard work were paying off!

Another unique emergency occurred on February 16th during the evening rush hour. Harry Hauer, a 30-year-old furrier, was crossing Broadway between 23rd and 24th streets when two "hobble skirt" street cars (trams with center door openings only eight inches from the street level that allowed women wearing fashionably long tight skirts to board the cars with ease) were approaching from opposite directions. Both cars reached him at the same time, pinning him between the cars.

Shrieking passengers alerted nearby police officers, who tried in vain to free the trapped man. Within moments of Hauer's first scream, 10,000 persons pressed close to watch the rescue. Eventually the fire department was notified. Hook & Ladder 24 arrived along with Deputy Chief Joseph Martin. A member of 24 Truck was lowered between the cars but was unable to free the man. An ambulance surgeon, Dr. Adair, then squeezed in and examined the trapped man, and administered pain medicine as Smoky Joe special-called Rescue 1.

"Hobble skirt" streetcar with very low center doors

Rescue 1's torches were brought in and used to cut away one of the car's window bars. Jacks were then positioned to force the cars away from each other. Ropes were dropped from the roofs of the cars and made fast about the pinned man. He was pulled up to the top of the car, then lowered to the street and medical care.

Hauer was said to have a fractured shoulder and was suffering from shock and possible internal injuries. He was taken to New York Hospital.

Later that day Rescue 1 responded to 88 Stanton Street, the Egg Cold Storage Company where ammonia pipes had broken in the cellar. Members using smoke helmets were able to enter the cellar, locate, and control the leak.

As the one-year anniversary of Rescue 1's organization grew near, *The New York Times* ran a large story in their March 5, 1916, issue. Under the headline: "First Year's Record of The Fire Department's Rescue Squad," the story chronicled the work of the new specially trained and equipped company. "During the year the squad 'worked' at many fires and gas and acid explosions, and not only saved lives but reduced the loss because it was able to get up close to the seat of the blaze."

The story also recounted the rescue of Fire Patrol Engineer Barney Myles, Rescue 1's work at ammonia fires, and leaks including the ones at Ruppert's Brewery. Their operational tactics, such as working in pairs and using a signal rope, were also explained. The testing of five or six different smoke helmets under extreme conditions at the Firemen's College was also featured. "The record which this picturesque body of 12 masked firefighters has made in the first year of its existence has swept away the last vestige of skepticism which existed in the minds of conservative old-timers."

On March 11th Rescue 1 responded to a second alarm at

Manhattan Box 518 for a smoky fire in the basement of the Hotel Gerard at 123 West 44th Street. The fire broke out at 6:30 in the morning and threw the 300 hotel guests into a panic. Twenty-five people, including a dozen children, were marooned on the roof for a while.

The fire that had begun in the kitchen quickly spread to a storeroom as the thick smoke made its way to the elevator shaft and soon filled the building. The flames also melted the elevator wiring, leaving it out of service. Guests had to use the stairs within the 13-story building.

Rescue 1 arrived and were sent by Deputy Chief Martin to find the seat of the fire in the cellar. Wearing their smoke helmets, they pressed the attack with a 2-½-inch hose and soon extinguished the flames. They also conducted searches on the floors that were heavily charged with smoke and helped evacuate many guests. While operating in the cellar Fireman Frank Clark of Rescue 1 was struck in the head and was taken to Polyclinic Hospital for treatment.

Fireman James Shaw holding tending line while wearing back up Draeger helmet 1916.

On March 20th at 4:32 p.m., Rescue 1 responded to an emergency at 12 Bond Street where a man named Albert Brandt was trapped between the elevator and the flooring. Members of Rescue 1 supported the man and provided oxygen, while using the acetylene torch to cut away metal sections of the elevator frame to free the trapped man.

Rescue 1 drilling with torch on elevator entrapments. Note the extinguisher.

Alarm bells rang March 21st at 3:54 a.m. sending Rescue 1 to 76 Pine Street, the laboratory of the Bielfoil Chemical Works. The owner of the company was making phosphorous trichloride, but was unable to control escaping chlorine gas as tubing of his apparatus became disconnected. The lab filled with the toxic gas and a fire started. Members of Rescue 1 wearing smoke helmets were able to control the leak and carry the defective apparatus outside.

March 29 10:50 p.m., 425-435 Eleventh Avenue Rescue 1 wore their helmets again to repair leaking ammonia pipes. They closed valves supplying the system.

Rescue 1 worked a small but smoky fire on March 22 at 7:34 a.m., 443 Greenwich Street. The company extinguished the fire on the third floor and vented the area.

On March 29 at 10:50 p.m. Rescue 1 responded to an ammonia leak at 425 Eleventh Avenue. They were able to shut off the supply valves and stop the leak.

Four alarms were transmitted for a fire in two old five-story buildings at 16 and 18 Beekman Street. The alarm was transmitted from Box 42 at 1:58 p.m. April 3, 1916, when flames were seen coming from the third-floor window of a paper warehouse. Within minutes, flames were raging from the top four floors of both buildings and extending to other nearby buildings.

Engine 32 arrived first due, and the radiant heat was so intense chauffeur Fireman William Plandon found his seat on fire a minute after stopping near the fire building. He burned his hand and arm beating out the flames before moving the rig. Rescue 1 arrived shortly after the second alarm and joined in stretching hose and protecting exposures. To make matters even more complicated, the street in front of the fire was being excavated for the new Beekman Street subway.

On April 5, 1916, a patrolman walking his beat near St. Patrick's Cathedral noticed the front of the church was illuminated by flames coming from the fifth-floor windows of the Clews Building across the street at 630 Fifth Avenue. The top four floors of the building had recently been renovated to convert the private home of Henry Clews, a prominent banker, to commercial property. This high-end shop now contained more than $2 million in jewelry, gowns, millinery, and art. The fire was rapidly extending to the floor above just as the alarm was being transmitted.

Manhattan Box 530 was received at 8:01 p.m. Lt. Moge of Engine 8 transmitted a second alarm upon arrival. Companies quickly stretched lines to the fourth floor but were driven back by thick smoke and extreme heat. A water tower was quickly positioned in hopes of knocking down some of the extreme heat on the fifth and sixth floors. Four alarms were transmitted bringing Chief Kenlon to the scene.

The steps of the cathedral provided an excellent vantage point and a huge crowd, many drawn from the nearby theatre district, assembled to watch the firemen battle the flames.

When hose lines were repositioned and ready to press the attack, the water tower was shut down. The firemen moved in but were quickly met by a wall of advancing flames pressed forward from the rear sections of the fire floors not reached by the earlier water tower streams. The building flames were again pushed back by the attack teams. Fireman J.J. Hamilton of Engine 8 was overcome by the dense smoke and was rescued by his officer, Lt. Moge.

When Lt. Moge appeared with the unconscious man over his shoulder the crowd cheered his efforts. As conditions deteriorated, the water tower was again operated. Lines were stretched to numerous vantage points and directed into the billowing flames. Rescue 1 was among the many companies taking turns on the nozzle until the flames were finally controlled after a one-hour fight.

The following night Box 102 was received at 4:57 a.m. for a fire at 21 Roosevelt Street, a six-story multiple dwelling in the heart of the downtown tenement district. Flames were pouring from the second-floor windows as Engine 12 pulled in.

Captain Kivenny led seven of his men to the top of the stairs with an attack line, only to be blown back down the stairs by a backdraft.

A second and third alarms brought Chief Kenlon and Rescue 1 to the scene. Kenlon ordered an exterior attack and Rescue 1 stretched and operated a line into the blazing building.

It was a few minutes after 6 p.m. on April 13, 1916, when Manhattan Box 238 was transmitted for a fire at 558 Broadway, between Spring and Prince streets. Most of the building was occupied by Schmickl & Company, manufacturers of travelling bags. When Engine Company 13 arrived first due, heavy smoke was pouring from the windows, but the flames seemed limited to the second floor in the rear.

With Battalion Chief Henry Helm in the lead, 16 firemen stretched a hose to the fire floor and began putting water on the fire. Suddenly, a backdraft toppled them all down the stairs. As Captain McKenna fell, his nozzle broke the glass window, showering him in glass and cutting his face. Captain Alonzo O'Brien and Fireman James Hughes of Engine 20 were also injured by the blast and the fall. Fireman Reynolds of Engine 55 was also cut by flying glass.

The backdraft pushed the flames throughout the building and a second alarm was transmitted bringing Rescue 1 as part of the assignment. Reinforcements arrived and saw nearly every window was filled with flames. The fire took two hours to control and tied up traffic, including the street cars on lower Broadway.

Rescue 1 was called once again to 76 Pine Street near Pearl Street for another chemical fire. It was 9:54 a.m. on April 29, 1916, when fire companies responded to the scene and quickly stretched a line and extinguished a small fire in the second-floor laboratory of Niagara Chemical. Water from the line apparently reacted with chemicals and immediately generated clouds of noxious gas that drove the few remaining tenants from the building.

Chemists from various neighboring companies gathered and began brainstorming. They informed and overwhelmed the chiefs on scene with chemical facts and conjectures. It was quickly decided Rescue 1 was needed. They arrived promptly and were briefed on the situation. They split into an inside team and an outside team, with the inside members donning helmets and attaching themselves to a rope that was tended by members outside ready to come to their aid if necessary.

The members of Rescue 1 were very familiar with the building, having worked a similar chemical job a month earlier. They carefully removed bottles of phosphorous trichloride to the street. Then continued removing other bottles, carboys, barrels and other containers filled with chemicals of all kinds. The dangerous products were cleared from the building and gone over one by one with the chemists and rendered safe or were disposed of.

The FDNY Annual Report for the year 1915 was published and distributed on May 1, 1916. The 170-page book featured a cover photograph of Rescue 1, and contained a six-page report, with additional photographs of the company at work. This new branch of the fire service had captured the imagination of the public and fire departments across the nation. Newspaper and magazine articles chronicled their exploits during their first year of existence, including *Fire Engineering* and *Scientific American*. This helped departments across the nation to establish their own rescue companies. Meanwhile, Rescue 1 continued responding, and writing the book on rescue work with each new job they faced.

1915 Annual Report with Al Dreyfous photo of Rescue 1 on cover.

Every fireman enjoys the challenge of stopping a difficult fire. The members of Rescue 1 were also getting used to operating at hazardous materials jobs, as a major part of their responsibilities. Another specialty they were developing was pure rescue work—emergencies where people got themselves trapped in places not normally designed for people to be. A case in point was the May 10, 1916, 5:10 p.m. response to 82 Beaver Street for a young man wedged between an elevator and a shaft wall.

Joseph Dinsenbacher was a 15-year-old errand boy working for Breuer & Son, on the fifth-floor of the 14-story building. Young Joe was the only passenger on an elevator being operated by Joseph Raddigan. It was a few minutes before 5 p.m., when the elevator started up toward the fifth-floor offices. The car stopped at the floor and Raddigan opened the door. Just as young Joe was stepping out of the elevator the car shot upwards. Joe leaned back as the floor struck him. The car travelled briefly before coming to a halt with Dinsenbacher's legs wedged between the wall and the elevator, his face and body were facing forward at the sixth-floor landing. The elevator boy's shouts brought help, and the fire department was called. Arriving at the scene Hook & Ladder 15 attempted to free the boy but realized special tools were needed.

Rescue 1 arrived and within minutes had their oxyacetylene torch set up. After a few tentative cuts were made, dropping sparks ignited a small rubbish fire in the base of the elevator shaft. The fire was quickly doused, and a small line was brought near the cutting operation to cool the metal touching the young man's skin.

For a half hour the men of Rescue 1 carefully cut and pried at the elevator's metal frame, while supporting the trapped youngster. An ambulance arrived and the doctor was brought in to examine the boy. Dr. Patisky held the lad's hand and occasionally rubbed a cocaine solution on the boy's legs to deaden the pain.

The last cuts were made at half-past six and the boy was carefully lifted clear. He had not uttered a cry or moan during the entire operation. At first it was feared he might lose one of his legs, but closer exams at Volunteer Hospital later revealed a fractured femur and ankle. He was expected to make a full recovery.

Three alarms were transmitted for a difficult fire in a four-story brick building at 546-548 West 57th Street in Manhattan at 11:12 p.m. on May 31, 1916. Engine 23 arrived first and smashed in the doors of Brown's Steam Laundry, which occupied the first floor. Thick black smoke rolled out across the sidewalk as the men pushed a hose inside. Within minutes firemen began dropping unconscious, overcome by the thick gas-laced smoke.

A second alarm was transmitted bringing Rescue 1 to the scene. A field hospital was set up on the sidewalk and ambulance doctors joined the members of Rescue 1 as resuscitation efforts began in earnest. Pulmotors were used on 18 unconscious firemen. Thankfully all were revived and returned to duty.

One of Rescue 1's original members, Fireman John F. Mooney left the company on June 16, 1916, when he was transferred to Hook & Ladder 137 in Queens. He served there briefly before retiring. Taking his place in Rescue 1 was Fireman John W. Donohue who crossed the floor from Engine 33. Donohue who'd received the Wertheim Medal in 1915, was the third member of Engine 33 to be assigned to Rescue 1.

A powerful thunderstorm rolled across the city on the afternoon of June 17, 1916. Heavy rainfall, strong winds and lightning left a path of destruction across the city including downed electrical wires. Lightning struck the corner of the roof of a five-story factory building at 637 West 55th Street, between Eleventh and Twelfth Avenues, igniting a fire. One employee working on the top floor was burned by the lightning flash. As the injured man was being tended to, the lightning-sparked flames were quickly spreading. Within minutes all the employees of Schloss Brothers, manufacturers of furniture and cabinets, were driven from the building as smoke and fire took hold of the top two floors.

The FDNY received Box 551 at 4:01 p.m. and were on

scene in a matter of minutes. Seeing that the rapidly spreading flames were threatening a nearby lumber yard, Deputy Chief Smoky Joe Martin transmitted a second alarm. Rescue 1 responded with the second alarm companies and went to work attempting to control the expanding fire. A third alarm was needed to hold the fire to the top three stories of the building.

It was nearing 7 p.m. on June 29, 1916, when several people sitting near the open exit doors of the Fox City Theatre on East 14th Street, saw smoke drifting by in the alley between the theatre and the six-story commercial building next door. Approaching the doors, they immediately felt the heat from flames blazing on the second floor of the building across the alley. The alarm of fire was quickly raised, and the theatre was emptied without incident. The FDNY was simultaneously summoned by the transmission of automatic alarm Box 343. Under the command of Deputy Chief Langford, the arriving companies found fire on every floor and a second alarm was transmitted.

As nozzle teams moved in on the blazing floors, others stretched lines up the theater's fire escape to be ready to use that elevated vantage point to attack the fire. Inside the commercial building, firemen were battling the advanced fire condition and had to contend with a thick noxious smoke. One by one men operating on different floors were being overcome by the dense smoke. The members of Rescue 1 moved in to search for the unconscious firemen.

Fireman Frank Blessing appeared holding Fireman George Heckel in his arms. He carefully placed the unconscious man on the sidewalk and returned for others. Rescue 1 members made several trips into the thick smoke and returned each time with another unconscious fireman. The sidewalk was filled with them. A young woman dressed in evening clothes stepped forward and offered her services to the ambulance doctor and members of Rescue 1 manning the pulmotors. She was Miss Margaret Clarke of Worcester, Massachusetts, a medical doctor.

The last of the firemen rendered unconscious was Captain John McElligott of Rescue 1, who'd made repeated trips into the smoke. Capt. McElligott and most of the firemen were placed on full duty. Firemen James Burke, George Heckel and John Johnsson, however, were transported to the hospital for additional treatment; they, too, would soon return to work.

On July 6, 1916, Special Order No. 123 announced that effective July 7th Fireman James Shaw of Rescue Company 1 was promoted to the rank of Engineer of Steamer and assigned to Engine Company 21. The same order transferred Fireman James Smith from Engine Co. 74 to Rescue 1. Smith, who lived at 351 Amsterdam Avenue, just around the corner from Engine 74, was a United States Navy veteran who was awarded the Medal of Honor for his heroic actions during the Boxer Rebellion in China in 1900. He left the navy in 1902 and was an iron worker before joining the FDNY on May 4, 1906.

The city was suffering through some extremely hot weather on July 13, 1916, and afternoon temperatures were expected to be in the 90s for the second day in a row. At about 10:15, an explosion shook Martin Schmidt's butcher store at 422 Sumner Avenue in Brooklyn, just as a trolley car stopped out front. Moments later a second more powerful explosion tore the four-story brick building apart. Formerly a private home, the building on the northeast corner of Sumner and Macon streets had been converted into a store on the ground floor. An ammonia refrigeration plant was in the rear of the cellar and had a 12-pound tank of liquid ammonia under 700 pounds of pressure when the explosion occurred.

"I heard an ear-splitting roar like the report of a great

cannon," said Mrs. Margaret Hehn who was standing on the opposite side of the street. "The whole building rose in the air while the ground beneath me trembled. The house across the street seemed to stand still for just a second, then it dropped again before the echo of the explosion was gone and as it dropped back it fell to pieces."

The mass of wreckage was partially hidden by a cloud of dust. The muffled silence gave way to the screams of the injured within the trolley car. Sharp edged shards of wood, bricks and glass had knifed through the air riddling the trolley like buckshot. Neighboring windows along the street were also shattered. Eight persons riding in the car were injured. One rider named Mr. Gerber stated: "I was standing in the car as we came to the corner. I heard a terrific roar. The next thing I knew some people were picking me up on the other side of the street." He'd been blown right through a car window.

Fireman Alfred Kelly of Engine Company 246 had just turned the corner a block away when the explosion occurred. Kelly dashed to the fire alarm box and pulled the lever. As fire companies responded, Kelly joined some civilians who were attempting to push the stopped trolley car out of the cloud of ammonia fumes that had settled across the scene.

Within moments Battalion Chiefs O'Hara and Goodison, Hook & Ladder Companies 111 and 132, along with Engines 214, 217, 235 and 234, were on scene. Due to the warm day, firemen tossed their coats aside as they plunged into the wreckage. Working their way through the mangled debris, they were forced back by the waves of ammonia fumes that seemed to bubble up from the wreckage. Realizing it was nearly impossible for his men to work in the ammonia cloud, Deputy Chief Lally special-called Rescue 1 to the scene.

As Rescue 1 was responding from Manhattan, Brooklyn Rapid Transit company sent a wrecker to the scene. Firemen holding their breaths would dive into the debris and sling a beam with a rope. The wrecker then pulled sections away from a distance. This went on until the bright red Cadillac rescue rig rolled up.

With a better report of who was missing and where they might be, Rescue 1 members donned their smoke helmets and worked their way into the debris pile. They began sawing away sections of wreckage and working their way deep into the pile. After an hour of punishing work, one of the rescue men slowly climbed up the ladder and motioned for helmets to be removed. He weakly announced they had found three bodies.

As the debris was being cleared onto BRT flatbed cars, the rescue men resumed their digging and clearing. Late in the afternoon it began to rain, as Rescue 1 continued working in the rubble. As the bulk of the first alarm assignment was fed sandwiches and coffee by neighbors, a shout from the rescue crew was heard.

"We've got them!"

Carefully the body of a young redhaired girl was lifted to the surface. Annie Byrnes was the only customer in the store when the blast occurred. Next, another young lady, Lily Stahl the cashier, was lifted and carefully carried away.

Five minutes later the store's owner, Martin Schmidt, was brought up. At 4:10 Schmidt's nephew Broder Johnson was removed and at 5:34 Charles Thompson, another employee was removed. In all five persons were killed by the explosion and collapse. Eleven people were also injured.

The following day Rescue 1 responded to a smoky fire at the National Guard Arsenal at 35th Street and Seventh Avenue in Manhattan. A few minutes before six in the evening on July 14, 1916, John Cummings, a private in the National Guard, was mopping the second-floor hallway inside the arsenal building at

35th Street and Seventh Avenue in Manhattan. Busy with his custodial duties, he was startled to see smoke pouring from a room along the south side of the building. As he moved closer to investigate, 50 rounds of ammunition discharged due to the building heat condition. Cummings dropped his mop and ran to warn the 62 other people working in the structure.

Charles Lenz, an engineer working on some rifles nearby, heard the detonation of the cartridges and went to investigate. Seeing the rapidly developing fire, he dashed directly to the magazine, hoping to avert a catastrophic explosion of the stored munitions. Swinging open the large steel door, he stepped inside and opened the main emergency water valve. Slamming the heavy door closed, he left the water to do its work as he hurried from the building.

Meanwhile, Major W.A. Niver received news of the fire, and telephoned the Manhattan fire dispatcher's office directly, then hurried to the street to meet the arriving fire apparatus.

As workers were evacuating the building, two men, Private Andrew Moran and Tom McNally, a truck driver, reentered the arsenal and began removing army trucks stored inside. The duo successfully removed several trucks and despite the severe conditions, entered the building once again to get more. Clouds of thick noxious smoke pumped throughout the structure, and covered the entire neighborhood in a choking blanket. Moran materialized through the miasma at the wheel of yet another vehicle and pulled it to the curb. Waiting in the street and watching the smoke-filled truck door, he realized McNally had not exited after their last foray, and quickly reported the missing man to his superiors. One hour later McNally was found by firemen, unconscious and wedged between a truck and a pile of barrels. He was dragged outside, then given the Last Rites after all efforts to resuscitate him failed.

Firemen had their hands full as the dense smoke refused

to lift. Deputy Chief Smoky Joe Martin transmitted second and third alarms hoping to gain an edge on the stubborn blaze. Fireman John B. Corrigan of Hook & Ladder 4 was venting windows along the third floor when he came across an unconscious fireman slumped on the floor. Corrigan dragged the man to a window and called for help. Below on a ladder Fireman Walter O'Leary of Rescue 1 was operating a high-pressure hose through a straight nozzle when he heard the call for help from above. Calling to the street to shut down the line O'Leary wasted no time and ascended the ladder with the writhing hose line tucked under his arm. Corrigan was able to lift the unconscious man out the window and into O'Leary's arms. (Corrigan was formerly a sergeant in the 12th Infantry and left the Guard to join the FDNY five years earlier.)

While controlling the twisting hose and managing the weight of the unconscious man at the same time, O'Leary started down the ladder. Each step was a challenge as the pressure of the hose threatened to topple them both at any time. Glancing up, O'Leary saw Corrigan, now unconscious, draped across the windowsill. When O'Leary and the unconscious fireman were about halfway down the ladder the correct high pressure hydrant connection was identified and shut down. The hose went limp, making his descent a bit easier. Upon reaching the ground, members of Rescue 1 moved in with a pulmotor and resuscitated the unconscious man. Fireman John P. McNamee of Engine 16 would suffer a throbbing headache but would live to fight many more fires.

The battle was interrupted several times as unconscious firemen were carried outside. Pulmotors were used to revive Firemen Anthony King of Engine 34, George Lantelme of Engine 16, James O'Reilly of Engine 1, and George Heckle of Engine 14.

The huge blaze attracted a tremendous crowd. As explosions

rocked the building, the crowd surged back and forth. These surging spectators were finally moved two blocks away by the police reserves manning the fire lines. The huge building was a total loss. One man, Tom McNally. was killed and several were injured.

It was 3:52 on the afternoon of July 26, 1916, when Rescue 1 responded to Pier 8, East River, where a fumigation inspector named Jeremiah Lalane was overcome by cyanide fumes, after falling through a hatchway into the hold of the steamship *Isle De Panay*. The inspector was removed from the hold, and Rescue 1 members worked unsuccessfully to revive him.

Rescue 1 was again special-called to Brooklyn, this time on August 6th at 4:47 a.m. when a 10-ton ammonia tank in the basement of the Hotel St. George burst. The hotel, located on Clark Street between Henry and Hicks streets, had 500 guests sleeping at the time of the explosion. The force of the blast shook the hotel and the entire neighborhood for a half-mile around. The night clerk remained at his post long enough to notify the fire department.

Inside the hotel the guests were in a panic, the explosion at Black Tom Island the week before still fresh in their minds. Members of the Brooklyn Robins (later renamed the Dodgers) baseball team: Edward Appleton and Sherrod "Sherry" Smith had rooms on the seventh floor, Edward Pfeffer and Duster Mails had rooms on the fourth floor. The pitchers left their rooms and immediately began helping residents make their way to the fire escapes. They'd then cover their mouths and return and help more people make their way to safety. At one point Sherry Smith fell down a flight of stairs injuring his pitching arm. (Despite the injury he had 14 wins and an ERA of 2.34 that season.)

As the first due fire companies arrived, they saw the 11-story fire escape on the Clark Street side of the building was swarming with excited men and women in their night clothes. Many clutching handkerchiefs or cloths across their faces for protection. Dozens had fled to the roof, and all were suffering greatly from the noxious fumes.

Battalion Chief Harrigan immediately transmitted a second alarm. On the Hicks Street side of the building firemen placed a dozen ladders, and helped remove those trapped on the roof. Meanwhile, with the thick blanket of ammonia vapors filling the building, Deputy Chief O'Hara special-called Rescue 1 and Deputy Chief Smoky Joe Martin to the scene as the ambulance crews from local hospitals began treating those fleeing the building, who were suffering with ammonia burns to the throat and nasal passages.

When Rescue 1 arrived on the scene, Chiefs Martin and O'Hara quickly devised a plan. Rescue donned their smoke helmets and entered the cellar. Charged hose lines were run through sidewalk gratings and pulled into the cellar by the rescue men. They searched the area for possible victims, then examined the ammonia plant. Rescue 1 found the cylinder head blown off allowing the gas to escape. (Later inspections determined a defective steam pipe had burst, directing live steam onto the ammonia tank of the ice making machine, causing the tank to explode.) Rescue 1 was able to shut off the ammonia feed valve and stop the flow. The members of Rescue 1 then completed a secondary search of the cellar and every floor of the building even before the ammonia fumes had been ventilated.

Four tenants of the hotel did require hospitalization for ammonia fume inhalation and burns.

September 10th at 4:17 in the afternoon, Rescue 1 was special-called to 148 Elizabeth Street in Manhattan. This was the location of the Knickerbocker Ice Company. A team wearing smoke helmets ventured into the ammonia cloud and shut off supply valves leading to the condensers. This solved the leaking problem.

It is interesting to note the Knickerbocker Ice Company was incorporated in 1855 after several upstate New York ice harvesting companies joined forces. The company owned dozens of steamboats, 75 ice barges and employed more than 3,000 workers. By 1882, Knickerbocker was the largest supplier of ice to New York City. An estimated 285,000 tons of ice per year. Most of this ice came from Rockland Lake, a spring-fed lake at the foot of Hook Mountain, about 25 miles north of the city, and near the Hudson River. The ice was stored in huge ice houses, before it was loaded onto barges and taken down the river to the city. (This model continued until it became possible to artificially manufacture ice. This led to the slow demise of ice harvesting, which was finally halted in 1924. Knickerbocker and other ice harvesting companies switched over to artificial ice manufacture to remain competitive.)

September 16, 1916, was a quiet and pleasant autumn day in New York City until 1:36 in the afternoon. That's when the FDNY was called to Tenth Avenue between 32nd and 33rd streets, the scene of a reported train crash. The Washington Express, which consisted of an electric locomotive and six cars: a combination baggage and smoker, two Pullmans, a diner, and two day coaches, started out from Pennsylvania Station at 10:08 a.m. Two minutes later it began entering the north tube of the Hudson River tunnel system.

At the same time Electric Locomotive 27, which had been moving Long Island Railroad cars in the yard, entered the tunnel and plowed into the passenger train. The dining car was smashed, crumpled and driven up and over the rear vestibule of the parlor car ahead. W.H. Pierson, the conductor of the express train was pinned in the tangled wreckage, which then plunged into a stone wall.

Deputy Chief Smoky Joe Martin arrived, and immediately special-called Rescue 1 to the scene. Train crews attempted to use jacks to lift and move the cars, but the actions were causing further injury to the trapped conductor. Rescue 1 moved in with their oxyacetylene cutting gear, and slowly began cutting away selected pieces of twisted metal.

At one point the air and metal around the trapped man became too hot, and he passed out. The torch was shut off and the cutting continued with hand saws as an electric fan was brought in to cool the work area. The torch was fired again and the cutting was renewed. The cutting was again halted as a priest was brought close to perform the Last Rites. Instead, the priest encouraged the trapped man as the cutting continued. For three hours the rescue men took turns alternating between saws and the torch until the conductor was finally freed and rushed to the hospital.

Rescue 1 responded to another ammonia leak this time at a brewery on Tenth Avenue on September 19th at 1:36 in the afternoon. Again wearing smoke helmets, they shut off valves at the condenser and engine.

The following day they responded to the apartment house at 644 Madison Avenue and were able to shut off both steam and ammonia valves to alleviate a dangerous condition.

When Manhattan fire alarm box 230 was received at 6:58 p.m. on October 25, 1916, none of the responding firemen had any idea this fire would require some of the most dangerous and daring rescues ever made by the FDNY.

Number 21 East Houston Street in Manhattan was a

seven-story loft building being used as a factory. It housed a clothing manufacturing company on the fifth and sixth floors, and a laundry company on the top floor. The building ran back 100-feet on the Lafayette Street side and 115-feet back on the Crosby Street side. This left the building with an "L" shape if viewed from above. To the rear was a five-story tenement building that faced the back of the fire building, across a 15-foot shaft.

As the first due units rolled in, including Rescue 1, who made the quick dash from their quarters on Great Jones Street only five blocks away, they were faced with a major fire with reports of 50 people trapped on the roof above the raging flames, on the stairway, clinging to iron window shutters and on two lower fire escapes. Battalion Chief Henry Helm arrived and sent Acting Battalion Chief John Farley and a group of firemen to the roof of the tenement on the Crosby Street side of the blazing factory.

This team dashed up the stairs with a few ropes in their hands. Their plan was to drop the ropes to the street to pull extension and scaling ladders up to the tenement roof. Reaching the roof they saw a breathtaking sight: thick clouds of smoke and heavy flames were pouring from third-floor rear windows of the factory. The frantic cries of the trapped workers echoed across the tenement roof.

Fireman Thomas Kilbride of Rescue 1 noticed a man, Harry Kauffman, clinging to the top of a fifth-floor window shutter. Heavy smoke was pumping out the window around him and flames were pouring from the nearby rear factory windows, sending scorching waves of heat toward the trapped man and the adjacent roof.

Nearby on the tenement roof, lay an old short wooden ladder. Kilbride grabbed the ladder and approached the roof's edge. He called up to Kauffman and explained his plan. The terrified man nodded.

Standing at the roof's edge, the firemen placed the ladder on the coping tiles atop the parapet wall, then lowered the ladder across the shaft to the iron shutter. With Acting Chief Farley and Fireman Richard Mangles of Hook & Ladder 3 holding the ladder in this angled position, Kilbride slowly ascended until he was just below the man. Facing a five-story drop, Kilbride directed Kauffman to reach down and place his hands on Kilbride's shoulders.

"Keep your arms straight ahead, straight ahead!" Kilbride commanded. Within a moving cloud of hot smoke, the trapped man struggled to follow the directions. The moment Kilbride felt hands firmly grab his shoulders, the fireman reached up and seized Kauffman's clothing and belt. He lifted the man's entire weight up, then eased him down onto the ladder. They carefully climbed down and dismounted onto the tenement's roof.

Thomas Kilbride helped Kauffman across the roof and started him down the stairs, as other firemen worked frantically around them lowering ropes to pull up additional rescue equipment. Back at the ladder another man, Joseph Farkas, became visible clinging to the top of the iron window shutter. This time, Fireman Mangles stood on the coping tiles and braced the butt of the ladder on his thighs. As Kilbride and Farley held him steady, Mangles lowered the ladder toward Farkas.

With searing waves of heat and clouds of smoke choking his breath, Farkas stepped onto the ladder, and slowly climbed down. Each step directed the man's weight painfully into Mangles' thigh muscles. As Farkas reached the bottom of the ladder, he and Mangles were pulled to safety.

As scaling ladders and a portable 35-foot extension ladder were pulled to the tenement roof, attention was shifted to a woman, Ida Goldberg, who was sitting on the seventh-floor window ledge, crying for help. Fireman John Walsh of Hook & Ladder 8, grabbed a scaling ladder, stepped onto the parapet wall and hooked it to the fifth-floor windowsill. Stepping onto the bottom rungs he and the ladder swung like a pendulum across the bricks. When the ladder stopped, he climbed up and straddled the fifth-floor windowsill.

Medal Day book photo of fire building and shaft of 21 East Houston St.

Fireman John Devine of Hook & Ladder 3 grabbed an iron window shutter and used it to swing across to Walsh's position. Together they raised the scaling ladder to the sixth floor, and Walsh climbed up with Devine following. They then raised the ladder to the seventh-floor window, as Miss Goldberg helped guide the ladder's hook across the windowsill. Fireman Walsh then climbed up and helped Miss Goldberg onto and down the ladder to the sixth floor. Fireman Devine then helped Miss Goldberg down another scaling ladder to the fifth-floor window. When they reached that position, they held fast as another fireman, Michael Sloane of Hook & Ladder 8, pushed them both, again in pendulum fashion across the brick face to the waiting hands of firemen on the tenement roof.

Meanwhile, only steps away from the shaft, a solid brick wall of over three stories, loomed above them. At the top, trapped workers were frantically waving and calling for help as flames rose around them. Lt. Hotchkiss of Rescue 1 stood back and fired the rope rifle from the tenement roof, up and over the roof of the blazing factory. As a rope was being pulled up, Firemen James North and Fred Moeller of Hook & Ladder 9 lifted and raised the 600-pound wooden ladder into position. It fell 15-feet short of the roof. Unfazed, North and Moeller climbed the extension ladder with a scaling ladder in hand.

Despite the heroic efforts of firemen to reach those trapped on the roof, panic set in, and one woman jumped from the roof and plummeted into the courtyard seven stories below. A second woman also jumped and landed on the tenement roof, narrowly missing firemen. She was rushed to the street with severe injuries and despite the best efforts of Doctor Harry Archer, she died from internal injuries.

The other people trapped on the factory roof were taken down the scaling and extension ladders to the tenement roof. In all two were killed, and six workers and three firemen were injured. As this fire, which went to 4-alarms, was being fought another 4-alarm fire broke out only blocks away at 205 Greene Street, a five-story loft building.

The scaling ladder rescues at the East Houston Street fire were among the most spectacular and dangerous ever performed by the FDNY. Seventeen members of the department were placed on the Roll of Merit for their actions at this fire. Six of them, Firemen John Walsh, Michael Sloane, John Devine, Richard Mangels, Thomas Kilbride and Captain John Farley, would receive Class 1 awards and would also later receive FDNY medals for valor. (Fireman John Walsh was awarded the James Gordon Bennett and Department Medals and later the first Archer Medal for the best rescue in a three-year period.)

Several days later, on October 30th, Rescue 1 responded just down the block from the firehouse when a man became wedged between an elevator and the third floor at 23 Great Jones Street. The torch and pulmotor were both used to free and treat Mr. Frank Kelly.

On November 7th Rescue 1 responded to a smoky subway fire that left 40 people unconscious, with many inside the tunnel near the emergency exit at 104th Street and Central Park West. As firemen guided and carried up victims, Rescue 1 set up a first aid station on the grass of Central Park. Using pulmotors, they pumped oxygen into the lungs of those overcome. Most were quickly revived and only three people required hospitalization.

It was shortly after 11 a.m. November 23rd when a roof collapse occurred during the construction of a three-story brick and concrete garage at the southeast corner of 64th Street and Third Avenue. Sixteen men were at work on the third floor, when the roof of the 100-square feet structure collapsed. Eight men were pinned under the reinforced concrete and Rescue 1 was special-called by Deputy Chief Hayes.

Rescue 1 used their torch to cut away the twisted pieces of reinforcement, and were able to remove James Carrol, a bricklayer, who was injured. They continued cutting and were able to free the second worker, who was killed by the collapse.

Another elevator pin job was responded to on November 25th at 385 Lafayette Street. A young woman, Evelyn Danny, had tried riding a small sidewalk elevator used to lift ashes to the street, when her leg became stuck between the elevator and the car's running rail. Under the direction of Lt. Hotchkiss, members used the torch to cut away the rail. A spray of water was needed to prevent the heated materials from burning both the young woman, and the wooden car flooring. Miss Danny was successfully removed after a half hour and was transported to the hospital with crush injuries and mild burns.

December 1, 1916, saw Edwin Hotchkiss promoted to captain. He apparently remained in Rescue 1 until Christmas Eve, when he started his new command at Hook & Ladder (H&L) 12. Taking his place was Lt. Benjamin F. Parker from Engine 14. Ben Parker was appointed to the FDNY on April 24, 1907, and was assigned to Hook & Ladder 16. He was placed on the Roll of Merit for a rescue on November 25, 1908. In 1913 he transferred to Engine 64 until he was promoted to lieutenant on January 1, 1916, when he was assigned to Engine Company 14. Parker was transferred to Rescue 1 on December 1, 1916.

On same order Fireman John C. Conners was transferred from Hook & Ladder 20 to Rescue 1. Conners, a former iron worker, was appointed to the FDNY on June 7, 1911, and was assigned to Hook & Ladder 20.

Rescue 1 worked a difficult 3-alarm fire on the night of December 3, 1916. Captain McElligott, and Firemen Ryan, O'Leary, Kilbride, Donohue and Conners rolled out at 1:43 a.m. to Chrystie and East Houston streets where a fire that began in the rear of the first-floor saloon, quickly spread upwards inside the six-story tenement. Numerous people were trapped by the rapidly extending fire. The members of Rescue 1 and Hook & Ladder 20 made several outstanding rescues. A member of H&L 20 would receive a medal for his bravery.

On December 9, 1916, at 12:30 p.m., Rescue 1 responded to 1510 Broadway, the Hotel Claridge, where an ammonia leak filled the subcellar with noxious fumes. Rescue 1, wearing smoke helmets, were able to close ammonia valves controlling the leak. A similar emergency occurred on December 21, 8:39 a.m., when Rescue 1 responded to 223 First Avenue a meat market. They were able to shut ammonia valves and gas meters in the cellar.

Then on December 27th at 4 in the afternoon, the FDNY was called to Columbus Avenue and 72nd Street where a fire had broken out in the subcellar of the Park & Tilford Building. First due, Engine 74 took a hydrant and stretched an attack line down into the subcellar. Seven members of 74 then moved in to battle the flames. They were making good progress and had driven the fire back into one corner. Suddenly several sharp explosions occurred, filling the subcellar with stifling ammonia fumes. Several carboys filled with ammonia for the ice-making plant had exploded. (Carboys are ridged glass containers used to hold or transport liquids.) The nozzle team staggered away unable to breathe, and one by one dropped to the floor unconscious. Teams from Engines 56 and 40, were also overcome while attempting to remove their comrades and operate the line on the growing flames. Members of Hook & Ladder 25, who'd found a different entry point, moved in with the same results. More than a dozen firemen now lay strangled and blinded by the fumes.

Deputy Chief Burns and Battalion Chief McKenna held additional crews back until Rescue 1 arrived with their smoke helmets. Under the command of Capt. John McElligott, Rescue 1 moved in with a 2-½-inch hose and began extinguishing the fire. The rescue men then shut off ammonia vales to prevent additional leaks and began a through secondary search of the affected areas.

The unconscious firemen were located and carried to the street where a first aid station was set up and resuscitation efforts began. As the fire was being attacked and the last of the rescues were being conducted, McElligott ran out of oxygen. Removing his helmet, McElligott remained in the fumes until the last firemen were removed, and the searches proved negative. At that point the Rescue captain collapsed, overcome with fumes and exhaustion. He dropped to the floor unconscious. His men lifted him from the two and a half feet of water filling the subcellar floor and carried him up to Doctor Archer.

More than a dozen firemen had been rendered unconscious but were successfully revived by pulmotors. Most were sent home to recuperate. McElligott was so severely affected, that upon his return to quarters he was detailed to a fireboat by Chief Kenlon to recuperate. McElligott would now be in command of the 117-foot fireboat *George B. McClellan,* also known as Engine Company 78. This fireboat, built in 1903, was moored at the foot of 99th Street and the Harlem River.

Park & Tilford Building Columbus Ave & 72nd Street

The year 1916 had ended, and Rescue 1 had once again proven their value. They'd responded to 253 alarms and went to work 182 times. Their actual fire and emergency time at work was 137 hours and 47 minutes. They were out of quarters for 175 hours. They'd responded to 167-First alarms, 46-second alarms, 5-third alarms, 32 special-calls, and 3 Borough special-calls.

They'd used the smoke helmets 21 times, the torch 7 times and the pulmotor 6 times. They'd also extricated 11 people from elevators. Rescue 1 was credited with 4 rescues at fires. (Not including the dozens of unconscious firemen they'd carried out of dense smoke and fumes.)

On December 29, 1916, FDNY Special Order No. 232 was delivered to firehouses across the city. One important piece of information was the transfer of Fireman Alfred Henretty from

Rescue 1 back to Hook & Ladder 15. Henretty had been a member of Rescue 1 for a year and nine months. He was cited for bravery three times in his career and retired January 16, 1926.

Chapter 5: 1917

The year 1917 saw New York City bracing itself for more waterfront sabotage as the war in Europe raged on. The docks of the city were bustling with ships loaded with munitions, food, and clothing, all heading to the western front. The number of ship fires was climbing, as German saboteurs and sympathizers hid explosives and firebombs onboard ships destined for Europe. These often ignited before the ship could leave port. The work of firefighting was becoming even more dangerous.

Rescue 1 would start the new year with Lt. Ben Parker in command. (Captain McElligott was detailed to a fireboat to recover from the Park & Tilford fire.) Rescue 1 also received a guest fire officer in 1917, when Lt. Daniel Hurley from the Boston Fire Department was assigned to Rescue 1 for specialized rescue company training. He rode with and trained with Rescue 1 in preparation for his return to Boston for the organization of a Rescue Company in that city. Boston Rescue Company 1 went into service on June 15, 1917, with Lt. Daniel Hurley in command.

On New Year's Day 1917, Rescue 1 responded to the 96th Street subway station when a 17-year-old boy was struck by a train. The young man had been trying to balance himself on the edge of the southbound local platform when the train entered the station and struck him. He was thrown to the track bed and run over by the passing cars. Rescue 1 arrived and when the power was turned off, they climbed under the train with their special tools and began the extrication. Part of the platform had to be chopped away, then the coach was lifted from the wheels by jacks. The young man's body was then carefully removed.

Another difficult fire was fought on January 24, 1917, in the subcellar of the five-story office building at 31 Broadway. This smoky fire would reach three alarms before being brought under control. As the initial attack was commencing, Acting Battalion Chief John Kelly was overcome by the dense smoke and toppled down a staircase into the raging subcellar. Fireman Luke Henry, Chief Kenlon's chauffeur, was able to locate and remove the unconscious officer. To reach the seat of the fire, walls were breached to allow hose stream penetration.

A seven-story loft building at 129 Crosby Street was the site of a dangerous fire on February 1, 1917. Deputy Chief Langford and his troops were unable to utilize the fire escapes as an attack point when they found the iron shutters locked. As they entered through the first and second floor occupancies they were informed of a large stock of chemicals, including a 500-gallon tank of sulphuric acid located under the sidewalk. Langford special-called Rescue 1 and transmitted a second alarm.

It was decided to maintain an exterior attack due to the dangers of explosions or chemically laced smoke. Sixty guests were taken from the Hotel Valdosta across the street as a precaution.

During the night, temperatures in New York City plummeted. From a high of 48-degrees on February 1st, to a low of 8-degrees the following day. That's when FDNY units were called to 18 Oak Street in Manhattan. (Oak Street ran from Pearl to Catherine streets. It was gone by 1947 with the addition of the

Alfred E. Smith Houses.) The five-story commercial building housed an iron and steel company, two different lithographers, and a bookbinding company. A fire broke out in the cellar and quickly spread through all the floors.

Arriving fire companies were faced with frozen hydrants that slowed the initial attack. High winds drove flaming embers across the neighboring buildings, as firemen struggled to free the frozen valves on the high-pressure hydrants. Teams of firemen were sent to the roofs of nearby buildings to extinguish flaming brands as they landed.

Flames soon filled the building as the adjacent buildings were evacuated. Men, women, and children, many in their night clothes, were hurried from their apartments and out into the freezing cold.

During the later stages of the fire, firemen had to contend with sheets of ice coating the streets and sidewalks, and accumulating on the front of the fire building and the adjoining structures. Battalion Chief Rankin and seven members of Hook & Ladder 9 were operating a hose line from a narrow third-floor ledge, when a tremendous backdraft toppled them, leaving them senseless. Members of Engine 29 and Rescue 1 helped move them to safety. The unconscious members were then taken to the first aid station. They were all revived by Doctor Archer.

On February 7, 1917, after speeches by several civic dignitaries, Fire Commissioner Robert Adamson introduced Chief John Kenlon to a crowd of more than 3,000 people filling Carnegie Hall. As part of a spectacular demonstration of how the fire department worked, the chief strolled across the stage and stood before a three-story "building" that would soon have flames projected upon it by a moving picture camera. The chief pulled a prop fire alarm box wired directly to the fire dispatchers for the occasion. Thirty-seven seconds later the crowd could hear

Engine 23 responding from their quarters on 58th Street and Broadway. Moments later a line was being stretched up the center aisle and within four minutes the auditorium was swarming with an entire first alarm assignment to the delight of the crowd.

Members of Rescue 1 appeared on the stage and cut away steel bars blocking the windows of the mock building. Other rescue men in smoke helmets, entered the building and performed a "rescue." The victim was turned over to other rescue men who revived him using pulmotors. Other firemen ascended the façade using scaling ladders, slid ropes, and jumped into life nets. The exhibition was given as part of a Civic Forum showing the department's role as a vital part of city life.

On February 13th an early morning fire broke out in the terminal equipment of the Mexican Telegraph Company, in the basement of 66 Broad Street. The building engineer led arriving firemen to the seat of the fire and within minutes the engineer and several firemen lay unconscious on the basement floor.

Members of Rescue 1 wearing smoke helmets, found the unconscious men and brought them to the street, as other firemen vented the sidewalk deadlights to help relieve the smoke. (Deadlights or vault lights are glass blocks or iron-framed glass bulbs that allow light to enter basements and cellars through sidewalks, before electricity was used.) When the downed men were all accounted for, the fire was knocked down with hose streams directed through the broken deadlights. Fire companies then moved in and extinguished the remaining pockets of fire.

Special Order No. 33, published on February 26th amended the FDNY Rules & Regulations by adding the following:

II—Section 136
Fire Cap.

Captains of Rescue Companies—Same as officers of engine companies, excepting that they shall have a white front with a blue border, one-half inch wide, number of company cut out in center of plain blue figure, three and one-half inches long, on background of white, with insignia of rank—two life guns above, barrels pointing upward, trigger facing trigger, painted in gold and shaded in red.

Lieutenants of Rescue Companies—Facsimile of Captain's with the exception that there will only be one life gun, placed horizontally above figure, barrel pointing to the right.

Firemen of Rescue Companies—Same as officers of Rescue Companies, excepting that they shall have a blue front, number of company, three and one-half inches long, in white on background of blue, and registered number of each member in white figures, one inch long, painted on line below.

Section 146
Insignia of Rank

Captains of Rescue Companies—Same as for Captain's of engine companies, excepting that smoke helmet be located in the center between two life guns, barrels pointing upward, with roof-rope and reel above helmet, life line and slug located below, with number of the company on the breathing bag of the helmet.

Lieutenants of Rescue Companies—Same as for Captains of Rescue Companies, excepting that there will be only one life gun, placed horizontally to the rear of smoke helmet, barrel pointing to the right.

Design for Rescue 1's captain's badge.

The janitor of the building at 9 West 28th Street decided to try improvised insect control when he set a can of chemicals on fire in the cellar. The space quickly filled with choking smoke driving the man outside. As the fumes filled the building the FDNY was called. The services of Rescue 1 were requested and wearing smoke helmets, they were able to locate and remove the smoking can.

Rescue 1 responded to a 3-alarm fire at 311 West 59th Street in Manhattan on March 7th. Five large drums of chlorine gas were damaged by the fire, and the escaping fumes soon reached the firemen, before drifting into a nearby theatre. Five hundred people were evacuated from the theatre without incident, but the firemen operating inside the building weren't so lucky as man after man fell unconscious. Dozens of men at a time were laid out on the sidewalks outside overcome by the gas. One fireman remarked they had their "first taste of trench warfare." (Chlorine was one of the deadly gases used during World War I.)

Upon their arrival, the rescue men, under the command of Acting Lieutenant Thomas Kilbride, put on smoke helmets and plunged into the gas-filled building. They immediately removed several firemen too weak to move and too injured to cry for help. On the roof several firemen were chopping a ventilation hole and were overcome by the escaping gas. They had to be lowered by rope to an adjacent roof. Many men suffered serious effects from the leaking gas but luckily none were killed.

On March 16th Fireman Francis Blessing was officially transferred to Rescue Company 1 from Engine 93. Blessing was a member of the company from day one, and his name appears in the earliest reports submitted to the Board of Merit. He continued his regular job of being the company's primary chauffeur.

Three young boys were playing marbles on the sidewalk near the electric plant at 14th Street and Avenue C on the sunny afternoon of May 2, 1917. Suddenly, the sidewalk beneath them collapsed, plunging the three lads into a huge water-filled hole that had been undermining the sidewalk for some time. A street cleaner, Marcus Sussman, was working nearby and heard the three crying for help. He immediately dashed to the gaping hole and looked down. Only two faces were looking back up. The third boy had vanished under the muddy water. Without hesitation Sussman jumped into the water and held the two boys above water.

Within moments a police officer, a civilian, and arriving firemen helped lift the two boys from the water. Rescue 1 was called and arrived quickly.

Informed a boy was still missing Fireman Frank Clark volunteered to attempt to dive under the water while wearing a smoke helmet. Clark donned the Draeger equipment and was lowered into the murky water. For several minutes he searched the muddy water trying to locate the youth without success. As his helmet began to fill with water, he was forced to abandon his search. (This was probably the first FDNY underwater rescue attempt.) A professional hard-hat diver later found the boy wedged under some bracing.

At 12:45 on the afternoon of May 10th, a fire that was accidently ignited by workers, destroyed the old wooden cupola atop City Hall. Fire Commissioner Robert Adamson was in the building at the time of the blaze and transmitted the alarm by telephone. For two hours FDNY units, including Rescue 1, attempted to extinguish the stubborn fire. A thick column of smoke drew a huge crowd who watched the firemen battle the rooftop fire. Many valuable and historic items in the building were saved from damage as the tower above burned. This was the second time the cupola was destroyed. The first was in 1858 when fireworks celebrating the laying of the trans-Atlantic cable ignited it.

Francis Blessing was promoted to lieutenant on June 1, 1917, and was transferred to Engine 93 on West 181st Street. On the same department order Fireman John Myer of Hook & Ladder 10, was transferred to Rescue 1. The former automobile mechanic joined the FDNY on November 28, 1912, and was assigned to Hook & Ladder 10.

The medal presentation of 1917 took place in the City College Stadium on July 6th with Mayor John Purroy Mitchel, Commissioner Adamson and Chief John Kenlon presiding. The new Doric-colonnaded amphitheater was located on a huge plot between Amsterdam and Convent Avenues, from 135th to 138th streets. The stands were filled with thousands of New Yorkers there to see the Fire Department's parade, demonstration and awards ceremony. They also heartily welcomed the guests of honor, Russian Ambassador Bakhmetieff and the Russian Commission to the United States.

The Fire Department Band led a contingent of uniformed

fire officers and men, including honor companies of previous medal recipients, and the group chosen to be decorated for valor. The lines of uniformed firemen took their positions. The heroes of the October 25, 1916, fire on East Houston Street were awarded medals for their bravery. Fireman John Walsh of Hook & Ladder 8 was awarded the Bennett and Department Medals. Fireman Michael Sloan of Hook & Ladder 8 was awarded the Mayor Strong and Department Medals. Fireman John Devine of Hook & Ladder 3 received the Wertheim and Department Medals, Fireman Richard Mangles of Hook & Ladder 3 received the Crimmins and Department Medals. Then Captain John E. Farley of Hook & Ladder 8 was awarded a Department Medal. Next, Fireman Thomas Kilbride of Rescue 1 stepped forward. Already on his chest were the Mayor Strong and Department Medals for a rescue he'd made in 1912 as a member of Hook & Ladder 1. When Mayor Gaynor pinned this second Department Medal to Kilbride's uniform, he became the first member of Rescue Company 1 to be awarded a medal of valor.

Fireman Thomas Kilbride

It's also interesting to note that the newest member of Rescue 1, Fireman John Myer, was also decorated at this ceremony when he received the Fire College Medal. As a member of Hook & Ladder 10, he and his company had completed their evolutions in the remarkable time of 15 minutes and 20 seconds. Myer joined his old crew for the award, then rejoined Rescue 1 for their demonstration.

The focus then shifted to a mock tenement dwelling erected across from the grandstand. The Life Saving Corps displayed various rescue tactics involving scaling ladders, ropes, nets, and life guns. Then members of Rescue 1 began a demonstration of their tools and equipment. First, they cut steel beams with their torch, then donned smoke helmets and disappeared into the smoke-filled temporary building and "rescued" trapped people.

Smoky Joe Martin joins Mayor, dignitaries and Rescue 1 members.

A two-alarm fire was battled on September 1st when a 35-gallon tank of acid exploded in the five-story loft building at 210 East 23rd Street in Manhattan. The explosion threw the members of Engine 16 and Hook & Ladder 7, including Assistant Chief Smoky Joe Martin, downstairs. All received burns. In the rear of the fourth floor, the explosion cut off Capt. McNamara and two firemen from the stairway. They fought their way to a fourth-floor window. The badly burned McNamara was draped over the sill when Fireman Gray saw his predicament. Fireman Gray immediately raised the butt of a 25-foot ladder to his own shoulders without assistance. This allowed McNamara to stand on the very top rung and escape the blistering heat. Perched atop the ladder, the captain then used his vantage point to dive through the broken window on the third floor. He then made his way to the street. Fireman Gray was later awarded a medal.

Rescue 1 responded to its first true confined space rescue on September 4, 1917. The Union League Club, a social and political organization, was formed in New York City in 1863 with the twin goals of cultivating "a profound national devotion" and "a love and respect for the nation." Early members of the club included the famed cartoonist Thomas Nast, John Jay (first chief justice of the supreme court), Teddy Roosevelt (26th U.S. President) and Ulysses S. Grant (18th U.S. President). Their building was located at 39th Street and Fifth Avenue.

On the evening of September 4th, an employee, John Garvey, was cleaning the boiler and became trapped inside one of the horizontal tubular sections. After working inside the hot confined space for a time, he found he could no longer fit through the 16 X 12-inch opening and the 105-degree temperature was having an ill effect on him. Other building workers arrived and suggested Garvey remove his clothes and cover himself in grease. After two attempts to pull him through the opening failed, the building engineer called the FDNY. After the members of the hook & ladder realized their axes and hooks were no match for the boiler, Rescue 1 was special-called.

The company arrived and sized up the job. Acting Lieutenant John Ryan called for the oxyacetylene cutting torch as a small audience of club members, each a former army or navy officer, watched with professional interest. Ryan wedged himself into the 36-inch space above the boiler to supervise the cutting. The flame carefully cut through the 5/8-inch steel to make an opening.

After two hours in the boiler, Garvey, exhausted and covered in grease, oil, and scales, stepped outside. After a quick check up by a doctor he was told he'd be okay.

Fifteen firemen and civilians were overcome by gas during a fire at 211 West 19th Street on September 12th. The fire was discovered within the 10-story building being used as an automobile garage and plant for the manufacture of auto bodies and accessories. When the alarm was transmitted, Engines 16, 3 and 19, with Hook & Ladder Companies 12 and 5, responded under the command of Deputy Chief Devanny. With flames in the vault below the sidewalk, the deadlights were chopped open, and ladders were placed down into the vault. Thirty-five firemen then descended into the vault with hose lines. As the attack began, men started dropping to the floor, overcome by illuminating gas that was escaping after the connections on the meter melted. With Captains Callagy, and Hotchkiss and Lieutenant Foley and 12 men lying unconscious on the floor, Deputy Chief Devaney special-called Rescue 1 to the scene.

Equipped with their smoke helmets, the rescue men descended into the vault and carried out their unconscious comrades. This included Ed Hotchkiss who'd been promoted and left the Rescue Company nine months earlier. Rescue 1 also rescued a gas company employee who'd been overcome while working to shut off the meter. All were treated with pulmotors and sent home.

Captain John J. McElligott, the company's original commander was officially transferred on October 9, 1917. He continued in Engine 78, the fireboat *George B. McClellan*. Continuing in command of Rescue 1 was Lt. Ben Parker.

On Halloween day 1917, the FDNY received Box 40 at 5:38 p.m., just as many workers were on their way home after a long day. Thousands of these workers were drawn to the scene of a major fire burning in the seven-story Electrical Exchange Building at 136 Liberty Street. The fire apparently began in an office on the seventh floor, and there were soon flames pouring from every window of the top two floors.

The building, designed for large companies, had been subdivided for many smaller firms with areas enclosed by numerous wooden partitions. This added to the fire load and made movement difficult for the first arriving firemen who found it impossible to find a clear path to the flames.

Within minutes two firemen were driven from the building with smoke blindness, two others had been cut by glass. Fireman after fireman staggered out choking from the noxious smoke. It was decided to utilize outside streams to knock down the flames. Battalion Chief McKenna transmitted a second alarm sending Chief Kenlon and Rescue 1 to the scene. Kenlon transmitted a third alarm on his arrival.

Kenlon started his attack from the Liberty Street side of the building. Within a few minutes, deck pipes from four hose wagons were directing their streams at the flame-filled windows above. As Water Tower 1 rolled into the block, Kenlon had it set up and fed by lines stretched from the fireboat *New Yorker*.

Forty-five minutes after the initial alarm, the flames were raging on the top two floors and extending to the cockloft and roof of the building. The long-distance attack was not reaching the seat of the fire. Kenlon ordered lines stretched up the fire escapes. Battalion Chief McKenna, Lt. Rocksberry and three firemen were the first to make a push. The gathered crowd watched as they moved closer and closer to the raging flames.

A second water tower arrived and was set up. The water tower was ordered to direct its powerful stream just above the men working their way up the fire escape. As they approached the sixth floor, the stream was charged and blasted directly on the firemen, who were clinging desperately to the thin iron railings until the stream was redirected.

The attack was taken over by handlines from fire escapes and other nearby vantage points. This newly directed attack began knocking down the fire. Despite being outside, the smoke was still debilitating, and Rescue 1 joined Doctor Archer at the aid station with their pulmotor and gave oxygen to several firemen. The fire was brought under control after two hours.

On November 1, 1917, Lieutenant Frank Blessing, who'd been promoted the previous June returned to Rescue 1. The 32-year-old Blessing had made quite a name for himself since joining the department in 1907. Blessing was already on the Roll of Merit three times, including a Class II for his scaling ladder rescue attempt and other actions at the Equitable fire in 1912.He was back on Great Jones Street and would share command of the company with Lt. Ben Parker.

On the afternoon of November 7th Rescue 1 was called to 505 East 75th Street, where a man was trapped between an elevator and the side of the shaft. William McDonald, a 21-year-old chauffeur from the Bronx, was at the Holender Fur and Dye Company to pick up a load of furs. After stopping on the third floor, McDonald stepped into the elevator and was waiting with another man to travel to the fourth floor. The elevator started suddenly without warning throwing McDonald off balance. He was jerked forward and fell headfirst between the car's edge and the shaft wall. As his head cleared the bottom of the car's floor, his legs were caught by metal frame of the elevator floor.

With a jolt, his body stopped.

William McDonald was now suspended in midair, upside down and seriously injured dangling beneath an elevator car stopped between the third and fourth floors.

The fire department was called, and Hook & Ladder 13 arrived quickly. They immediately called for Rescue 1 and an ambulance. The dangling man was conscious and helped direct his rescuers actions. Members of Rescue 1 set up their torch and were about to begin operations when McDonald requested a priest. When Father John Cunningham arrived, members of Rescue 1 and Hook & Ladder 13 lifted the priest up into the fire department jumping net they'd suspended beneath the car. The priest carefully moved into the net and was able to reach the pinned man. Suspended 75-feet above the elevators base the priest anointed the man and provided prayer and consolation as the torch work began.

When the last cut was made, firemen carefully lowered the injured man into the life net. Rescue 1 men then passed the injured man to the ambulance doctor and crew on the third floor. McDonald, suffering crushed legs and possible internal injuries, was rushed to Flower Hospital in serious condition.

The war in Europe was in full swing, and German saboteurs were very busy in the United States trying to stop materials bound for the Western Front from ever leaving American cities. Their destructive efforts were testing the abilities of the FDNY and other fire departments across the nation.

A fire of mysterious origin broke out underneath the Municipal Pier at the foot of East 24th Street, where hundreds of thousands of dollars of naval supplies were stored. The fire was discovered, burning under the flooring of the pier 400-feet out from the shoreline, and a first alarm was transmitted. It was late Thursday evening November 8, 1917. Some pier personnel and Marines, stationed to protect the stores, attempted to fight the fire while help was summoned. Due to the difficult location of the fire, the Marines, the first arriving land units and even the fireboat could not hit the flames directly with a hose stream. Rescue 1 with their cache of torches and hand tools, made their way to a position above the seat of the fire and were able to cut through the steel flooring and wooden pier below to expose the fire.

Days later the New York City Fire Department faced a serious fire on November 11, 1917, when the five-story Washburn Wire Works was the scene of a five-alarm blaze. Four separate fires in different locations were set within the five- and six-story factory buildings located at 117th Street and 118th Street along the East River. Just after midnight the flames tore through the huge complex and Rescue 1 was assigned to the fire which quickly reached five-alarms. Early in the fire an explosion caused a wall to collapse, narrowly missing several firemen. Many were injured, however. The falling bricks also demolished the hose wagon of Engine 58 and Water Tower 3.

To the firemen of New York City, it felt like the war was getting very close to home.

As the company's unique abilities became better recognized by the chief officers of the department, their roles at fires and emergencies became greater. The city, and especially the firefighters, suffered through one of the coldest three-month periods in its history, between December 1917 through February 1918. The average daily temperature was 25.7-degrees in Central Park. For 67 consecutive days the temperature averaged less than 20-degrees, and on more than one occasion, touched 15-degrees below zero. This brought about unusual congestion on piers and railroad terminals. Many vital sprinkler systems across the city were frozen and rendered useless for firefighting.

The nation, and New York City, were also suffering from a serious lack of coal. Burning coal was the primary source for heat in these frigid temperatures. It was also necessary to fuel the steam engines that the department still relied upon to develop water pressure in areas not served by the high-pressure hydrant system.

Chapter 6: 1918

When a huge ammonia pipe inside the Bellevue Hospital powerhouse burst on January 2, 1918, Rescue 1 was special-called to the scene. The temperature inside the hospital had dropped to 15-degrees, and extra blankets were being placed on the patients, as the Rescue Company devised a plan. The chief engineer of the plant, Wilmer McInzer, donned a smoke helmet and led members of Rescue 1 through a labyrinth of pipes to the location of the damaged pipe. The rescue men shut off the flowing ammonia, and vented the space before the fumes could reach the hospital.

Beginning at 8:30 p.m. January 4, 1918, Manhattan fire companies started what would become one of the longest and coldest nights in department history. Units battled a two-alarm fire in a six-story loft building at 444 Broadway under freezing conditions. As this fire was being brought under control, another major fire, in a six-story building on Mulberry Street was called in. This huge building was filled with cardboard boxes. Chief Kenlon, Deputy Chief Binns and the members of Rescue 1, already coated in ice, responded to the fire. Upon arrival, Kenlon transmitted a fourth alarm and began efforts to keep the flames from spreading to nearby buildings.

A crossfire of water sprays showered the fire ground causing ice to coat the structures, fire apparatus and the firemen. The situation was becoming so bad that firemen had to literally chip the ice off each other, to keep from freezing in place where they stood. In addition, water pressure problems prolonged the operation until 11 o'clock.

Upon their return to quarters on Great Jones Street, Chief Kenlon and the men of Rescue 1 were so encrusted in ice that jets of steam were used to free them from their fire coats. The newspapers quoted the new Fire Commissioner Thomas Drennan the next day remarking, "It is difficult to appreciate the terrible conditions under which firemen work. This has been an eye-opener. The job of a fireman is certainly not enviable. The men I have seen working tonight are heroes."

All the fire apparatus south of 42nd Street was called to a fire that destroyed a six-story loft building at 387 West Broadway, near Broome Street on the evening of January 14th. The fire brought street traffic to a halt and interrupted the elevated Sixth Avenue subway line. Moments after the first rigs rolled in, flames began pouring from all the windows of the adjoining six-story loft building number 383. Firemen now had two large structures ablaze.

Capt. John Norton and Fireman Thomas Fox of Hook & Ladder 20 climbed the fire escape on the West Broadway side of the building, venting windows and examining for fire extension as they went. Near the roof level, fire conditions changed rapidly, and the two men became trapped by the rapidly extending flames. Firemen Paizak and Laffan grabbed scaling ladders and were able to rescue their captain and comrade.

During this long and difficult battle, a number of firemen were knocked unconscious by the thick smoke and were revived by members of Rescue 1 with their pulmotors.

Just after noon on January 16, 1918, a member of the department was walking past the six-story brick building at 343-345 West 36th Street, when he noticed smoke coming from the structure. The alarm was transmitted, and companies rolled in quickly. Fireman John F. Kocher of Engine 54 pulled the nozzle and a line of hose off his rig and moved toward the fire building, as members of his unit continued the stretch behind him. The team waited by the door, as the remaining hose was flaked out. Lieutenant John Donaghey then called for the line to be charged.

Neighbors had smelled smoke since 8 a.m. that morning, and now watched as thick smoke pumped from the warehouse. The nozzle team prepared to enter the warehouse, which was filled with stored theatrical scenery. Joined by Acting Battalion Chief Murtagh, the officer nodded to his men, and they all crawled forward disappearing into the smoke. After pressing in about 30-feet, the floor began to collapse beneath them. Members of the nozzle team clawed at the sloping wood floors, calling to each other and shouting for help as they slid toward the blazing fire below. Members of Rescue 1 moved in and pulled the closest members to safety.

Fireman Frank Clark of Rescue 1 was able to reach the engine officer who was hanging on desperately as the pitch of the collapsing floor below him increased. Rescue officer Lt. Benjamin Parker directed his men into position and called for a hose line as he pulled one of the trapped firemen clear of the blazing collapse area. Conditions were becoming so severe, that the continuing rescue effort was conducted under the covering spray of a hose stream. With a fireman holding his legs, Parker was lowered headfirst down to where he could reach Murtagh. With extraordinary effort Parker dragged the acting chief up the steep incline. Lt. Parker returned for another rescue attempt, but the complete collapse of the first floor and the growing fire conditions forced him back. Sadly, one member, Fireman John F. Kocher of Engine 54, was killed as he slid into the blazing cellar.

The members of Rescue 1: Firemen Frank C. Clark, John Mayr, James Smith, John W. Donohue and John C. Conners were placed on the Roll of Merit with Class II awards. Lt. Benjamin Parker was given a Class I and was later awarded a Department Medal and the Thomas A. Kenny Memorial Medal. This was the first time this medal was ever awarded.

The 1914 Cadillac Rescue rig at the scene of a fire.

The company's special training and equipment came into play on April 11, 1918, when Rescue 1 was special-called to Charles Street and the North River. Moored just offshore was the USS *Frank H. Buck*, a 6,076 gross ton tanker built in 1914, owned by the Associated Oil Company until acquired by the Navy in 1918. Two pipe fitters were lowered into the ship's hold and began making repairs. A navy quartermaster, Felix Taskowsky, who'd become concerned when the workers were not heard from, lowered himself into the hold. Several tense minutes later he signaled to be hauled up. Just as he approached the deck his strength gave out and he slipped from the noose of the rope.

The fire department responded, and wearing smoke helmets, members of Rescue 1 under the command of Acting Lt. John Ryan were lowered into the hold. Searching, they found a compartment separating the engine room and the oil tank. The compartment, filled with deadly fumes, is where the overcome workers were located on the floor. The men were dragged back to the rope, and each was hoisted to the deck, but all three could not be revived. For their dangerous confined space rescue operation Firemen John W. Donohue, John C. Conners and John P. Ryan were placed on the Roll of Merit with Class II awards.

On May 1, 1918, Fireman Walter A. O'Leary, an original member of the company, was promoted to lieutenant and assigned to Engine Company 14. On the same order Fireman William T. Hutcheon of Engine 33 was transferred to Rescue 1.

A fire followed by a series of explosions of ammonia fumes, rocked the new 11-story Merchant's Refrigeration Company, a concrete refrigerating plant on 16th Street and the North River (Hudson). It was 7:32 p.m. on May 11, 1918, when James Vincent, an assistant engineer in the plant, turned in the alarm. He became asphyxiated by the fumes when a 225-ton compressor exploded, rupturing an ammonia pipe. The first arriving units were faced with a huge building covering an entire square block. Inside, a major fire was burning, compounded by a serious uncontrolled ammonia leak in the basement. To add to the difficulty, the assistant engineer had not escaped and was believed to still be inside.

Assistant Chief Smoky Joe Martin immediately transmitted a third alarm and special-called Rescue 1 to the scene. Under the command of Lt. Ben Parker, the men used smoke helmets, split into teams, and prepared to enter the basement from three different sides. Before they could begin, a huge explosion tore through the building. The blast threw a 12-foot square 300-pound door across Eleventh Avenue injuring members of Ladder 12 and a score of soldiers who had been guarding the military stores within the plant.

Heavy ammonia fumes blanketed the street. Many firemen were overcome where they stood, and operations were suspended for almost an hour before Chief Martin would allow Rescue to enter the building. The company was then able to shut off the flow of ammonia and locate and remove the dead worker.

The following day Rescue 1 was special-called to Staten Island for a stubborn fire aboard a new freight ship moored at the pier of the Atlantic Dock Company in Tompkinsville. The company was taken by fireboat to the scene and members again wearing smoke helmets, climbed down into the hold of the ship. Searching below decks, rescue men located a difficult to reach fire burning in the coal bunkers. Thick clouds of hot smoke were pumping under pressure from the bunkers. Flames roared across the face of a glowing mountain and out across the ceiling of the ship's hold. All the while heat was radiating downward, the fire burrowed deep into the huge piles of super-heated coals. Rescue 1 stretched a line of hose and attacked the blazing coal bunker. Clouds of steam soon joined the already toxic brew. When the flames were knocked down and the searches were complete, the company took up and returned to Manhattan by fireboat.

A late afternoon fire raced through the seven-story Spears furniture warehouse that occupied nearly the entire square block on Tenth Avenue, between 39th and 40th streets. It was June 15, 1918. The smoke during the initial attack was so thick, it was impossible to even make out the building's windows. The operators of 16 hoses and deck nozzles found it difficult to direct their streams as the thick clouds of smoke blanketed the burning building.

Smoky Joe Martin had transmitted five-alarms, bringing nearly 300 firemen to the scene. Soon after Chief Kenlon arrived, the outer wall of the top three floors toppled onto 10th Avenue. Forty firemen working below scrambled as the weakened walls came tumbling down.

Members then rushed to Engine 34's high-pressure hose wagon where Fireman Mathias Fox had been operating the deck pipe. The fireman was completely buried beneath bricks and rubble. They uncovered and rushed the seriously injured man to an ambulance. Fox struggled with his rescuers, claiming he was uninjured as he was carried to safety.

The collapse also buried Water Tower 3 and destroyed several lengths of hose that briefly whipped about showering the area with water. Firemen successfully struggled to keep the flames from extending to the brewery next door. This was one of the smokiest fires the FDNY had battled in several years as clouds of thick smoke enveloped the city as far as Avenue A on the east side.

On June 24th a 19-year-old young man named Meyer Belski was working at the Le Roy Shirt Company at 114 Fifth Avenue, unloading stock from an elevator. The car was half filled with bolts of fabric and Belski was handing them out to the elevator operator Joseph Pemberton. Unaccountably, the elevator moved upwards and Belski slipped while holding a roll of cloth and fell between the car and the wall. The bolt of cloth, which was larger in circumference than the boy, became jammed and stopped the elevator's movement. The cloth itself was being cut by the elevators frame.

A police officer answered the first calls for help and notified the FDNY. Arriving on scene were Hook & Ladder 3 and

Rescue 1 under the command of Acting Lt. John P. Ryan. The trapped boy, now losing consciousness was mumbling "Save me, save me..." as the members of Rescue 1 set up their equipment. They slowly cut away at the metal work with the torch, keeping the boy's clothing wet to absorb the heat. After 45 minutes of cutting metal and chipping away at the brick work, the young man was freed.

He was handed to Doctor Allen of New York Hospital, who'd been treating the lad as the rescue men did their work. The young man was rushed to the hospital with serious injuries but was expected to survive.

A crowded subway car from Long Island City and bound for Grand Central Station, ran into a dense cloud of smoke in the under-river tube just before noon. The train's motorman slowed and finally stopped as the smoke obscured his vision. The passengers on the crowded train began to panic but were quickly quieted by FDNY Deputy Chief Reid. The chief ascertained the problem was burning third rail insulation and ordered the motorman to continue toward Grand Central. Reaching the station, the chief transmitted the alarm and took the next train back to the Jackson Street station. He then led Rescue 1 with their smoke helmets and extinguishers into the tunnel. They found a short circuit had ignited an insulation block supporting the third rail, and extinguished the small, but smoky fire.

One of the most difficult and dangerous fire rescue operations undertaken by members of Rescue 1 in their early years, or perhaps any year, took place on Saturday October 5, 1918. The Brooklyn Navy Yard was in full swing, its piers crowded with ships of all types, most of these laden with ammunition. At Pier 12 the submarine USS *O-5*, (SS-66), under the command of skipper Lt. Commander George A. Trever, was tied up alongside

Lt. Commander Robert H. English's *O-4* (SS-65), back from the European war zone for repairs to its conning tower.

Lt. Commander Trever had reported to the yard commander's office to get his sailing orders and returned to the boat to observe engine trials. The plan was to use the *O-5*'s diesels to recharge the sub's acid storage battery cells, dozens of which lined the keel of the 173-foot-long submarine. Each battery was as tall as a man and weighed more than a thousand pounds. The boat's twin, air-breathing diesels, located in a large compartment near the stern, were designed for surface propulsion with simultaneous battery charging. Once underwater, the batteries provided power to electric motors for propulsion. The risk during battery charging operations was the generation of volatile hydrogen gas that if not controlled by ventilation, would build up inside the sub and possibly cause an explosion.

The USN Submarine *O-5*, Hull No. 66 in April 1918.

After a successful 20-minute run of the starboard engine while charging batteries, the port engine began operations. Four minutes later the diesel was shut down to allow repairs to a faulty valve. Then the battery test resumed, and everything was looking normal. The storage batteries were fully charged and began emitting hydrogen gas. Blower fans and exhaust ventilation lines were working to remove the dangerous gas from the boat. Unknown to the crew, engine vibrations had caused a quick-closing, spring-loaded flapper valve over the main exhaust line to close. It only took a few minutes before Ensign William J. Sharkey, who was working near the aft battery to become alarmed.

"Do you smell that gas? There is a lot of gas in here. You better get it out of here," he ordered Crewman J.I. Still, an electrician second-class, who was working in the compartment.

After checking that the blowers were running properly, Sharkey ordered them to be sped up.

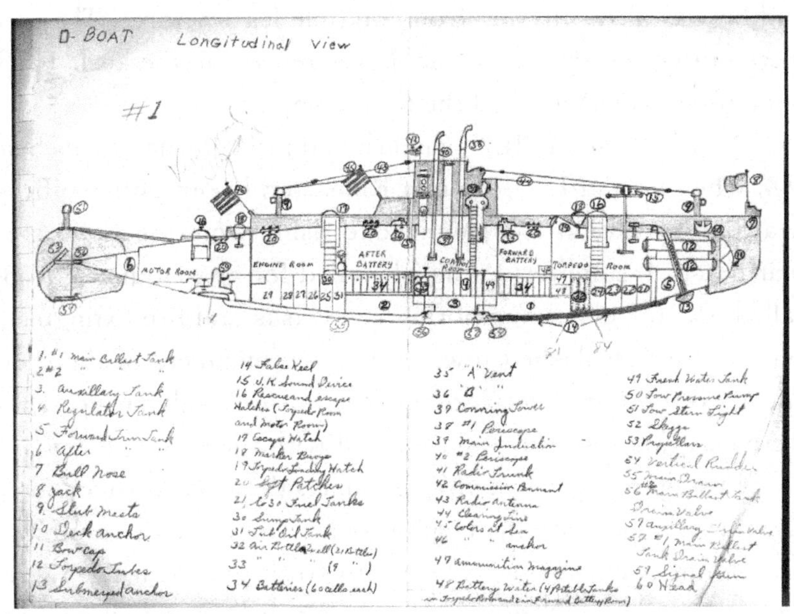

A crew member's training notes on the Submarine *O-5*.

Sharkey had also summoned Captain Trever from the control room. As he stepped through the bulkhead door and into the after battery, he too smelled the accumulating hydrogen gas. Assured the blowers were working properly Trever inspected the gas intake lines and found them open. Next, he checked the exhaust pipe that led through the overhead to discharge gas from the boat. The commander was startled to find the main flapper discharge valve closed.

"Here's your trouble!" he shouted, reaching up to open the valve.

His actions were too late. A fireball erupted over the batteries, thrusting steel decking on which the men were standing up against the overhead. Both Trever and Sharkey were thrown violently to the deck. Sharkey's skull was broken, both of Trever's legs were broken below the knees, and his scalp was cut and bleeding. Electrician Still lay nearby, his head was bleeding, and he was also suffering from multiple leg fractures. The men were buried beneath debris as flames burned in the keel. Thick noxious smoke soon filled the tight compartment.

Nearby, Captain R.H. English had just returned to his boat *O-4*, when he and Lt. Benjamin Kilmaster, his executive officer, heard an explosion and saw smoke rising from the *O-5*'s open rear hatch. Instinctively, English yelled for an ambulance to be called and for his crew to bring gas masks and fire extinguishers. As English dashed toward the *O-5*, members of the crew and yard workers began to exit the burning submarine. They were carrying the badly injured Still with them.

Disregarding his own personal safety, English climbed down the ladder into the engine room. The extreme conditions drove him back up the ladder into fresh air. Hearing Trever and others were still inside the sub, English strapped on a gas mask and re-entered the burning submarine. He was able to pull Trever from the burning debris and drag him back to the ladder. Other sailors and workers opened the bulkhead door and pulled English and Trever through before closing the door again. Trever was handed up the ladder and taken to an ambulance.

After several minutes navy officers decided to call the fire department. Upon their arrival, Deputy Chief O'Hara of Division 10 and Battalion Chief Kirk of Battalion 31 entered the submarine through the aft hatch and reached the battery platform. They attempted to reach the trapped crew members but were driven back by a series of explosions. They then moved to the conning tower but could not penetrate the dense cloud of smoke and gases.

Deputy Chief Patrick Maher of Division 11 arrived and after conferring with the other fire chiefs and naval officers, special-called Rescue 1 from Manhattan. While Rescue 1 was enroute, O'Hara and Kirk tried to re-enter the blazing sub through the torpedo compartment but were again driven back by explosions.

The on-duty members of Rescue Company 1: Fireman Thomas Kilbride, John Donohue, John Ryan, Frank Clark, James Smith, and John Myer, with Lt. Francis Blessing at the wheel, raced from their quarters on Great Jones Street, Manhattan in the company's original rig, the 1914 Cadillac touring car. While Rescue 1 was heading toward the Brooklyn waterfront, additional attempts were made by Capt. English and various teams of sailors to reach the switchboard, disconnect the batteries and control the fire. But deteriorating conditions prevented their efforts.

When Rescue 1 arrived, they assembled with their gear and were briefed by Rear Admiral John McDonald and Capt. English, Fire Chiefs Maher, O'Hara, and Kirk. Fire was now raging in the battery and dynamo rooms, and flames were venting from the front hatch, exposing a nearby powder magazine. The door of the main hull leading into the torpedo compartment had been blown open by the first explosion and was so warped that it could not be closed. There were also 20,000 gallons of diesel fuel, 8 large torpedoes and ammunition for the submarine's gun stored within the cramped quarters of the O-Class submarine.

Newspaper artwork showing Rescue 1 approaching the fire.

Admiral McDonald warned that if one of the torpedoes let go, the effect would be disastrous. He believed the building heat or any of the constant explosions currently rocking the boat, could detonate one of the torpedoes at any time. He also added the fire would have to be fought using chemical fire extinguishers, as water from a hose could cause further short circuits in the already damaged wiring systems.

The admiral had ordered that all the available extinguishers and navy breathing gear be made available. Coupled with the smoke helmets, the members of Rescue 1 and the naval officers accompanying them, would have some breathing protection in the miasma of gases being created. In addition, although not completely understood at the time, the contents of their fire extinguishers—carbon tetrachloride can burn or decompose and produce poisonous phosgene gas. Yet another dangerous addition to the already deadly atmosphere.

Now fully aware of the dangerous conditions they faced within the cauldron-like submarine, Lt. Blessing broke his company into teams. He would take Firemen Tom Kilbride, John

Ryan, and John Myer and enter the submarine through the aft hatch with Lt. Commander English guiding the way, while Firemen Jim Smith, John Donohue, Frank Clark and naval officer Lt. Ben Kilmaster donned respirators and attempted to enter through the conning tower hatch.

Hurrying down the hot metal ladder into the submarine, they were driven to their stomachs by the intense heat. Inching ahead on their bellies, they set up a chain that passed hand extinguishers from the aft hatch ahead to the closest rescue men who would aim the carbon-tet stream at the flames and glowing wiring. Lt. Commander English inched forward hoping to reach the switchboard and disconnect the circuits to the batteries. Conditions proved too hot to reach the switchboard.

Drawing of Rescue 1 fighting the fire using hand extinguishers. Believed to have been drawn by Chief Kenlon's son.

The hull of the submarine was becoming increasingly hotter as the metal absorbed the heat from the growing fire. Blessing and his men battled the flames with hand extinguishers and searched the ship, as naval personnel attempted an alternative method of disconnecting the batteries. Firemen John Donohue and Jim Smith entered the conning tower and descended the red-hot ladders down to the control room. The rescue men and several sailors, including English, inched ahead, flat on their bellies, trying to reach the forward battery. Fireman Smith, overcome at one point, took a brief ten-minute breather where he was. Smith began inching forward until he reached the ammunition magazine in the torpedo room. Smith and Donohue set up another chain of men who handed the ammo from the room, up a ladder and out of the submarine.

In the after-battery area another team with Fireman Kilbride at the lead, located Ensign Sharkey's body and were able to remove him up a hatch by rope. While one team of Rescue 1 members fought the flames, other teams searched for fire extension, injured sailors, and a way to remove the ammunition stored beneath the flooring. (Fifty carbon tetrachloride handheld fire extinguishers had been used to gain control of the fire.) Meanwhile Lt. Commander English and his team's tenacious efforts had paid off. Under extreme conditions they were finally able to disconnect the batteries that had been generating the gases that were feeding the fire.

This allowed a water-fed fire hose to be used to fight the remaining pockets of fire and cool off the red-hot metal sections of flooring and bulkheads. Finally, after a two-and-a-half hour battle the fire was declared under control. Blessing and his men were sweaty and exhausted after their tremendous firefighting and rescue operation. They gathered their gear on the dock and were congratulated by the fire chiefs and naval officers.

A statement of Rear Admiral McDonald of the Brooklyn Navy Yard showed the dangers involved and the bravery of the firemen:

> The heat of the burning material, as well as numerous small explosions of hydrogen gas from the batteries rendered the work performed extremely dangerous to the men at work owing to the fact that either the explosions of hydrogen gas or the heat of the fire within the submarine might have detonated the explosives there at any time during the entire period that this work was being performed.
>
> The members of the Fire Department were acquainted with these facts and performed the work with full knowledge of the risk involved.

Lieutenant Commander George A. Trever died from his injuries nine days after the explosion and fire. He was awarded the Navy Cross.

Ensign W.J. Sharkey was also posthumously awarded the Navy Cross for his brave attempt to avert the explosion.

Lt. Commander Robert Henry English was awarded a Navy Cross for actions as submarine commander in the Atlantic during World War I. He was then awarded a gold star in lieu of a second Navy Cross by the President of the United States for his heroic actions onboard the *O-5*. By World War II, English had been promoted to Rear Admiral, commander, submarines, Pacific Fleet. He was tragically killed in the crash of a Pan Am

Clipper near San Francisco on January 21, 1943.

Due to their heroic actions the FDNY Roll of Merit included:

Lt. Francis Blessing Class I, with Bennett and Department Medals

Fireman Thomas Kilbride Class I, with Department Medal

Fireman John Donohue Class I, and Department Medal

Class II awards were given to the following:

Deputy Chief John O'Hara

Battalion Chief Henry P. Kirk

Fireman John Mayr

Fireman Frank Clark

Fireman James Smith

Fireman John Ryan

World War I ended on November 11, 1918.

On November 13, 1918, Fireman John B. Milward of Hook & Ladder 24 transferred to Rescue 1. Milward, born in Ireland in 1880, joined the FDNY on January 25, 1909, and was assigned to Engine Company 3. After his initial training was completed, he transferred to Hook & Ladder 24 on March 1, 1909. While he worked there, his name appeared on the Roll of Merit twice. As a Third Grade Fireman, he received a Class II for a rescue attempt he made on January 31, 1911. With a strong wind blowing, units arrived at the fire building on the northwest corner of Sixth Avenue and 37th Street and saw a woman standing on a fourth-floor fire escape with flames closing in on her. A ladder was quickly thrown up and Milward raced toward the top as the frantic woman, her clothes now catching fire, hurled herself from the flame-filled fire escape.

Milward stopped climbing, wrapped his leg around a rung, and attempted to catch the 250-pound woman now plummeting toward him in flames. She broke through his arms nearly pulling him from the ladder. She continued falling and was killed as she hit the ground.

The same department order detailed Rescue 1 Fireman John Myer to be the chauffeur for Chief of Department John Kenlon, a position Myer held until Kenlon retired in 1931.

In the early morning hours of December 8, 1918, a two-car subway shuttle car jumped the switch at 142nd Street and Lenox Avenue, left the track and smashed into four steel pillars before bursting into flames. Heavy smoke quickly filled the tunnel adding to the difficulty of evacuation and rescue. Newspapers reported Rescue 1 responded from Great Jones Street to the scene of the crash in 14 minutes. As police reserves held back the growing crowd, Rescue 1 moved in and began a prolonged operation to free the trapped motorman. Grant Cooper, the motorman, was pinned within the crumpled wreckage. As lines were stretched, and injured passengers were removed by FDNY companies, Rescue 1 began the delicate task of cutting away the twisted metal imprisoning the dead men. After an hour's work the oxyacetylene torches had cut away enough of the steel to release the body. Four other people were also treated and taken to the hospital.

Two weeks later, just after midnight on December 16th, a chemical fire was discovered in the basement of Havemeyer Hall at Broadway and 118th Street, Columbia University. First arriving units moving in on the fire were quickly driven back by the noxious smoke and building heat condition. With the fire threatening to extend to the upper floors, Battalion Chief Webber special-called Rescue 1.

Upon arrival Rescue 1 faced a serious situation. Besides the fire extending from the basement, two men, Lt. Michael

McCarthy of Hook & Ladder 22 and Fireman Charles Rinschler of Engine 47, were missing and believed unconscious in the basement of the fire building.

Donning smoke helmets, members of Rescue 1 entered the cellar, located both men, and carried them outside where other Rescue 1 members and Doctor Archer had set up an aid station. Both men were successfully resuscitated. Smoke-helmeted rescue men re-entered the cellar only to be driven back time after time. After an hour-long battle, the fire was extinguished.

Overhead shot of the 1914 Cadillac shows bench seats and central compartment where the smoke helmets and special tools were stored. Stretchers are seen just beneath the Dalmatian's paws.

Chapter 7: 1919

The FDNY now had 5,321 men, organized into 304 companies. There were still 356 horses in service pulling apparatus to fires. The department would respond to 15,152 alarms during the year with 235 reaching multiple alarm status. The population of the city had grown to 5.5 million people.

It was 1 a.m. January 19, 1919, when FDNY units responded to Box 769 at 423 East 104th Street, a two-story building operated by the Delivery Auto Truck Company. The fire quickly grew to three-alarms, as flames raced throughout the building. At the height of the fire, members of Engine 44 were stretching a line to the roof a one-story shed. They were going to use this vantage point to attack the flames, now threatening to spread to the surrounding properties.

Suddenly, without warning, the rear wall of the fire building collapsed onto the one-story shed, burying several members in hot bricks and flaming debris. Firemen, including members of Rescue 1, dashed to the collapse area and began digging through the flaming rubble in hopes of reaching the trapped men. The rescuers were able to remove Lt. Alfred Stapleton of Hook & Ladder 26, Fireman John Shelton of Engine 44 and Fireman Joseph Callahan of Engine 78 (the fireboat *George B. McClellan*), all seriously injured. They were rushed to nearby hospitals. The other men, Firemen George J. Scanlon and Joseph G. Schmitt, trapped by the debris, were dead. A priest was brought in to deliver the Last Rites, before their bodies were recovered.

Sadly, George Scanlon, aide to Deputy Chief Thomas Hayes for the past seven years had returned to his spot in Engine 44 a week earlier so he could be closer to his home. Probationary Fireman Joseph Schmitt had only joined the FDNY ten days earlier.

A four-alarm fire was battled on February 9, 1919, at Third Avenue and 133rd Street in the Bronx. The fire was in the Muehlstein & Company tire and scrap rubber company and was threatening to spread to the Hurlburt Motor Truck Company next door. With the Harlem River only a block away, water supply was not an issue. Acting Chief of Department Smoky Joe Martin was concerned about the dense smoke and the large cache of gasoline and kerosene stored next door.

Rescue 1 arrived and with the assistance of other firemen, over 100 barrels of gasoline were rolled from the adjoining building's loading dock and taken to the river.

The lack of breathing protection would hamper firefighting efforts on February 17, 1919, when 30 firemen were overcome while fighting a fire in a four-story warehouse on East 48th Street. The building, formerly used by a flour company, was now being used by the federal government.

Three employees that opened the warehouse in the morning found the interior of the building in flames. The spontaneous-combustion fire originated in bales of jute piled to the ceiling of the first floor. (Jute is a coarse fiber used to make ropes or sacks.) The second floor was filled with bags of Sulphur and the floors above were filled with other chemicals. The burning jute had apparently heated the ceiling and second floor enough to ignite the Sulphur, which gave off dense fumes.

First due units were taking a beating, as they attacked the fire on the first floor. The smoke and gases from the various products being burned were knocking out the firemen. The gases built up to dangerous levels inside the building and caused an explosion that blew off the second-floor shutters. Several firemen working on nearby ladders were knocked to the ground by the blast. Inside the building, men began dropping unconscious.

Rescue 1 arrived and immediately went to work. They were able to remove several unconscious firemen, who were taken to a first aid station set up by Doctor Archer, Robert Mainzer and members of Rescue 1. These firemen were treated with pulmotors until they regained consciousness.

Meanwhile, the smoke-helmeted rescue men reached the second floor and were trying to control the Sulphur fire and the debilitating fumes being generated. By the early afternoon the fire had reignited, and the attack was renewed. This time Chief Kenlon reduced the number of firemen being used and rotated them frequently. Fresh members of Rescue 1 again operated using the smoke helmets and were finally able to douse the flames and vent the smoke and gases.

As stated in the official report to the Board of Merit: "mask equipped, they operated under the most hazardous and trying conditions until weakened to a point of exhaustion, in stretching and operating lines . . . for five and a half hours. Fireman Smith was removed to the hospital." For their bravery, Acting Lt. John P. Ryan, and Firemen John W. Donohue, John C. Conners, William Dorritie, William T. Hutcheon and James Smith were all placed on the Roll of Merit with Class A awards. Also awarded Class As for this job were Lieutenants Thomas Kilbride and John Donohue who joined the company at the scene and worked this difficult fire. Several days later Chief Kenlon promoted both Doctor Archer and Robert Mainzer to Honorary Deputy Chiefs for subjecting themselves to unusually severe hazards while resuscitating 30 firemen who had been overcome by the noxious fumes.

Doctor Harry Archer, possibly Fireman John Delaney and Robert Mainzer

A spectacular fire in the heart of the grocery warehouse district required three-alarms to control on February 20th. The alarm was received at 9:20 a.m. for a fire in a five-story spice factory at 64 North Moore Street. Rapidly extending flames threatened the surrounding buildings as firemen moved in on the fire. Attempts to penetrate the noxious smoke and extreme heat proved impossible even for members of Rescue 1. They eventually manned exterior lines and helped battle the flames from a distance.

It was 12:30 on the afternoon of May 20th when flames broke out on the sixth floor of a nine-story loft building at 640 Broadway near Bleeker Street. The huge building ran through to Crosby Street and was occupied by 92 jobbing and manufacturing firms. (This was the site of the Empire Bank building fire 20 years earlier.)

Three alarms were quickly transmitted, as the workers on the upper floors scrambled to find a way to escape the smoke and flames. When the fire spread from the sixth floor to the seventh and eighth, a man and a woman became visible on the top floor calling for help. The members of Hook & Ladder 20 went into action. Moving from the position on the adjoining roof they lowered themselves to the roof of the fire building by ropes. They then crawled to the edge of the roof and lowered a rope to the trapped couple.

The woman was removed first, and the man soon followed. As this rope rescue was underway Lt. John Coffey of Engine 33 came from the building carrying and unconscious woman he'd found on the ninth floor. (In less than a year, John Coffey would cross the floor and become a member of Rescue 1.) Rescue 1 members manned hose lines and set up an aid station as the fire was battled into the afternoon hours.

On June 12, 1919, the members of the department lined up in their traditional positions before the steps of City Hall. After the presentation of the medals Mayor Hyland made a brief speech announcing that on June 15, he would be putting the two-platoon system into effect, so that men had more time home with their families.

I have always felt that the firemen ought to have the two-platoon system. I hope as soon as possible to give you men of the Fire Department exactly the same opportunities that the employees of all other departments have. You are entitled the two-platoon system, and you are not getting it as a favor, but because it rightfully belongs to you.

At City Hall From left: Chief Kenlon, Lt. Blessing, Coffey, and Parker. Firemen Kilbride and Donohue are fourth and third from the right.

The Bennett and Department Medals were then awarded to Lieutenant Francis Blessing, of Rescue 1 for his heroic actions on Saturday October 5, 1918, at the submarine fire in the Brooklyn Navy Yard the year prior. Also decorated with Department Medals were Firemen Thomas Kilbride and John Donohue for their parts in the sub fire.

Mayor Hyland pins the Department Medal on Fireman Thomas Kilbride. Fireman Donohue, seen in the middle of the second row, awaits his award.

On June 16, 1919, Rescue 1 underwent a personnel adjustment. Leaving the company was Fireman James Smith, who had taken a beating at several difficult fires including the submarine fire the year before. He was being transferred to Engine Company 57, the fireboat *New Yorker*. Also leaving was John W. Donohue who'd joined the company in 1916. Donohue was promoted to lieutenant and assigned to Engine 18.

Joining Rescue Company 1, were Firemen:

James A. Devine from Hook & Ladder 3, a former chauffeur who joined the FDNY in 1913. He was also a veteran of World War I.

Paul C. Maron from Hook & Ladder 12, a former steamfitter who joined the FDNY in 1912.

Joseph Horacek from Engine 55, a former driver who joined the FDNY in 1913.

Walter L. Lamb from Hook & Ladder 26, who'd joined the FDNY in 1913.

John Kistenberger from Hook & Ladder 124, a former carpenter who joined the FDNY in 1913.

Charles C. Roggenkamp from Hook & Ladder 10, a former steamfitter who joined the FDNY in 1913.

William R.P. Fletcher from Hook & Ladder 2. A former iron worker who joined the FDNY in 1914.

The addition of these men was due to the establishment of the two-platoon system in the FDNY. Prior to this, firemen worked a continuous tour of duty with four hours off per day and one day off per week. With the addition of the second platoon, firemen would work a 9X6 day tour and a 6X9 night tour with 24 hours off every sixth day. Basically, firemen went from working more than 100 hours per week to only 84. In Manhattan the system went into effect from 59th Street south to the Battery.

This included nine battalions. In Brooklyn seven battalions were chosen. The new system was further expanded in 1920.

A spectacular fire in lower Manhattan swept through the superstructure of the South Ferry elevated railroad terminal during the afternoon of July 2, 1919. Apparently, a hot box underneath a wooden train car ignited flames that quickly spread throughout the five-car train and extended to the ferry house and elevated train structure and tracks.

Huge clouds of thick smoke rose into the sky, attracting a large crowd of onlookers. The oil-soaked terminal was a ready fuel, and the flames began spreading with remarkable speed. A second and third alarms were quickly transmitted bringing all the downtown fire companies to the scene.

To add to the problems already facing the firemen, the Staten Island Ferry had just landed and had discharged its passengers who found their exit blocked by smoke and flames. They retreated and found another exit. Sixty sailors who were confined to their beds in the sick bay on the second floor of the ferry house, were helped to the street by firemen, police officers, and members of the Coast Guard.

Rescue 1 joined the fire attack as lines were stretched and moved in on the spreading flames. The growing crowd was making fire operations even more difficult, until 40 mounted policemen and scores of cops on foot moved in to push the crowd back. Hundreds of passengers and employees were rescued as the fire swept through the station. Six firemen were injured.

On July 24, 1919, at 6:45 p.m., FDNY units were dispatched to Pier 6 at the foot of West 20th Street for a reported fire on board the White Star Liner *Cedric*. There were 400 men on board the ship at the time of the blaze and the ship's fire crew was notified. They found smoke coming from Holds 5 and 6. After removing the hatch cover, such a cloud of pent-up smoke and heat emerged that one sailor, Seaman Edwards was immediately overcome and fell into the hold. The other sailors made several attempts but were unable to reach him before firemen arrived.

Five firemen then descended into the smoky hold but after a few minutes were not heard from. Fearing for his men, Chief Charles Murray ordered three additional men to find the first five. They were lowered by a crane into the hold. As soon as they reached the bottom they signaled to be pulled back up as it was too hot and smoky to remain in the hold without breathing protection.

Moments later Rescue 1 arrived and assembled at the hold opening with their masks and electric lights. Four members of Rescue 1: Acting Lt. John Ryan, and Firemen Charles Roggenkamp, Paul Maron, and Joseph Horacek donned masks and were lowered into the hold. Advancing while attached to their search rope, they were able to locate and remove the missing seaman and the five firemen, all found unconscious. Rescue 1 then regrouped and extinguished the deep-seated fire.

For their efforts at this dangerous fire, the members of Rescue 1 who worked in the ship's hold were placed on the Roll of Merit was Class B awards. It was later determined that a large shipment of mattresses was the cause of the dense smoke.

It was noon on July 25, 1919, when Hook & Ladder 15 was sent to the Standard Arcade Building at 50 Broadway in lower Manhattan for an elevator repairman caught between an elevator car and the shaft wall. Battalion Chief Walsh and Lt. Walter Morris sized up the situation and realized Rescue 1 was needed with their torch. A 15-inch beam was cut, and they also removed part of the concrete floor to the free the trapped man. The injured man was then transported to the hospital.

Thomas Kilbride, one of the original members of the company was promoted to lieutenant on August 1, 1919. Kilbride remained in Rescue 1 taking the place of Lt. Ben Parker who was promoted to captain on the same order. Parker would assume command of Hook & Ladder 16. The officers of Rescue 1 were now Lt. Frank Blessing and Thomas Kilbride.

Now Lieutenant Tom Kilbride wears a smoke helmet telephone system headset.

Also joining Rescue 1 on that order was Fireman Frank Joseph of Engine 77. Joseph had joined the FDNY on November 1, 1913, and was assigned to Hook & Ladder 10. The former driver also worked in Hook & Ladder 76 and Hook & Ladder 3 before being assigned to the fireboat *Abraham S. Hewitt*. His name appeared on the Roll of Merit for a rescue he made in 1914 while a member of H&L 3.

The steamship *West Indian* was moored at the foot of West 23rd Street on August 4, 1919. Two workers were lowered into the ship's aft peak tanks (peak tanks were used to store ballast or fresh water) to begin their scaling work (cleaning deposits left by hard water.) The first man was immediately overcome by fumes left by disinfecting the tank. The second man raised the alarm before he too fell unconscious. One by one additional members of the crew were lowered into the confined space attempting to rescue the other downed workers. Within minutes there were five unconscious men within the tank.

Rescue 1 under the command of Lt. Frank Blessing, responded to the scene and set up their gear: smoke helmets, ropes, and pulmotors. Blessing and Fireman John Milward were lowered into the tank and the unconscious men were quickly removed to safety. These men were treated with the pulmotors and regained consciousness. One of the original workers was then taken to the hospital, the others were treated by physicians at the scene. Both Blessing and Milward were placed on the Roll of Merit with Class A awards.

One of the most difficult and dangerous conflagrations in the history of the New York City Fire Department occurred on September 13, 1919, within the sprawling Standard Oil Company plant in Greenpoint Brooklyn. This huge fire required the transmission of two Borough Calls above a 5th alarm. Plus, special-calls for extra companies and a recall of all off-duty members. The huge fire started in Tank Number 36 and spread quickly. The plant held vast quantities of naptha, gasoline, oil and alcohol. The fire burned relentlessly for four days and required the services of over 1,000 firemen.

The members of Rescue 1 who worked this fire were: Lt. Francis Blessing, Firemen Al Kinsella, John Kistenberger, William Fletcher, Walter Lamb, James Devine and Charles

Roggenkamp. They joined more than 400 other firefighters that were all placed on the Roll of Merit with Class A awards.

The FDNY battled the flames at the Standard Oil Yards for four days.

The company responded to another elevator entrapment on the afternoon of October 15th. Rescue 1 was special-called to 615 West 162nd Street in the Bronx, where a 28-year-old-woman was pinned between the elevator car and the shaft wall in her home. Despite suffering a fractured hip, the young woman helped direct the firemen as they worked to free her. She was extricated after spending nearly two hours pinned with her body above the car and her legs dangling below.

Lt. Thomas Kilbride and Firemen Paul Maron, Al Kinsella, and William Dorritie all were placed on the Roll of Merit for their actions on October 17, 1919. Under punishing conditions, they entered ammonia-filled rooms, shutting off valves on compressors and condensers to control the leaks.

As Rescue 1's first five years of service was ending it was becoming clear to the department and the public that this special unit had become a very important part of the FDNY firefighting force. The need for the use of the smoke helmets and special tools carried by the company was becoming more and more frequent. The job was changing from the reliance on leather-lunged firemen, to the beginnings of a specialized branch of the fire service that handled both technical and heavy rescue.

Action shot of Rescue 1's arrival at an alarm in their 1914 Cadillac touring car.

Chapter 8:
1920

With the institution of the two-platoon system, the number of firemen and officers in the FDNY had risen to nearly 6,000 in 1920. There were still 304 companies, but the number of fire horses was down to 296. Rescue 1 was still responding in their 1914 Cadillac touring car. At the start of 1920, Rescue 1 had no captain. Frank Blessing and Thomas Kilbride shared command as lieutenants.

Front- Firemen William Fletcher, Jim Devine, Lt Tom Kilbride, Lt John Donohue, John Conners, Walter Lamb, Frank Joseph. Rig Front- William Dorritie, Paul Maron,Frank Clark, Charles Roggencamp, John Milward Back- William Hutcheon, Joe Horacek, John Kistenberger.

It appears that Lt. John Donohue was brought into the company between 1919 and 1920 possibly to fill openings when both regular officers were off. His name does not appear on the Department Orders as a transfer, but he is mentioned in 1919 on the Roll of Merit as part of Rescue 1. He also appears in several photographs taken at that time.

A difficult and dangerous fire was fought on January 22nd at the famed Ritz-Carlton Hotel at 46th Street and Madison Avenue in Midtown Manhattan. At 8:30 p.m., a wedding reception was being held in the Grand Ballroom, when suddenly smoke began pouring into the room from the ceiling paneling. The guests left their food and resumed partying in another room as the fire department was called.

Arriving first were Engine 65 and Hook & Ladder 2, and they immediately began searching for the source of the thick noxious smoke. Believed at first to be wiring inside a wall, the smoke soon took its toll on the firemen who began dropping to the floor unconscious. Acting Battalion Chief Murtha, special-called Rescue 1 to the scene.

Under the command of Deputy Chief Ross, Rescue 1 went to work. Lt. Frank Blessing split his company, with several members resuscitating the downed firemen as other smoke-helmeted rescue men began to search for the seat of the fire. They eventually located a 40 X 40-foot vault of refrigeration pipes that extended over a section of the ballroom ceiling where burning insulation was generating thick smoke and heat. Temporary lighting and fans were set up by hotel employees to help the firemen.

It seemed that as soon as an affected fireman was back to work, he'd be knocked out again. Lt. Robert Jackson of Hook & Ladder 2 required the use of a pulmotor to be revived. The conditions were so bad, non-smoke-helmeted firemen had to work in relays, while Blessing's helmeted men had to work in blistering heat cutting six large holes in the ballroom ceiling.

Conditions became so bad, that a battalion chief was sent home suffering temporary blindness due to the thick, hot smoke. Tank after tank of oxygen were changed out as members of Rescue 1 continued working despite the conditions. It was reported that it took seven hours for the fire to be completely extinguished. In all, the rescue men changed out 22 tanks for the smoke helmets. Several members of Rescue 1 also suffered blisters and burns to their necks and ears due to the extreme heat generated by the confined space fire.

Winter was hammering New York City as January became February in 1920. With temperatures below zero, FDNY units had to contend with snow filled roads, frozen hydrants, and strong winds. Companies were called to Manhattan Box 318 at 1:58 a.m. in the early morning hours of February 1st. The location of the alarm was 57 West 12th Street, where flames were racing through a four-story brownstone dwelling. More than 40 people were inside when the fire started, but 20 escaped before the first engine arrived. Capt. Stephen McKenna of Engine 72 was told that many people were still trapped inside as they rolled in. He could see three women, clinging together on a fourth-floor window ledge.

McKenna split his company into teams, sending Fireman Robert Tierney and Probationary Fireman Matthew Crawley into the building next door to attempt to rescue people visibly trapped and calling for help while Fireman Charles Amato started climbing up the front of the building like a human fly. There was no ladder company on scene yet. Other members stretched hose lines and prepared to battle the flames.

Amato worked his way to a ledge between the fire building and the building next door and straddled across the distance. Inside the adjoining building, Tierney and Crawley had just reached his level and appeared at the window. As Tierney held his right-hand, Amato swung his body across to the fire building window and began to grab people with his left hand. Amato swung them in pendulum fashion, one by one, back to the adjoining building where Crawley had wrapped his leg around the fire escape railing and received each of them.

Six times this dizzying feat was completed as the growing crowd below held their breath. The last woman, now frantic with flames closing in, jumped. Amato leaned out and grabbed her, but almost pulled himself and Tierney from their perches. Crawley was able to extend his limbs through the railing, stretch out, grab the dangling woman and squeeze her to the fire escape railing taking her weight from Amato. Probationary Fireman Crawley now held the woman dangling in midair while Amato and Tierney repositioned themselves and completed the rescue.

Newspaper photo diagram of Engine 72 pendulum rescues.

As the multiple alarm companies, including Rescue 1, arrived they quickly joined the battle. Deputy Chief Martin arrived and assumed command of the fire. Moments later Martin received a frantic call from the manager of a Con Edison substation across the street from the fire. He reported that thousands of gallons of water were pouring into the building through holes in the wall. Members of Rescue 1 were sent to help.

Department pumps were quickly set up as the accumulating water rose and threatened to flood the dynamos. This would have resulted in the loss of power to all of Manhattan below 14th Street. Rescue 1 found that an old wooden conduit ran across Gold Street directly under the fire building and the sub-station. It apparently had been buried since Dutch Colonial times, when it was used to feed water to a farm. Rescue 1 was able to divert the flow. With the flooding situation under control, they returned to fighting the fire.

Sadly, the flames took seven lives, but responding firemen rescued 40 people from the blazing building. Numerous firemen were placed on the Roll of Merit for their heroic work at this blaze including Firemen Charles Amato, Robert Tierney and Probationary Fireman Matthew Crawley who received Class I awards and later were awarded medals. (Both Robert Tierney and Matthew Crawley would later become members of Rescue Company 1.)

The brutal winter weather was taking its toll on civilians, when on February 6, 1920, two massive canopies of the Playhouse Theatre on West 47th Street near Seventh Avenue, and the Rivoli Theatre at Broadway and 49th Street collapsed under the weight of accumulated snow, ice and sleet. Walking under the Playhouse Theatre's canopy at the time of the collapse was Lt. Col. Fred Davison of the 22nd Infantry who was stationed on Governors Island. Arriving quickly Hook & Ladder 2 special-called

Rescue 1 as they dove into the collapse area and freed the army officer. Davison, a decorated WWI veteran, suffered a fractured skull and later died in the hospital.

Rescue 1 arrived and helped with a secondary search and inspected the building for other hazards. Rescue 1 then responded to the second collapse, where a 50-year-old woman, a 30-year-old porter, and several other people were trapped or injured by the collapse of a second large canopy.

The FDNY and the city faced blizzard-like conditions on February 11th. The streets were filled with deep snow and were impassable in certain areas. Chief Kenlon said, "New York was facing the greatest fire hazard ever confronted in the history of the present department." The streets, especially in lower Manhattan, were not only snow-filled but blocked by numerous vehicles stuck in the snow.

A third alarm was transmitted for a fire at 321 Broadway at 7 p.m. Only one-third of the assigned units arrived at the blaze. Later that evening a three-alarm blaze in a loft building at 145 Spring Street was battled as four engines, two ladder trucks and the rescue wagon responded. Only one engine made it to the scene. The remaining companies were stalled in streets blocked by trucks, cars and snow. Members jumped from the trapped rigs, grabbed tools and ladders, and plodded on foot to the fire.

Members of Engine 55, their rig blocked by abandoned vehicles, pulled off lengths of hose and headed to the fire. Members of Hook & Ladder 20, trapped at Mercer and Prince streets carried their hand tools and two 35-foot extension ladders three blocks to the blaze. Other companies were forced to do the same.

As the frequency and severity of fire duty on the lower west side of Manhattan increased, Rescue 1 was relocated from Great Jones Street to the quarters of Engine Company 30 at

278 Spring Street. (This building is now the home of the Fire Museum.) This three-bay firehouse was one mile closer to the dry goods district where some of the most difficult fires were occurring. This area would become known to New York City firemen as Hell's Hundred Acres. Rescue 1 was moving closer to the eye of the brewing storm.

On February 18, 1920, Rescue Company 1 moved into their new quarters. This firehouse had once held three separate sections of Engine 30. The third section was disbanded in 1911, and the second section had closed in 1918. (The second section would be re-established in 1925 and continue to respond until 1939.) This left a huge amount of space for Rescue 1's growing array of tools and specialized equipment.

Rescue 1 joined Engine 30 in their Spring Street firehouse in 1920.

In the beginning of March, Rescue 1 Company Commander Francis Blessing was admitted to St. Lawrence Hospital in

Brooklyn with pneumonia. Sadly, he would pass away two weeks later on March 15, 1920. The 35-year-old fire officer was the first member to join the company after the original members were chosen. An expert motor mechanic before joining the department, Blessing was brought to the company for his driving abilities. He had been the chauffeur of Chiefs Kenlon, Croker and Martin. According to the N.Y. *Evening World*'s article about his death:

> He was assigned to the Rescue Squad as first chauffeur when it was organized six years ago and continued to drive for the squad after he was promoted to lieutenant and commander. He had a record of taking the apparatus seven miles into the Bronx in ten minutes one night last winter.

Frank Blessing's name appeared on the Roll of Merit seven times including the Bennett Medal. Newspaper reports of his illness and death said the 35-year-old fire officer was taken ill in early March, having exposed himself to the elements while attending his mother's funeral. Blessing lived at 366 Cypress Avenue in the Bronx.

Thomas Kilbride was then designated as Lieutenant in Command.

A fire broke out in the three-story brick warehouse at 288 South Street on the night of March 28, 1920. The flames began on the top floor and were soon shooting through the roof and burning downwards to the second floor, as the first alarm companies rolled in. The warehouse was filled with coffee and spices and at first the flames were producing a pleasant aroma that drifted across the neighborhood. Thousands of people were drawn to the blaze and filled the streets and sidewalks near the fire building.

As the fire consumed bag after bag of spices the smoke

being produced also changed in nature. The sweet smell soon became acrid as bags of pepper caught fire. Firemen working inside were driven back and Chief Martin called Rescue 1 over and asked them to break out the smoke helmets.

The rescue men entered the building and set up a relay handing back bags of coffee and spices to prevent their exposure to the flames, as other smoke-helmeted men moved deeper into the building with a hose line. At the height of the fire, Honorary Chief Mainzer worked with Doctor Archer as a medical station was set up and firemen after fireman was treated for eye irritation or smoke inhalation.

Mainzer and Archer soothed the pepper irritation with glasses of milk and eye wash solutions. Mainzer raced around the neighborhood and purchased every bottle of milk he could find and returned to the medical station. Conditions became so severe, that at one-point Mainzer fell over unconscious from the noxious smoke. He was quickly revived and returned to helping injured firemen.

The peppery smoke drove away the crowds and the streets were soon empty. Stores of fireworks then began igniting and spreading the fire within the warehouse. Chief Martin pulled all his men from the building before it eventually collapsed in on itself and the smoldering ruins continued pumping acrid smoke into the air.

An explosion of magnesium flash-lamp powder (used in photography) tore through the top floor of a four-story building at 251 West 42nd Street at 5:50 p.m. on April 2, 1920. Two workers were seriously injured, a large section of the roof was torn off, and the rear wall was left unstable. Arriving fire companies under the command of Battalion Chief Curtain immediately went to work. Captain Seiferth of Engine 54 and Lt. Heller of Hook & Ladder 21 were the first in the building and a line of hose was quickly stretched to the top floor.

Just as the water was started, a second explosion occurred, toppling the firemen. Members of Rescue 1 and other companies scrambled to the top floor and pulled their injured comrades to safety.

It was just after midnight on April 10th when a fire was reported in a five-story loft building at 116 Wooster Street. The building housed a paper box company and a doll company. The place was loaded with excelsior (slender curled wood shavings used for stuffing furniture) and other flammables and was soon a mass of flames. Several firemen including John Milward of Rescue 1 were severely cut on the hands and wrists by falling glass.

Shortly after this job another fire broke out in the basement of the Consolidated Stock Exchange, at Broad and Beaver streets. The flames originated in an area used for storage by painters and carpenters. It was 3 a.m. when the first due Engine 10 moved in aggressively with their line, until they were stopped by a wall of heat and smoke. Engine 4 took over the line until they, too, were driven back, and Engine 32 took their turn. One by one firemen dropped to the floor unconscious, only to be pulled from the fire building and taken to the medical station where they were treated for smoke inhalation.

On May 1, 1920, Lt. John Coffey of Engine 33 transferred to Rescue 1. Coffey joined the FDNY on March 4, 1912. His name appeared on the Roll of Merit with a Class I award, for his rescue of a woman and her child in 1918. For this daring rescue he was also awarded the Hugh Bonner and Department Medal.

Rescue 1, nine engines and three hook and ladder companies

responded by ferryboat with Chiefs Kenlon and Martin from Manhattan, to a major fire in the National Lead Company on Staten Island. This May 2, 1920, blaze went to three alarms and destroyed the original fire building, a hotel and two homes. This was the first time Manhattan fire companies responded to Richmond (although Rescue 1 had responded to a Staten Island ship fire back in 1918).

The smoke helmets were used again on May 11th when FDNY units responded to a ship fire, at the foot of West 12th Street in Manhattan. The fire was in the forward hold of the 405-foot freighter *El Alba,* where hundreds of bales of cotton and a quantity of rubber were stored.

The alarm sent three fireboats, *New Yorker, Willard,* and *Duane,* under the command of Acting Deputy Chief McKenna, and two land companies, Engine 3 and Hook & Ladder 5, under the command of former Rescue 1 officer and now Battalion Chief Ed Hotchkiss. The land companies and members of the fireboats followed Hotchkiss into the hold with a hose line and attempted to reach the seat of the fire.

The smoke condition became so severe, that firemen began dropping to the deck unconscious. Deputy Chief McKenna dropped unconscious and was carried back to the pier. Rescue 1 was special-called and upon arrival entered the hold with their smoke helmets. They pulled out the remaining unconscious firemen, who were found in the water accumulating in the bottom of the hold. These men including Chief Hotchkiss, Lt. Foley of the *Duane,* Lt. Farr of the *Willard,* and Lt. Calvary and Fireman Dollard of Hook & Ladder 5, Capt. Henry and Fireman Bowen of Engine 3, were then treated at a first aid station. Acting Battalion Chief Smith and Fireman Seavers of the Marine Division were also treated at the scene and were sent home to recuperate. Members of Rescue 1 were not able to extinguish the deep-seated fire, so fireboats moved in and flooded the hold to extinguish it.

A fire that was ignited by a hot saw that fell into a whale oil tank, required a second alarm on May 27, 1920. The fire was in the cellar of the two-story brick and corrugated iron building at 2 Sheriff Street. (Sheriff Street used to run from Houston to Grand streets in Manhattan's Lower East Side. Housing developments in the 1940s left only one small block between Stanton and East Houston streets.) Smoke from the fire forced the early dismissal of students in a nearby school. Rescue 1 helped extinguish the flames and checked for extension.

Chlorine gas leaking from one of 15 tanks in the Thompson warehouse at 521 Broome Street, drove more than 200 families from their homes on June 23, 1920. It was 11 p.m. when the alarm was received from a police officer who noticed people having difficulty breathing. Handkerchief to his mouth, the officer notified the Beach Street precinct and the FDNY was called.

Deputy Chief Helm arrived and ordered all houses in the immediate area evacuated and special-called Rescue 1. As soon as the front door was forced, Chief Helm stepped inside the warehouse, only to stagger back out shouting to Rescue 1 to adjust their gas masks. Members of Rescue 1 searched inside under the command of Lt. Kilbride and located a tank with a one-inch hole and set about plugging the leak.

Meanwhile, Acting Chief of Department Smoky Joe Martin and Doctor Archer arrived. Archer set up his medical aid station as Martin coordinated Rescue 1's operations and the work of Hook & Ladders 20 and 5 evacuating the nearby apartments.

Inside the warehouse, despite having gas masks, the

members of Rescue 1 were having a difficult time controlling the leak and operating within the greenish-yellow cloud of noxious gas. Four members wearing gas masks stumbled from the building suffering the effects of the gas. Firemen Walter Lamb, Joe Horacek, and John Kistenberger were treated briefly by Dr. Archer before being rushed to the hospital.

Rescue 1 men with Draeger smoke helmets.

Rescue 1 Firemen Frank Clark, Charles Roggenkamp, Frank Joseph and John J. McEntee of Engine 30 detailed to Rescue 1, were able to control the leak and removed the tank to the street. The tank was placed in the rescue truck and taken to the Canal Street dock and tossed in the river.

When the gas in the neighborhood dissipated, the families were allowed back into their homes. The members of Rescue 1 piled into their rig and drove to the hospital to check on their injured men. All of the Rescue 1 members and McEntee were placed on the Roll of Merit.

The exploits of Rescue 1 were good copy for the city's many newspapers. They were frequently referred to as the Rescue Squad, but their work becoming known across the city—especially in Manhattan, where there was a heavy concentration of people and businesses in the same area. People lived above stores, next to factories, near warehouses, around the corner from the huge oil tanks, across from the bustling waterfront. There were drug warehouses, chemical plants, power plants, cold storage plants, lumber yards, and tenements.

One particular article in the *The Sun* and *New York Herald* on July 5, 1920, stated:

> A.J. Brown, superintendent of the 12-story apartment house at 600 West End Avenue, smelled ammonia leaking from the 50-pound ammonia refrigerating tank in the subcellar yesterday. He closed all the doors and windows that might have let the fumes up through the building and called the fire department. Mr. Brown said he obtained a prompt telephone connection and noticed the time at which the call was put through. Nine- and one-half minutes later, he said, Rescue Squad No. 1 arrived and its members, with masks donned as they jumped from the car, went into the subcellar. The squad had travelled from Engine 30, in Spring Street.
>
> Mr. Brown said it was the fastest work he ever had seen. The cellar was filled with stinging gas by that time and an explosion was imminent, but the gas helmet men found

> the leak and stopped the operation of the tank. Before leaving they opened the windows and aired the place.

The company operated at a similar call on July 25th when they responded to an ammonia leak at 318 West 57th Street, in the basement of the West Side Young Men's Christian Association. Rescue men were able to patch the leak before the fumes reached the upper floors, where several meetings were in progress.

Two days later they were called to 21 West 34th Street where a seven-year-old boy, John Kenneally, was wedged between the floor of the elevator and the ceiling of the first floor. (The youngster's father, John Kenneally, was captain of Engine Company 37.) The youngster was with his mother shopping for clothes, when he wandered away and stepped into the freight elevator. It rose immediately and as he tried to jump out, his body became caught.

The members of Rescue 1, with help from Engine 24 and Hook & Ladder 8, succeeded in freeing the boy after an hour of careful cutting. He was removed to Bellevue Hospital suffering a badly cut head and internal injuries.

On August 17, 1920, four-alarms were transmitted at Box 338, for a fire at 48 West 14th Street in Manhattan. Clouds of thick noxious smoke pumped from the building blanketing the street and sidewalks outside. Assistant Chief Martin arrived as Engine 20 pushed a line into the cellar. A backdraft drove most of the firemen out of the cellar, that was when Probationary Fireman Dennis Donovan was immediately missed, and two volunteers from Hook & Ladder 12 re-entered the cellar in search of the missing man. He was located unconscious in the cellar and carried out by Firemen Charles Costello and Frank McGrath.

Fireman Donovan was worked on by Doctor Archer for more than an hour, but despite his best efforts with the pulmotor the young fireman could not be revived. Dozens of firemen were rendered unconscious as they battled this difficult blaze. The flames were finally extinguished by members of Rescue 1 utilizing smoke helmets as they attacked the flames with a hose line. The conditions were so extreme and deadly that Firemen Costello and McGrath were both awarded medals, with the Bennett going to Costello.

On August 31st Rescue 1 was called to a major elevator incident in the Clarendon Building at 18th Street and Fourth Avenue. It was just after 6 p.m., when 18 workers leaving their jobs on the 12th floor, squeezed into the elevator. One last employee hurried up just as the car door was closing and heard one of his colleagues say, "Next trip!"

Two seconds later the elevator car plunged to the bottom of the shaft.

As it fell, the counterbalance in the lifting machinery, weighing several hundred pounds, came off the guides and smashed through the roof of the car.

For several minutes the injured struggled trying to free themselves from the tangled wreckage, their screams and cries for help echoing within the elevator shaft. Chief Martin arrived and refused to allow any of the firemen to enter the wrecked car until the massive wreckage on top of the car was secured by ropes.

Members of Rescue 1 moved in, and with the help of the first due engine and truck, removed the injured who were not pinned first. They then tried to use jacks, ropes, and levers to free the imprisoned people, but had to resort to the torch to cut away the mangled steel. Martin ordered a hose line stretched to protect the firemen and the trapped passengers.

As the last of the living people were removed Rescue 1 shifted their sights on removing two dead men from beneath the wreckage. It took two more hours of difficult and dangerous work to free the bodies and remove them from the mangled elevator. In all, three people lost their lives and one of the injured women lost her leg.

On September 1, 1920, Fireman Alfred Kinsella was promoted to lieutenant and was assigned to Engine Company 74.

The company was called to 460 Riverside Drive on September 7th to free the body of a man caught between the first floor and the roof of an elevator. The torch was used the cut away metal to release the trapped body.

A broken ammonia pipe in the basement of the Marlborough Hotel at Broadway and 36th Street drove 100 patrons from the hotel's dining room as it filled with the noxious fumes on September 10th. Rescue 1 responded and repaired the leak, allowing the hotel and restaurant to return to normal business.

In an era before modern refrigeration, New York City's needs for fresh food were met differently than they are today. For instance, live cattle and other animals were delivered to the city in train cars, and then made ready to eat. The live animals arrived in the city and were penned briefly before being herded to slaughterhouses and packing plants. The area of the west side of Manhattan between West 16th Street to the north, Ninth Avenue and Hudson Street to the west, and Gansevoort Street to the south, became known as the Meatpacking District. By 1900 there were 250 slaughterhouses and packing plants.

Also included in this neighborhood were the poultry and dairy industries. The area became so tightly crowded that by

1929, as part of an improvement plan, the New York Central Railroad built an elevated railway specifically for these businesses, called the High Line.

Another major location for this industry was West 39th Street, close to the Hudson River. This block (now filled with Port Authority bus ramps and parking for the Javits Center) was known as "Abattoir Row." Abattoir (derived from the French verb "abattre," meaning to strike down or slaughter) is a fancy name for a slaughterhouse. It was a common sight to see the streets in the neighborhood closed to vehicular traffic, while cattle were herded from their pens, taken to the slaughterhouses and packing plants, and turned into beef. There were even cow tunnels and bridges built, to help move the animals without disrupting local traffic.

Flames broke out in a meatpacking plant at 635 West 40th Street on September 11th and within minutes threatened to spread to the entire neighborhood. As the first alarm units rolled up, flames were already bursting through the roof. Chief Martin arrived on the first alarm, and seeing a strong breeze whipping up the flames, sent in a second and then third alarms. Rescue 1 rolled on the multiple alarm and joined the firefighting efforts.

Chief Kenlon arrived on the third alarm and saw that a huge pen of pigs was trapped by a wall of flames. Large streams from a fireboat were played on the pen as firemen and employees moved the squealing animals from danger. To add to the excitement, the occasional porker would break free and make a mad dash into the street.

The huge flames attracted a large crowd of local Hell's Kitchen tenants and visitors to the Theatre District only blocks away. The entire scene was illuminated by the flames, as hose streams were directed toward the growing fire. Searchlight trucks were moved into position as the smoke grew and the flames darkened. It took four alarms to extinguish the fire, which was held to the original fire building.

It was noon on September 16, 1920, the echoing sounds of the Trinity Church bells were just fading when a powerful explosion tore through a crowded street in lower Manhattan. A wagon loaded with dynamite and packed with sash weights was detonated on Wall Street just outside of the J.P. Morgan Company building. The first FDNY units rolled into a devastating scene. The streets and sidewalks were covered in dust, debris, splintered wood, shards of glass, burning automobiles, and the mangled bodies of the dead and dying.

Wall Street terrorist explosion Sept. 16, 1920, 44 killed, 100 injured.

A second alarm was immediately transmitted. As the vehicle fires were extinguished, members of Rescue 1 and other companies began treating the injured who were strewn across the street and sidewalks. First aid stations were organized, and ambulances hurried the injured to nearby hospitals. This act of terrorism took a heavy toll: 44 people were killed and more than 100 were seriously injured.

The next day, a fire in a five-story brick building occupied by the United Dressed Beef Company caused some serious damage and drove hose teams from the building. The fire started in a ventilation fan motor and soon spread to bags of fertilizer packed for shipment. Strong ammonia fumes were generated and mixed with the thick smoke. This caused 200 steer and calves to stampede in their adjoining concrete pens.

A second alarm was transmitted, and members of Rescue 1 donned their smoke helmets and pushed a hose line into the blazing building. They were able to bring the fire under control after an hour of punishing work.

It was a few minutes after 2 p.m. on October 8, 1920, when an explosion tore through the oil tanker *G.R. Crowe*, where it was undergoing repairs at the Shewan & Sons shipyard at the foot of 27th Street in Brooklyn. There were 300 men working on the ship, with about 20 working in the hold when an explosion rocked the vessel. The blast triggered a fire, trapping the men at work in the hold. The FDNY was immediately called.

The first unit to arrive, was Engine Company 239, under the command of Lt. James McWilliams.

> The first thing that struck my eyes in entering the yards was the spectacle of men trying to get a breath of air through the anchor hoist. Their faces were streaming with blood. I noticed their hair was burned away. As I approached nearer to the ship, I saw others trying to get some air from eight-inch portholes. There seemed at first no way of getting to them and rescuing them. The forward part of the ship where the men were trapped was a roaring furnace.

The members of Engine 239 stretched a line onto the deck of the blazing ship and began to drive back the flames. Even with the Rescue Company already responding it was clear some action had to be taken immediately. Fireman William Boyce was lowered into the hold and began to grope around, trying to find some of the trapped men. Boyce located John McCoy, dragged him back, and signaled with the rope to pull them up. Before the rescue could be started Boyce dropped to the deck unconscious.

As soon as Lt. McWilliams and Fireman William Perrine saw Boyce fall, they slid down the rope into the hold to rescue him. McWilliams grabbed Boyce and firemen on the deck hauled them up. Fireman Perrine grabbed McCoy and they, too, were hoisted to the deck and attended to by an ambulance surgeon.

A few minutes later Rescue 1 arrived and assembled beside the hold with their smoke helmets. Rescue members were lowered into the hold by rope. Searching for the trapped workers, the helmeted firemen dragged the unconscious workers to a point where they could be pulled up to the main deck. In all, five men were killed by the explosion. Twenty others were injured, six of them seriously.

For their heroic efforts Lt. McWilliams and Firemen Boyce and Perrine of Engine 239 were placed on the Roll of Merit with Class II awards. Ten other members of Engine 239 and Hook & Ladder 109 also received Class B awards.

On the afternoon of December 1st Rescue 1 responded to 113 East 14th Street, the Irving Lunchroom, where a tank of ammonia had exploded in the basement. Rescue men expected to find several children in danger, when they heard cries and whimpering as they fought their way into the dense fumes in the basement. Their search found no children, but did locate six kittens huddled together in a pile of rags, suffering from the fumes less than 10-feet from the leaking tank. The helmeted rescue men carried them to the street where the 75 guests had fled. The kittens recovered.

Later that day, a major collapse occurred at the nine-story Strathmore apartment house on the northeast corner of Broadway and 52nd Street. The brick building was undergoing renovations, as the structure was being converted into office spaces. It was just after 4:30 when the rear wall collapsed with a thunderous roar that blasted out the windows of the adjoining buildings. A six-foot-high pile of debris rolled out into 52nd Street.

First arriving companies made several exciting and dangerous rescues from the first-floor automobile dealership. Several people were pinned beneath the wreckage and were dug free by members of Hook & Ladder 4 under the command of Lt. George Polsenski. They removed two men and a woman to safety, as Rescue 1 arrived and began their search. The rescue work had been going on for almost two hours, when a large secondary collapse occurred. Firemen barely escaped and regrouped as a shoring crew was brought in.

As the evening grew dark, huge theatrical lights were set up to illuminate the scene. While the shoring crews were hard at work, another tremendous crash brought down the remainder of the rear wall. Deputy Chief Ross examined the collapsed building and declared it unsafe. It was deemed too dangerous to continue operations inside. The Building Department called for a wrecking crew to clear away the most dangerous overhead debris, cornice and wall.

When it was deemed safe again Rescue 1 renewed their search. Making their way into the workers locker room, they found three suits of street clothes. This led them to believe there were still three additional workers, trapped within the collapse area. The following day the searches were completed and proved negative. Amazingly, only one worker died in the collapse.

On December 9, 1920, Rescue 1 was again special-called, this time to Broadway and Vesey Street where a man was wedged between two trolley cars. Traffic came to a stand still while two police officers attempted to cut the man free with hacksaws. He appeared to be hopelessly entangled so Rescue 1 and a hook and ladder were called to the scene. Rescue 1 broke out the torch and within a few minutes, the badly injured man was freed and rushed to the hospital with serious chest and shoulder injuries.

On December 16, 1920, Rescue 1 received two new members, when Firemen Bela Varga and Edward Schneider were transferred into the company. Varga joined the FDNY on March 4, 1912, and was assigned to Engine 30. Born in Bridgeport, Connecticut, on December 19, 1885, Varga was a former electrician. Ed Schneider would only remain in Rescue 1 for several months before transferring back to Engine 31.

Rescue 1 pulled in first due, at a fire in a loft building at Broadway and Canal streets on December 29, 1920. Believing people were still in the building, Lt. John Coffey split his company as he took off for the front fire escape. Coffey ascended toward the fourth-floor window that was billowing thick clouds of smoke. Close on the rescue officer's heels was Fireman Paul Maron. When they arrived at the fire floor, a huge backdraft blew out the windows and sent a cloud of hot thick smoke and gas directly at the officer, toppling him to the fire escape landing unconscious.

Fireman Maron tried to get to Coffey, but he was overcome and also dropped to the landing unconscious. Fireman William Hutcheon grabbed a scaling ladder and climbed from the third floor to the fourth and grabbed Maron, who was the closest. As Hutcheon held Maron and began his descent, the unconscious fireman regained some of his senses and barked, "For God's sake, don't mind me—get Coffey!"

Meanwhile a large ladder was positioned and as Coffey was being removed from danger he muttered to his rescuers "Never mind me boys, get Maron!"

As soon as Hutcheon had Maron safely on the ground, he returned to the fourth-floor fire escape landing thinking there might be other members of Rescue 1 there. Within seconds, he, too, was overcome and had to be removed to the street. Doctor Archer had arrived in his specially designed auto and set up a medical first aid station in a nearby storefront. The members of Rescue 1 were revived and taken to Volunteer Hospital for further examinations.

It was New Year's Eve, five hours until 1921, when Rescue 1 was called to 278 West Broadway, a crockery store on the fifth floor of the building. First due units rolled in just after 7 p.m. and worked their way toward the top floor fire. Hook & Ladder 8 took the rear fire escape as Engine 31 stretched a line of hose up the interior stairs. Both teams were moving in on the fire when it became apparent it wasn't an ordinary fire. They all tumbled backward, choking on acrid fumes. Members of Rescue 1 using smoke helmets, entered the caustic atmosphere. They found that the gas pipes in the occupancy had melted, and the escaping illuminating gas was feeding the flames. The members of Rescue 1 controlled the leaking pipes, then turned their attention to a drum of sulphuric acid that was attached to the apparatus used in the finishing process for the crockery ware.

Rescue men disconnected the drum and carefully carried the hazardous material from the fire area. Companies then commenced an aggressive attack on the flames and had things under control in several minutes.

How's this for a fire-fighting face? It is Paul C. Maron's, the hero of many a daring rescue.

Paul Maron in newspaper photo.

Chapter 9:
1921

By 1921 the population of New York City had reached 5.8 million. The FDNY was swiftly motorizing their firefighting fleet, and of the 299 land-based fire companies only 20 still were horse drawn.

It was time for Rescue 1 to get a new rig. Fire Commissioner Drennan sent the following report to the New York City Board of estimate:

City of New York, Fire Department,
September 22, 1920

Hon. John F. Hyland, Mayor, and Chairman of Board of Estimate & Apportionment:

Sir—At a meeting of the Board of Estimate and Apportionment, held on March 26, 1920, permission was granted to this Department to purchase a motor-driven water tower at $18,500, the cost to be charged against account CFD No. 10-E.

The Board of Purchase fixed June 10, 1920, as a date for opening bids on this tower, but no bids were presented on account of the inability of manufacturers to furnish the type of water tower specified.

I now find that a motor-driven wagon for Rescue Company No. 1 and an automobile for the Chief of Department are required, and for that reason it is requested that the $18,500 allowed for the water tower be set aside for the purchase of the rescue wagon and the automobile.

> The wagon now assigned to Rescue Company No. 1 has been in use since 1915, when the rescue squad was organized. This wagon is now out of commission owing to difficulties in obtaining parts required for much needed repairs. This wagon is no longer fitted for the purpose for which it was intended. This wagon consists of a second-hand chassis and the body was made and mounted by mechanics of this Department.
>
> A new up-to-date motor-driven rescue wagon is required to replace that now in service. Rescue Company No. 1 not only responds to fires where dense smoke or the prevalence of gas or other fumes prevent firemen from entering the building, but also in rescue work in cases of emergency, as, for instance, people imprisoned in elevator shafts, railroad wrecks, etc. It is, therefore, imperative that a wagon capable of quickly reaching the scene of the fire or emergency be obtained as speedily as possible to replace that now assigned to the rescue squad. The activities of this squad are not confined to any one borough, as it goes to all parts of the city when required. (It then further explains the need for Chief Kenlon's automobile.)
>
> Respectfully,
> Thomas J. Drennan, Fire Commissioner

The following resolution was offered:

> The Board of Estimate and Apportionment hereby approves and expenditure by the Fire Department not to exceed seven thousand five hundred dollars ($7,500) for a new and completely equipped rescue wagon for Rescue Company No. 1. [They also approved $8,800 for the chief's car.]

On February 11, 1921, the Board of Estimate approved a contract for a new and completely equipped rescue wagon for Rescue 1 at $9,000.

Rescue 1 would receive a new rig built on a White chassis. The 2-ton vehicle was quite similar in size and appearance to the original rescue rig. The new truck was equipped with a 50-horsepower engine. The open cabbed rig was slightly longer than the Cadillac and did not have cab doors or windshield.

Rescue Car for New York City

Rescue Company No. 1 of New York City fire department has acquired a White rescue car equipped with a 50-horse-

Rescue Car for New York City

power motor. The wheel base is 156 inches, the wheels being of steel with pneumatic cord tires. The car is equipped with a 30-gallon gas tank.

An article in the April 20, 1921, edition of *Fire and Water Engineering* reported that the FDNY had recently acquired a two-ton White rescue truck, equipped with a 50-horsepower motor.

> This apparatus is furnished with every appliance and auxiliary that is required for this service. It is one of the most complete of its kind ever installed in a fire department. The list of tools and equipment is as follows:
>
> One tarpaulin to cover the seat, dashboard and engine
> One tarpaulin for the body of wagon
> One 5-ton trip jack
> One 10-ton trip jack

One motor driven air pump with power taken off from the engine
Two stretchers (with tarpaulin cover)
Two jimmies (prying tools)
One life gun, one canister containing cartridges and cord
Two 100-foot lengths of Manila rope
Two hand lanterns
One increaser 2-½" to 3"
Two reducers, 2" to 2-½"
One 1-1/4" controlling nozzle
One high-pressure wrench
One hill pump for tires
One long handled auto jack
One K&G cutting torch, with O2 tank and acetylene gas
25-feet of copper-covered-hose
25-feet rubber hose
Gauges for O2 and gas
One jet and four tips
Two pairs of rubber gloves
Two pulmotors
Four breathing helmets
Two telephone helmets, 150-feet of telephone cable
Six extra cylinders for helmets
Three wading pants
One Grether searchlight (battery flashlight used with helmet)
One hand searchlight for fires (battery powered flashlight)
One 30" Stilson wrench
One nickel plated fire bell mounted on the rig

Grether searchlight.

Collapse on January 21, 1921, Throop Ave. Brooklyn.

Rescue 1 was special-called to Brooklyn on the night of January 21, 1921, to a fire and collapse at 492 Throop Avenue, Brooklyn. Companies were making an aggressive interior attack, pushing hose lines deep into the first floor of the four-story brick factory building, when the floor above them collapsed. Amazingly, the way the building collapsed the timbers formed an arch over the firemen and no one was injured. One man from Engine 235 was found unconscious, knocked out by the thick smoke. He was quickly removed and revived.

A four-alarm fire was battled on February 8th on the first floor of 158 Duane Street, a five-story brick building occupied by the Merriam Shoe Manufacturing Company. With heavy flames threatening the adjoining buildings, multiple alarms were transmitted in quick succession. These calls for extra help came in at just the right time, when the day and night platoons were being shifted, and the men of both platoons all responded to the fire.

On April 1, 1921, Fireman Charles A. Kennedy of Hook & Ladder 26 transferred to Rescue 1. Kennedy was appointed on November 27, 1913, and assigned to Hook & Ladder 24. He had also worked in H&L 44 in the Bronx.

On May 18, 1921, Fireman Joseph D. Sullivan of Hook & Ladder 12 transferred to Rescue 1. The former longshoreman joined the FDNY on June 16, 1916.

Rescue 1 responded to a fire onboard the *Panhandle State,* a 10,500-ton oil burning steamship, moored at Pier 7 at the foot of Rector Street. The ship had just arrived from France, and the old crew was replaced by a new one. The fire was discovered at about 8:30 p.m. on May 19th and members of the crew used fire extinguishers without success. A police officer patrolling the pier, sent in the alarm sending two fireboats, engines, hook & ladders, and the Rescue.

Assistant Chief Martin and Deputy Chief Helm were among the first to arrive and found the engine room ablaze. As several hose lines were directed into the hold, Chief Martin and the rescue officer agreed entering the engine room was too dangerous, as the flames were impinging directly on the ship's fuel tank. As two tugs attached lines to the ship, firemen chopped the pier mooring lines and the ship was towed away to prevent the fire from extending to other ships or the piers.

On May 20, 1921, Rescue 1 was called to Ninth Avenue and 34th Street, where a 16-year-old boy had fallen beneath an elevated subway car at the station. Rescue 1 brought a priest to administer Last Rites to the trapped boy, as they freed him from beneath the wheels of the first car. Sadly, the boy died.

Later that evening a crowd of more than one thousand people, watched as Rescue 1 work for 20 minutes to extricate a 35-year-old man from beneath the trucks of the Third Avenue trolley car at Canal Street and the Bowery. This operation was under the command of Deputy Chief Binns. While the rescue men worked to free the man, an ambulance surgeon joined them under the car and administered first aid to the pinned man. The man was then rushed to Gouverneur Hospital in critical condition.

At this point in the company's history, they were being assigned to all reported ship fires in Manhattan. The use of their smoke helmets or gas masks proved extremely effective especially battling flames in the hold of a ship. May 23, 1921, was another ship fire, this time on board the US Navy's training ship *Granite State*.

Manhattan Box 729 was transmitted sending companies to the US Navy warehouse and offices at the foot of West 96th Street where the 206-foot-long, three masted vessel was moored. Commissioned in 1864, the vessel served as a ship of the line during both the Civil War and the Spanish American War. After World War I, its name was changed from USS *New Hampshire* (BB-25) to USS *Training Ship Granite State*.

Oil leaking from a nearby transfer pipe created a large slick across the water, which was ignited by a passing Navy gig. The *Granite State* was soon ablaze with flames spreading to the pier and adjacent ships. Unlike most of Rescue 1's ship operations, there was no need for smoke helmets as the huge wooden ship was quickly filled with flames. Rescue 1 joined the other units stretching lines and trying to stop the spreading fire.

Luckily, before abandoning ship, the crew was able to flood the powder magazine and prevent a major explosion. Among the vessels saved from the flames, was the Presidential Yacht *Mayflower*, which had just transported President Harding to New York City earlier that day.

Fire companies under the command of Battalion Chief William Clark, soon had several streams attacking the flames through port holes. As the body of fire increased, additional lines were stretched and additional alarms were transmitted. The major attack was soon taken over by fireboats. The ship was a total loss.

Engine Company 24 arrived at 453 Hudson Street at midnight on June 19, 1921. The basement of the building contained the ice plant of the New York Milk Products Company. Five families were driven from the building by the strong odor of ammonia. Capt. Mullaly special-called Rescue 1 to the scene. Rescue men donned masks and were quickly able to locate a small leak and repaired it. The tenants were then able to return to their apartments.

On July 1, 1922, Fireman Frank Joseph transferred from Rescue

1 to Hook & Ladder 79. He had spent three years in Rescue 1.

Gas leaks, especially ammonia and illuminating gas, were still common in the 1920s. But what about breathing protection advances? The Army gas mask was developed during World War I to provide protection against all the poisonous gases, vapors, and smoke encountered on the battlefield. After the war, when these masks were advocated for use by people in chemical, metallurgical, and other industries where noxious fumes and gases occur, the Bureau of Mines immediately pointed out that these masks give no protection against ammonia gas used in refrigeration, or against carbon monoxide.

In the early 1920s, special gas masks with canisters containing absorbents designed for protection against ammonia or carbon monoxide were developed. These masks however provided little or no protection against other gases. A "fireman's" canister was also developed, which was smaller and lighter than the "Universal" gas mask, making it ideal for concentrations encountered by city firemen. The fireman's gas mask canister weighed only 4 pounds (3 pounds lighter than the Universal.) All the filter type gas masks, however, were useless in oxygen-deficient atmospheres and the smoke helmet had to be used.

The *New York Herald* reported in its July 9, 1921, issue:

FIREMEN USE MASKS STOP BASEMENT LEAK

Fumes Cause Excitement in Ice Cream Parlor.

The rescue squad of the Fire Department, situated at Spring and Varick streets, made the record run of its career

> last night when it reached 149th Street and Third Avenue, the Bronx, in 22 minutes. The squad was called because of an ammonia leak in the basement of Coune's Ice Cream Parlor, which had driven about 20 patrons and half a dozen clerks, sneezing and coughing, to the street, and had also emptied several stores on either side.
>
> A big crowd collected when the fire apparatus arrived, but backed off again when the fumes got a bit of a breeze behind them. Business in what is known as "the Hub" of the Bronx was suspended for an hour until the rescue squad got the leak plugged.
>
> A patrolman who met the sneezing and coughing patrons of the place on their first exodus turned in the fire alarm, but the regular firemen, not having gas masks, dared not venture into the basement. Waiting for the rescue squad, however, they sprayed it liberally with water and thus absorbed a good portion of the fumes. (*NY Herald* pg. 16)

The same job was covered by the *NY Tribune* story that also mentioned Lt. Coffey and his men wore gas masks and wading trousers when they entered the basement to shut the pump stopping the flow of vapor. A defective gasket was responsible for the blowing out of the cylinder head.

On July 13, 1921, the department was faced with another dangerous gas related emergency on board the liner *Mincio*. Hydrocyanic acid, which is a solution of hydrogen cyanide in water, is a colorless and extremely deadly poison and was being used to fumigate the hold of a ship moored at the Italian-American pier foot of West 30th Street. One worker was overcome and soon the hold was filled with his heroic shipmates trying to save him. Rescue 1 arrived, immediately donned their masks, and dove into the dangerous ships hold. Under the command of Acting Lieutenant John Conners, the rescue men removed five crewmen from the dark depths of the ship and hurried them to the main deck. Three of them were dead, but two were rushed to Bellevue Hospital.

Four days later, July 17th, a serious fire was fought in the five-story building occupied by the Phoenix Cheese Company at 345 Greenwich Street. At about 9 p.m. the night crew of the cheese company began coughing and sneezing. The foreman, John O'Malley believed it was due to the refrigeration plant on the second floor. The ammonia traveled through pipes from the main plant several blocks away, so O'Malley had them shut off the ammonia. He also had a fireman from Engine 27 sent to the location, but no fire could be found. But by 2:15 a.m., the fumes were so strong Rescue Company 1 was dispatched under the command of Lt. Thomas Kilbride. Rescue 1 members went through the building but could not find a cause for the fumes or a fire. The firemen, however, were becoming so groggy they had to work in relays.

Shortly after 3 a.m. rescue men were examining parts of the refrigeration unit and found pockets of intense heat and realized there was a fire within the insulation materials surrounding walk-in boxes on the second and third floors. Engine 27 was called to the scene. Lt. Stapleton directed Firemen Mike Brosnan, John Flynn and James Melville to stretch and operate a hose line into the big ice box.

After a few minutes it was noticed the line had gone slack, alerting the other firemen that the hose team was down. Kilbride called for volunteers and Firemen Charles Roggenkamp and Charles Kennedy stepped forward with smoke helmets. The men made their way into the ice box and found the heat so intense it nearly cracked the glass in their smoke helmets. Inside, Kennedy found Flynn and Roggenkamp located Brosnan. They called for help and despite the noxious smoke and fumes, Capt. David Oliver and Fireman James Mulvaney of Hook & Ladder 1, Fireman James Simonetti of Engine 27 and several members of Rescue 1 arrived without breathing protection. Under extreme conditions, this group was able to remove all three unconscious firemen.

For their heroic actions rescuing brother firefighters, they were placed on the Roll of Merit with Class II awards. Fireman Charles Roggenkamp of Rescue 1 also received the Prentice Medal, Fireman James Mulvaney of H&L 1 received the Brookman Medal, Fireman James Simonetti of Engine 27 received the Crimmins Medal, and Capt. David J. Oliver of H&L 1 received the Scott Medal.

Lt. Thomas Kilbride, Fireman Charles A. Kennedy Jr. of Rescue 1, and Fireman James Melville of Engine 27 also received Class II awards, but no medals.

On July 31, 1921, Rescue 1 responded to another ammonia leak, this time at 277 Broadway. They found the engineer, Al Frost, unconscious and removed him to safety. As members of Rescue 1 controlled the leaking ammonia system, Acting Lt. Frank Clark grabbed a pulmotor and worked on Frost until he regained consciousness.

On August 5, 1921, it was 1 a.m. when two men were working to free a hose that had become stuck beneath a freight elevator in the Municipal Building. While the men tried to free the hose, the elevator car pitched forward suddenly. Both workers fell into the shaft, with the broken elevator following them down. Despite their fall both men scrambled to their hands and knees and arched their backs against the slowly descending elevator. Their cries for help brought other workers who called the FDNY. Hook & Ladder 1 arrived along with Battalion Chief John Gunn who special-called Rescue 1.

When Rescue 1 arrived they descended into the elevator pit with their torch and jacks. They cut some steel free, then used the jacks to raise the elevator car and release the trapped men. Both were carefully taken to a waiting ambulance and transported to Volunteer Hospital in critical condition.

On the afternoon of August 12, 1921, a seven-year-old boy named Bernard Gates had just received a penny for running an errand. He showed his reward to a friend who tossed the coin into the hose connection of a nearby fire hydrant. Young Gates dove toward the hydrant driving his small arm deep inside to retrieve his penny. He'd grasped the coin but realized his arm was now wedged inside the hydrant. His cries for help brought a blacksmith from his shop several doors away. The man worked for nearly an hour but was not able to free the youngster. Hook & Ladder 5 was called to the scene, and they promptly requested Rescue 1.

The members of Rescue 1 arrived to find the boy, now unconscious and being supported by his distraught mother. As a crowd of about 1,000 people gathered close, Rescue 1, using their torch, were able to disconnect the hydrant from its base and lifted it up. The boy's hand, still clutching the penny, was seen as they carefully dislodged the lad's arm from the hydrant opening. An ambulance surgeon declared the boy okay so the lad, and his penny went home with his mother.

On the morning of August 16th, the merchants in Manhattan's produce district (the area around Washington and Murray streets) were doing business with tears in their eyes, while breathing through wet handkerchiefs held over their mouths and nostrils. This situation occurred when a gasket head on an ammonia compression machine burst in the produce house of Henry Behrman & Sons at 257 Washington Street.

As conditions worsened, everyone was driven from the building, and then from nearby buildings. Battalion Chief O'Donohue arrived after an alarm box was pulled. While breathing through his own handkerchief, Chief O'Donohue telephoned for Rescue 1.

Rescue 1 with Acting Lt. John Conners in command arrived quickly. Connors and Firemen Kennedy and Varga donned masks and entered the toxic atmosphere. They made their way to the cellar and located the leak. They were able to shut down the still running machine, then closed the main valve to stop the leak. Even though Rescue 1 solved the problem within minutes, it took an hour for the neighborhood and the affected building to be safe to enter.

On the night of September 16, 1921, at 9:30, a blow-out in a refrigerating plant machine released 600,000-cubic-feet of ammonia gas that quickly engulfed the surrounding neighborhood. The Knickerbocker Ice Company located at 77th Street and East End Avenue was nearly surrounded by tenements and in a matter of 15 minutes, a radius of half a dozen blocks filled with fumes. One newspaper reported more than 5,000 persons were driven from their homes, choking and gasping for breath. And things were going to get worse.

As the first FDNY units rolled in they found 60 people unconscious in the street and the fumes so caustic it was almost impossible for even the toughest fireman to handle. Rescue 1 was called and raced uptown at top speed.

Recognizing the danger to the entire neighborhood, Lt. Roth in command of Engine 14, without the benefit of breathing apparatus, attempted to enter the plant and shut off the ammonia pipes feeding the huge ice maker. Roth's hands were badly burned before he and his men all dropped to the floor overcome by the fumes.

On their arrival Lt. John Coffey split his company into teams. One team entered the plant and began a search. Inside they found the cylinder head of Ice Machine No. 2 had blown off and that the machine was connected to 20 drums, each containing 100 pounds of liquid ammonia that was being fed through the system at 180 psi. The members of Rescue 1 located and shut down the feeder valve stopping the escaping gas, then searched the plant for possible victims.

The second team spread sheets on the East End Avenue sidewalk between 69th and 70th streets, seven blocks south of the leak and began tending to those overcome or affected by the fumes. They were forced to stay low, as the layered fumes hung about four feet above the sidewalk, even at this distance from the leak. Firemen and police officers, without benefit of breathing protection, used wet pillowcases wrapped around their noses and mouths to provide some protection, as they carried victims to the first aid station.

At the first sound of the explosion a group of veterans from a nearby VFW post grabbed gas masks and sprang into action searching the 14 tenements. These men, former soldiers, searched the building under the direction of Lt. Coffey and his men. A dozen partially overcome women and children were carried from their apartments by gas-masked firemen and soldiers. Two hundred patients were treated at the first aid station. These coordinated efforts averted a potential catastrophe.

A week later, September 21st, another ammonia emergency occurred, this time in a bakery at 517 West 59th Street. The outcome was slightly different due to the bravery and perseverance of the engineer Thomas Lemmey. It was 8:30 a.m. when a nipple on one of the ammonia tanks on the fourth floor blew off. The escaping gas immediately drove the tenants of the building and of the adjoining tenements to the streets seeking fresh air.

Engineer Lemmey wrapped a wet towel around his face

and plunged into the dense layers of fumes. Crawling into the freezing room, he was able to stop the leak from one of the two 10-ton tanks.

The arriving members of Rescue 1 were met by the weeping and coughing engineer who explained that he had been able to stop the leak. Impressed by Lemmey's toughness the rescue men donned their masks, double-checked his work, and then completed a secondary search.

A week later, September 24th, a similar ammonia leak occurred at a butcher shop and grocery store at 958 Madison Avenue. The engineer at this plant attempted a similar heroic attempt but with different results. George Ose, attempted to control a leaking 10-ton machine only to burn his hands and was knocked unconscious. Rescue 1 arrived, donned masks and went into the basement and stopped the leak. They then removed and treated the injured engineer until an ambulance arrived.

On September 30th at 6:30 in the morning Rescue 1 responded to yet another ammonia emergency in the basement of the Loft candy factory at 400 Broome Street. The masked members of Rescue 1 worked for a half hour transferring 500 gallons from a defective tank into another empty tank. The first due members of Engine 55 were nearly overcome prior to the arrival of the Rescue.

It was just before midnight, on Sunday October 9th, when Rescue 1 was sent to 130 West 42nd Street near Broadway where the cap blew off the ammonia condensing machine inside the Bush Terminal Building. Rescue 1 donned their masks and quickly controlled the leak before any of the fumes could reach the streets and sidewalks of Times Square.

Monday October 10, 1921, was a most unusual day for Rescue 1. The week began with two huge Fire Prevention parades, one in Manhattan and another in Brooklyn the following day. The parades featured a half-million dollars' worth of new motorized fire apparatus, including the new 1921 White rescue truck. The parade moved south on Broadway from 116th Street at 10:30 a.m. and ended in lower Manhattan.

A special-call after the parade sent Rescue 1 speeding back northward to 668 East 188th Street in the Bronx. An eight-year-old girl had become wedged, by her neck in a dumbwaiter shaft. Rescue men cut away woodworking and were able to free her. Sadly, she did not survive.

A small fire in the cellar of the Golden Shoe Store at 116 East 14th Street, proved to be extremely dangerous for the first due company on the afternoon of October 15, 1921. Engine Company 72 and Hook & Ladder 3 arrived first. Hook & Ladder 3 forced the sidewalk elevator door and Engine 72 quickly stretched a line down into the smoke-filled basement. Acting-Battalion Chief Arthur Kellagy and Capt. Stephen McKenna were directing operations in the corner of the cellar when they were overcome by leaking illuminating gas. Kellagy and McKenna went down close to the meter with gas pouring from melted connections overhead. Two of the nozzle team men fell nearby, but closer to the exit.

At the front of the cellar, near the sidewalk elevator opening where the hose was dropped down, other firemen became aware of the danger and yelled for help. A second alarm was transmitted as the number of men dropping unconscious in the cellar grew. Chief Martin arrived and special-called the gas company emergency crew, and an extra engine and truck. Rescue 1 arrived and donned their masks and with Lt. Kilbride in the lead, plunged into the smoke and gas-filled cellar. They located the downed men and carried them back to the sidewalk elevator, where they were lifted to the street. Gas workers then teamed up with Rescue 1 and shut the flow.

Meanwhile, a first aid station was set up in the lobby of the Fox Theatre next to the fire building. The audience of 1,000 people was unaware of the life-saving work being conducted only feet away. Bottles of milk from Luchow's restaurant were brought in, a common remedy for smoke inhalation. Seventeen unconscious firemen were successfully rescued and revived. Acting-Chief Kellagy and Capt. McKenna were transported to a nearby hospital as a precaution.

Aid station set up in adjoining building.

On October 24th Rescue 1 responded to 406 East 79th Street when a man who was lowering a taxicab inside a parking garage got his head wedged between the safety doors. Engines 39 and 44 arrived and special-called Rescue 1. The company then used torches and tools to release the dead man's body.

Rescue 1 left Manhattan on special-call to Brooklyn at 5 p.m. on the evening of November 1, 1921, when a worker got his foot stuck between the freight elevator and the shaft wall in the Mundet & Company cork factory at 65 South 11th Street. The flooring of the elevator car was constructed of heavy timbers and steel bands and defied every effort of the first responding firemen. The trapped 22-year-old man helped direct the rescue men, as they made cuts with the torch. The iron bands, however, were becoming so hot that they burned the trapped man. Rescue 1 then concentrated on chopping away wooden sections. He assured Lt. Kilbride he would not faint as the operation commenced. True to his word, a half-hour later as the last of the metal was bent away, he was lifted onto a stretcher and thanked each of his rescuers before heading off to the hospital.

The Atlantic Fruit Line steamship *Tanamo* arrived in New York on November 20th, after steaming from Puerto Rico, with Governor Emmet Montgomery Reily and 19 other passengers. A fire in the hold was discovered during the trip, and at the direction of the ship's captain Herbert Hudson, the hold was sealed and flooded with steam to extinguish the flames. The ship was then moored at the pier at the foot of Rector Street, and the passengers disembarked. Governor Reily was taken onto a police department launch and secreted away from the growing crowds gathering near the pier. Then, believing the fire extinguished, the captain ordered the hatch opened.

The moment a rush of fresh air entered the hold, volumes

of thick smoke began pumping out, spreading over the waterfront. Flames were soon seen shooting up from the cargo of tobacco, fruits and coconuts. Realizing the fire was beyond the control of his crew, the captain dashed to the pier and called the fire department.

The fireboats *New Yorker, Zophar Mills,* and *Mayor Gainer,* were soon alongside and were pumping water into hold numbers 1 and 2, the flames having eaten through to a second hold. The ship began to settle down with a starboard list as the weight of the firefighting water grew. Deputy Chief Ed Worth of the Marine Division conferred with Deputy Chief John Binns and additional land units were requested.

With the idea of fighting the flames at close quarters, Rescue 1 was called in at 11 a.m. The members of Rescue 1 assembled on the deck with their masks, tools and guide ropes, ready to descend into the hold and commence firefighting when Chief Kenlon arrived. Kenlon, a Master Mariner himself, did not like what he was seeing and ordered Rescue 1 to stand fast. It was too dangerous to enter the hold. The ship's crew had already removed all their belongings, and the engine room was being abandoned as the lower sections of the ship became dangerously hot.

The fire, apparently ignited by a firebomb placed in the hold while still in Puerto Rico, was slowly taking over the ship. Crowds of native Puerto Ricans who carried signs protesting Governor Reily's administration, continued crowding close to the pier and jeering the firefighting efforts. Kenlon and his chiefs decided it was safest to tow the ship away from the pier and let the fire burn itself out.

A story in the November 12, 1921, issue of the Brooklyn newspaper *The Standard Union,* stated that a new rescue company would be established by Commissioner Thomas Drennan within the next few months. They even speculated the new company would be housed at the Jay Street firehouse.

Fire Service Magazine ran a similar story stating that since the FDNY purchased a new rig for Rescue 1, this would immediately allow the department to organize Rescue Company 2 in Brooklyn. Both articles cited the recent incidents when Rescue 1 responded across the river to perform rescue work in Brooklyn and other boroughs.

Sadly, just like when the establishment of a rescue company was mentioned after the Equitable Fire in 1912, it would be some time later that the company would be put into service. This second rescue unit would not happen until March of 1925.

Forty-eight men were busy constructing the New American Theatre at 779 Bedford Avenue near Park Avenue in the Williamsburg section of Brooklyn. It was 12:30 p.m. on November 29, 1921, when disaster struck the site. Four steel girders, each weighing several tons, slipped from the brick columns supporting them, sending an avalanche of steel, bricks and lumber onto a score of men working below. The falling beams also toppled an entire 40-foot-high brick wall onto the unsuspecting workers. A nearby fire alarm box was pulled sending Engines 209, 211 and 230 and Hook & Ladders Companies 102 and 104 to the scene. Captain Maurice Foley, the Acting Chief of the 34th Battalion, immediately called for more help. Hook & Ladders 108 and 119 were sent and Rescue 1 was special-called from Manhattan.

While the rescue work was being accomplished, the Brooklyn District Attorney, Harry E. Lewis and investigators from his staff arrived at the scene. Eager to determine if any laws were broken, Lewis ordered a team of police officers to clear the building of everyone except the cops and firemen. The construction workers, foreman and construction management were escorted from the site and held for questioning.

As the DA's investigation commenced, the dangerous and laborious task of lifting the mangled steel, cutting the fallen timbers, and removing the collapsed brickwork piece by piece was continued. Several trapped workers were rescued by the firemen and hopes were high that others would be recovered. By 6 p.m. a steam shovel was brought in to lift the heavy debris. Under illumination from the FDNY Searchlight rig, the work to remove all those imprisoned in the rubble continued late into the night. By midnight, six dead workers were in the King's County Morgue and the building's owners and general contractors were under arrest, charged with manslaughter for their improper building methods. Seven workers in all were killed in the collapse and more than 20 were injured.

New American Theatre collapse, Brooklyn, Nov. 29, 1921

Members of Rescue 1 locate trapped victims.

Special Department Order No. 110, dated June 19, 1922, cited the following:

> Class A, service rating, awarded to each of the following for their work at the collapsed theater building: Rescue Co. 1: Lt. John Coffey, Firemen William Hutcheon, William Dorritie, John Conners, Joseph Sullivan, James Devine and Joseph Horacek.
>
> Also included were all the members of Engines 209, 211, 230, and Hook & Ladders 102, 104, 108 and 119. Acting Battalion Chief Maurice Foley, Fireman Harry Gray H&L 12 (Chief Martin's aide) and Fireman Daniel Healy of H&L 24 (Chief Martin's driver "Daredevil Dan.")

Chief officers and the firemen of New York City had vast experience with heavy smoke conditions laced with various chemicals. They were found in commercial buildings across the city. Leaking natural gas could generally be expected in cellar fires that burned near the gas meters or fittings. But they did not expect these unique hazards while operating in office buildings.

The first arriving units that responded to the Vanderbilt Building at 132 Nassau Street at 9 a.m. on December 17, 1921, did not find a fire on the fifth floor, but rather a cloud of chlorine gas. The gas seemed to be coming from Room 520, the offices of a welding manufacturer, and nearly overwhelmed the first due firemen. Battalion Chief Patrick Walsh special-called Rescue 1. The company grabbed their smoke helmets and located the source of the leak. The rescue men then carefully removed a 60-pound tank that was ready to be shipped to Manila. Leaking acetylene was also found and removed.

The *Evening World* newspaper reported that Rescue 1 responded so quickly from their quarters, that a small automobile attempting to get out of their way ran into a store window on Varick Street.

Rescue 1 member carrying out shipping boxes containing leaking acetylene from the fifth floor of 132 Nassau Street on December 17, 1921.

Left: Lt. John Coffey, Firemen Roggenkamp, John Conners taking a break after removing storage boxes of leaking acetylene at 132 Nassau Street.

Postal employees working in the mailroom of the Federal Building (also known as the Old Post Office) just south of City Hall, noticed smoke and called the fire department. Responding fire units were directed to the Park Row side of the building at 6:45 p.m. on December 18, 1921. The fire, smoldering in a subcellar vault, soon filled the huge structure with thick choking smoke. First to arrive was Engine 32 under the command of Capt. Anthony Jirreck. They quickly stretched a line into the building. Thick clouds of smoke were pumping from a sidewalk grating on Park Row when Chief Martin sent in a second-alarm, special-called Rescue 1, and ordered the grating area to be vented by truck companies.

The smoke was taking its toll, as fireman after fireman dropped to the floor unconscious. Rescue 1 arrived, and members donned their smoke helmets before plunging into the heavy smoke. Lt. Coffey led them on a search for the downed men, then on the attack on the deep-seated fire. Ten firemen were knocked out before the fire could be extinguished and the smoke cleared from the building. Doctor Archer set up a first aid station and was able to revive all the men.

It was 7 p.m. on December 30, 1921, when a southbound four-car train of the Ninth Avenue elevated subway line crashed into the rear of a four-car train stopped at 40th Street. The noise from the crash echoed through the streets below, and was followed by the cries of those trapped in the wreckage. Arriving fire companies placed ladders to the elevated tracks and found the train cars had telescoped into one another.

Rescue 1 arrived and went to work freeing the people trapped in the twisted wreckage. The motorman was trapped in his control box but was able to escape through a window. He was then helped down a ladder by fire personnel. One person was killed, and 20 others were injured. The motorman of the second train was later arrested by the police.

Chapter 10:
1922

The year 1922 started off with a cold snap that immediately affected the members of the FDNY. From midnight Monday January 2nd until the sun came up that morning, firemen responded to 21 fires in Manhattan and the Bronx, and then to 63 alarms in Manhattan alone during the daytime. Most were small fires, but several fires in tenements drove about 60 families into the bitter cold streets, clad only in their nightclothes.

A fire in the old east building of the Frederick Loeser & Company department store at Fulton and Bond streets in Brooklyn quickly went to three-alarms on January 24, 1922. Glowing embers driven by high winds threatened to spread the fire from the old five-story building across the entire neighborhood. The cold temperatures also hampered firefighting efforts as water froze as soon as it touched anything. Despite the cold, a large crowd assembled to watch the action as flames burst through the roof.

The multiple alarm brought many Brooklyn companies to the scene and prompted the response of Assistant Chief Martin and Rescue 1 from Manhattan. The flames were held to the top floor and despite water damage on lower floors, the rest of the building was saved.

Another elevator entrapment sent Rescue 1 to 409 Lexington Avenue on January 28, 1922. A 16-year-old boy working for a manufacturing company, attempted to operate the building's freight elevator, and somehow became wedged between the floor of the elevator and the sixth floor of the building. Rescue 1 was special-called and worked for an hour and a half using the torch, saws and axes to free the body.

1922 Rescue 1 from left front: Lt. Kilbride, Lt. Coffey, Firemen Conners, Fletcher. In rig: Firemen Varga, Dorritie, Tierney, Horacek, Kistenberger, Milward and Clark.

Another smoky fire in lower Manhattan broke out just after six o'clock on the evening of February 21, 1922, in a warehouse filled with cotton, cotton goods and woolens at 55-57 White Street. While employees were investigating the source of the smoke, the automatic alarm summoned the fire department. Deputy Chief John Binns arrived, and after sizing up the level of the smoke and the nature of the flammables involved, transmitted a second alarm. The acrid smoke from the burning cotton compelled the firemen to work for only brief periods, before being relieved. Twelve firemen fell, knocked out by the dense smoke. They were removed by their comrades and members of Rescue 1 using smoke helmets.

Companies made very slow progress. When they reached the stairs to the basement, the heat from the blazing cellar was so hot, that not even the smoke helmeted rescue firemen could descend. Binns sent Rescue 1 and several truck companies to vent the cellar by opening the sidewalks. As thick clouds of smoke chugged upwards, hose streams were directed into the blazing cellar.

For more than two hours FDNY companies struggled to extinguish the fire, protect the building's contents, and remove each other as they were overcome by the smoke. Acting Battalion Chief Crawley checked the first floor, where several companies were trying to save a large quantity of baled cotton. The chief decided the floor was unsafe and ordered everyone out of the building. Moments later, the floor collapsed into the blazing cellar, luckily the chief had just cleared the last of his men.

It was around 7 p.m. March 14th when a man jumped in front of a northbound Ninth Avenue elevated subway train. The man, a Canadian army veteran and steward onboard a steamship, was killed as the front wheels rolled over him. Rescue 1 was called to extricate the man's body. In his pocket a note was found requesting his sister and a friend be notified of his death. It also said: "May God have mercy on my soul."

Heavy fumes from a broken pipe in an ice making machine, spread throughout the Hotel Belmont on April 2, 1922, at 3 a.m. The fumes spread quickly via elevator shafts and ventilators and mushroomed down from the 19th to the 14th floors. Many of the upper floor guests were driven from their rooms within the

42nd Street and Park Avenue hotel. It was feared there were still guests in the affected rooms above, when Rescue 1 arrived. Lt. Thomas Kilbride's priority was the search for life. With a potentially deadly atmosphere filling the occupied upper floors, they donned smoke helmets and gas masks and made a primary search.

After the search on the upper floors was completed, Lt. Kilbride split his company. Kilbride and a team then headed downstairs to find the leak, as other masked rescue men set up 20 large electric fans to disperse the ammonia vapors.

The rescue men were able to penetrate the engine room, four floors below grade, and plug the leak.

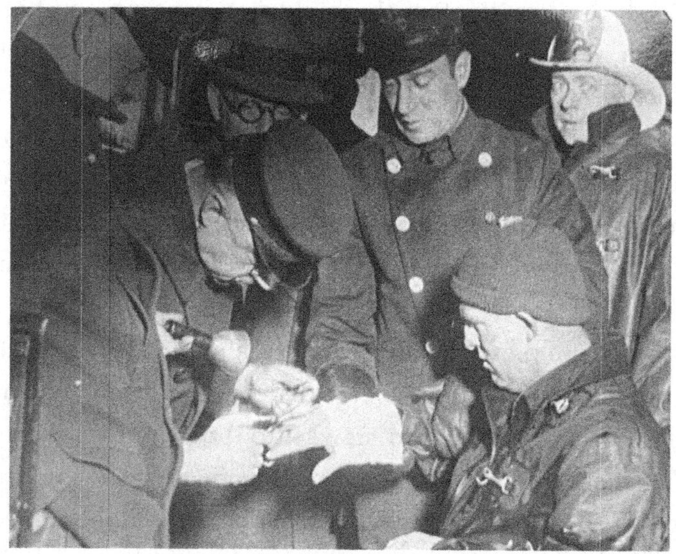

Doctor Archer stitching up a lacerated hand, a common injury to gloveless firemen.

The following day, April 3rd, Rescue 1 worked a second alarm fire at 408 Broome Street. The late-night fire was in a seven-story loft building, across from NYPD Headquarters. Chief Kenlon was showing Mayor Hylan the progress of the battle, when a loud crash of breaking glass was heard from the Lafayette Street side of the building. Three firemen were then seen staggering toward Broome Street with blood streaming from cuts on their hands and faces. They were Lt. Thomas Kilbride and Fireman Bela Varga from Rescue 1 and Fireman Louis Chacken of Engine 55.

They reported to the first aid station set up by Doctor Archer who treated their wounds. Cleaned and bandaged, they were asked if they wanted to report sick. They all laughed and hurried back to work.

Although Rescue 1 was routinely handling ammonia and other leaking gas problems, they never took the work for granted. On April 26, 1922, the FDNY was called to 409 West 14th Street, where two machinist's helpers were overcome, as they attempted to stop a leak in a large ammonia tank in the building's basement. The two workers, wearing gas masks, had removed the old flange and were attempting to replace it with a new flange, when the pressure of the ammonia gas became so great it dislodged their masks and sent them reeling toward the stairs. Attempting to adjust their masks, they met the night watchman who helped them through the vapors and out to the street. All three fell to the sidewalk unconscious.

Rescue 1 was called and arrived under the command of Lt. John Coffey. The rescue men assembled their gear and devised a plan. Lt. Coffey, and Firemen John Milward and Charles Roggenkamp donned their smoke helmets and entered the noxious atmosphere. The gas concentrations were so severe, that Coffey and his men were burned despite their breathing protection.

The remaining members of Rescue 1 then took turns entering the basement and working on the leak. It took a half hour to bring the leak under control. Newspaper stories covered this job and reported that Lt. Coffey, and Firemen Roggenkamp and Milward were burned by the ammonia fumes. The stories also stated that the other members of the company entering the basement were also burned. Those named were Firemen Joseph Hughes, William Bergen, Timothy Devine, and William Herrick.

This particular job and the news articles covering it help unravel just how Rescue 1 was operating in those early days. Several newspaper stories covered this job and mentioned those injured. The names or the spelling seems to be slightly off in the case of Lt. Coffey the articles spelled it "Coffee." Milward was spelled "Milwood," and Roggenkamp was "Rogencamp." They also mention Timothy Devine, who was probably James Devine (Jim not Tim), William Bergen, William Herrick and Joseph Hughes.

It seems members were working in Rescue 1 who were not officially transferred into the company on the department orders. But instead, they were bringing in prospective members on temporary details, prior to an official transfer.

Usually, a phone call from the chief or one of his trusted aides would request the temporary detail of the fireman. A letter to the commander of this fireman would follow—the so-called "Onion Skin," referring to very thin old-time paper. This is the way new members are brought into the Rescue to this day. This detail phase gives both the company and the prospective member time to see if they fit into this new kind of firefighting. Most stayed in the company. Some returned to their original companies. Another possibility is they were just detailed for the day or night tour to adjust manpower and fill in, when men were off sick or on vacation.

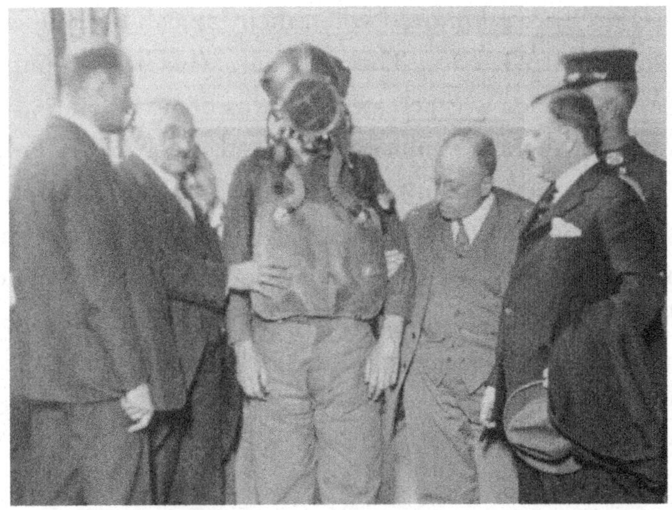

Lt. Kilbride, the mayor and other officials examine a rescue man and his smoke helmet.

Two days later, on April 26th, Rescue 1 was special-called to 174th Street and Macomb's Road in the Bronx, the site of an excavation cave-in. One man was killed, and five others were injured, when the side of the excavation, under an apartment house, caved in. The injured avoided being buried, but were hurt by tumbling rocks.

The trench extended from the curb line to the center of the street where sewer pipes were being placed. Rescue 1 waited to free the dead man until the medical examiner was sure of the cause of death. After the injured were removed, it took Rescue 1 20-minutes to dig out the buried man.

A short while after the completion of this rescue another trench collapse, this one in Brooklyn, injured a worker who was buried beneath four-feet of dirt. He was dug out by a steam shovel and the members of a hook and ladder company.

On May 6, 1922, a bank teller, a bank guard, a police officer and his prisoner, were all injured when their taxicab became jammed between two street cars. The prisoner, who had attempted to pass forged checks, was arrested and was being taken to the local stationhouse when the collision occurred. At Third Avenue and 122nd Street, a taxi attempting to avoid a traffic jam, moved into the wrong lane and became violently wedged between the two passing street cars. The impact exploded the taxi's gasoline tank and shattered the windows of the street cars. The driver and the prisoner were able to scramble to safety. The teller, police officer, and the bank guard were pinned in the mangled wreckage. Members of Hook & Ladder 14 extinguished the fire, which had extended to the trolley cars and special-called the Rescue.

Upon their arrival, Rescue 1 set up their oxyacetylene torch and cut away the steel entrapping the passengers. The injured were taken to the hospital and treated for their injuries. The prisoner disappeared.

Remnants of the crushed taxi after Rescue 1 cut away wreckage.

On June 3, 1922, Fireman James A. Devine transferred to Hook & Ladder 9 after almost three years in Rescue 1. The same order sent Fireman William J. Anderson from Hook & Ladder 143 to Rescue 1.

Fireman James G. Brown of Hook & Ladder 9 also transferred to Rescue 1. Brown had previously been on the Roll of Merit and received the Bonner Medal for his actions at the Equitable fire in 1912 while a member of Hook & Ladder 1. Brown joined the FDNY on July 6, 1906.

Fireman Robert Tierney transferred to Rescue 1 from Engine Company 72. He'd joined the department on December 24, 1916, and was awarded the Brookman Medal in 1921 while a member of Engine Company 72.

Fireman Thomas Larkin from Hook & Ladder 10 also transferred to Rescue 1. Larkin joined the FDNY on February 1, 1920, and was only a fireman second grade when he joined Rescue 1. In 1922 he was awarded a College Efficiency Medal as a member of Hook & Ladder 10.

Several thousand people living in the crowded tenements on Essex Street between Hester and Grand streets, were driven from their homes when the valve cap of a 50-gallon tank of ammonia exploded on June 4th. The tank was part of an ice making system in the cellar of a seven-story sausage factory. First due units immediately called for Rescue 1, and they arrived in short order. Under the command of Lt. Coffey, his men masked up and quickly plugged the leak.

A construction site accident on June 10, 1922, killed one worker and injured two others. A crane lifting a 10-ton metal beam into position in the main balcony of a new motion picture theatre collapsed and dropped the huge beam onto the workers below. Rescue 1 responded to the West Houston and MacDougal streets location and used their jacks and hand tools to lift the beam and free one dead man's body. The injured workers were transported to the hospital for treatment.

Rescue 1 joined many other members of the Fire Department, as they assembled in front of City Hall on the morning of June 20, 1922. This was the annual FDNY medal day ceremony. Mayor John Hylan remarked about the medals about to be awarded:

> These marks of honor, donated by public-spirited and generous-hearted citizens are mute symbols of duty well done and are intended to indicate in tangible form of gratitude, esteem and affection in which the people of this city hold the recipients.

Captain David Oliver and Fireman James Mulvaney of Hook & Ladder 1, and Fireman James Simonetti of Engine Company 27 each stepped forward and were awarded medals for their heroic efforts on July 18, 1921, at the Phoenix Cheese Company fire. Capt. Oliver, who'd recently been injured while responding to a false alarm, had been sitting in a chair near the steps since the start of the ceremony. Oliver was helped up and stood at attention as the mayor pinned the Walter Scott Medal to his chest. After a brief salute and handshakes, Oliver sat back down, before being taken back to the hospital to continue his convalescence.

Medal Day booklet photo of Fireman Charles Roggenkamp.

The Prentice Medal was then awarded to Fireman Charles Roggenkamp of Rescue Company 1, for his part in the heroic rescue of a brother fireman.

The mayor then used a new a new portable telephone transmitter, attached to a fire alarm box, to call the dispatcher and request Rescue 1 respond to City Hall. The company arrived and gave a demonstration of their special tools and equipment.

Commissioner Drennan and members of Rescue 1 at 1922 Medal Day ceremony.

Several days after receiving his medal, Fireman Charles Roggenkamp was enjoying a day off. The special training received by each member of Rescue 1, could help make a difference in a fire operation, even if the company was not at the scene, or if the members were off duty. On the evening of June

23, 1922, Roggenkamp came across Brooklyn fire companies working a smoky blaze in a three-story building on South 11th Street. Suddenly, two unconscious firemen were dragged from the fire building and placed on the sidewalk.

Roggenkamp identified himself and sprang into action. The rescue fireman began administering first aid to the downed men. His efforts were of such high quality that Deputy Chief Helm recommended him to the Board of Merit for his capability. Roggenkamp was subsequently awarded a Class A.

Diners in the Apthorp Cafeteria at 60 East 14th Street, were startled to see three masked members of Rescue 1 walk through the restaurant and descend into the cellar below them on the night of July 4th. Rescue had been called when a leak was discovered in the restaurant's ammonia plant. Lt. Kilbride and Firemen Sullivan and Connors were able repair the faulty valve. Dinner was not interrupted.

A smoky fire in the Lexington Avenue subway, caused huge problems at 11:17, on the morning of July 6, 1922. Three hundred riders were imperiled and more than 150 were injured by the smoke from burning insulation mixed with the noxious gas from fire extinguishers used to fight the fire. When a short circuit stalled a train at 60th Street, a flash of fire was seen from the motorman's car. Dense smoke began pumping from beneath the stalled 10-car train. A subway train guard began squirting a Pyrene carbon tetrachloride fire extinguisher upon the flames. This added a noxious gas to the already toxic smoke that made breathing even more difficult and sent subway passengers into a panic.

An off-duty police officer used the subway's emergency telephone to call for help. Engine Company 39 arrived quickly and Capt. Howard Ruch was the first to enter the subway. He was overcome by the gas fumes after making several rescues. Scores of passengers were dropping as well.

First aid stations were set up and hospital surgeons were joined by members of Rescue 1 with pulmotors. A notice had been sent to all hospitals in Manhattan to send help. Patients were worked on with the resuscitators, and those that did not respond were hurried off to the hospital. From his hospital bed, Capt. Ruch later stated, "We were gassed with the poisonous fumes from the moment we entered the tunnel. These extinguishers are efficient for any place except a subway."

Doctor Archer added, "This mixture (in the Pyrene extinguisher) contains tetrachloride of tin, and this breaks down into carbon dioxide when exposed to air . . . Pyrene should never be used in a confined space."

Until the late 1950s, carbon tetrachloride was routinely used as a fire extinguishing agent. Its fire stopping capabilities were excellent, but this chemical, also used in dry cleaning and refrigeration units, was found to be extremely dangerous, especially if inhaled or absorbed through the skin. To make matters worse, when carbon tetrachloride is exposed to heat, it decomposes into deadly phosgene and hydrogen chloride gases.

Phosgene was used extensively in World War I as a choking agent. Phosgene, or the related agent diphosgene, was responsible for 91,000 deaths, or 85% of the total gas warfare deaths.

It was 10 a.m. on July 14, 1922, when workers at the Knickerbocker Ice Company at Broome and Elizabeth streets, accidentally broke an ammonia pipe inside the freezing room on the second floor. This break allowed vast quantities of ammonia vapor to escape. The fumes drove all the workers into the street. Rescue Company 1 was called. As the company arrived, one of the workers put on a gas mask and attempted to close the valves. He was joined by Firemen Sullivan and Hutcheon of Rescue 1. Together the team was able to stop the leak and ventilate the building.

Firemen Sullivan and Hutcheon leaving Knickerbocker Ice Company after controlling ammonia leak. Note boy holding handkerchief to face.

The morning of July 18, 1922, started as a beautiful day in New York City. The summer sun was just peeking over the top of the Manufacturer's Transit Company's seven-story warehouse on Jane Street in Greenwich Village.

A little after 8 a.m. warehouse workers were busy loading wooden cases of powdered magnesium into the building's freight elevator. Several of the cases were stacked on the sidewalk adjacent to the opened elevator. Even though the air was still relatively cool, the workers were building up a good sweat as they moved the heavy crates into the building. The huge warehouse, formerly an automobile parking garage, ran through to the next block, and contained large quantities of combustible materials. Stored in the basement and on various floors were crates of photographic flashlight powder, bonded whiskey, tons of rubber and quantities of rolled paper.

For some unknown reason—maybe a spark caused by friction—one of the cases of magnesium powder suddenly exploded, throwing several of the workers across the cobblestone street. Scrambling to their feet, they were horrified to see flames spreading among the stacked wooden crates. Most of the workers ran for their lives, while several brave men dashed back toward the fire and tried to smother the flames with pails of sand.

The sand had no effect, and the fire spread from the crates on the sidewalk to those in the freight elevator. A second explosion toppled the remaining workers, spreading the flames to other parts of the warehouse. A Greenwich Avenue merchant, watching the activity from his store across the street, decided he'd better call for help. He hurried to the nearest fire alarm box and pulled the handle.

At 8:15 a.m. the alarm was received in the Manhattan Fire Dispatcher's Office. The first firemen to arrive found the flames were already out of control. The wooden crates of magnesium powder were burning briskly on the sidewalk, and spewing fountains of white sparks. Meanwhile, the fire was roaring up the open elevator shaft of the seven-story building.

With wailing sirens, one after another, fire engines descended on the scene. The engines stopped at hydrants, where the men quickly connected to the water supply. Hose lines were dragged into position and water quickly filled the hoses.

The Acting Chief of the New York City Department, Joseph Smoky Joe Martin, arrived on the scene and took command of the firemen. At first, he encouraged his men to bring their fire hoses as close to the flames as possible. Heavy streams of water bored into the wall of flames, but whenever the firemen moved the stream to another part of the burning building, the flames returned to the place they had previously doused. Sparks and sheets of white-hot flame continued to pour from the wooden crates on the sidewalk, endangering nearby buildings. At times the plume of burning magnesium, which resembled pyrotechnics, reached over the roofs of the three- and four-story houses fronting on Jane Street.

Chief Martin directed his men to hose down nearby buildings. This prevented the fire from spreading, but within the burning warehouse the fire seemed unaffected by the torrents of water that firemen were pouring into it. With flames bursting through the roof of the warehouse a dense, black, acrid smoke arose and settled on each side of the building. It became so dark on Jane and West 12th streets, that firemen had great difficulty finding their way forward.

At about 8:45 a.m. Lieutenant John Schoppmeyer of Engine Company 13 led a group of men with a hose line into the warehouse, through a door on the 12th-Street side of the building. Suddenly, there was an explosion that far exceeded the magnitude of any of the previous blasts. A huge section of the wall, 15-feet wide and extending from the fifth floor to the roof, was blown out, and the entire roof was lifted off by a massive gush of white flames.

Chief Martin found himself slammed against a building across the street, his face burned, and the wind knocked out of him. Lieutenant Schoppmeyer and his men were also hurled backwards by the explosion. A large section of elevator machinery and roofing blew into the sky, falling to the street crushing Schoppmeyer. He was pulled from the debris, but never regained consciousness and died several minutes later.

Across the street Rescue 1, under the command of Lt. Kilbride, were operating a line from the roof of a nearby building. Fireman Charles Roggenkamp on the nozzle, was arching the stream across the street into the blazing building when the explosion occurred. Kilbride, Roggenkamp and four other members of Rescue 1 were blown back across the roof to the edge of the coping. They lost control of the hose but were able to scramble to their feet and hurry downstairs and into the street to help those injured. Martin ordered more manpower and resources to the scene.

July 18, 1922, this Jane Street fire became known as the Greenwich Village Volcano.

The detonation had driven cases filled with merchandise through the warehouse windows and walls, littering the street with an eclectic assortment of dolls, toys, fancy electric light bulbs, dried peas and other small items. These items were quickly washed away by the rivers of fire-hose water, cascading down West 12th and Jane streets.

Companies scramble to regain control after Jane Street explosion on July 18, 1922.

The thick acrid smoke of the Jane Street fire was so dangerous, that city officials ordered 2,000 people evacuated from the neighborhood. Despite this precaution, several residents were sickened by the smoke. They were treated at first aid stations set up around the fire area by the local chapter of the American Red Cross.

Scores of firemen and police officers were also overcome by smoke and were treated at Red Cross stations. A battery of six pulmotors were in use at one time at the corner of Greenwich and West 12th streets, with a score of unconscious and semi-conscious persons laid out on the sidewalk. The street resembled a battlefield.

As Martin's men held their hoses close to the fire, they were being pelted by hot ejected materials and risked being scorched by bursts of flame. To protect his men, Martin ordered them to remove doors from nearby buildings and use them as wooden shields. His men continued fighting the fire in this manner for several hours.

The constant eruptions resembled volcanic activity, and the fire quickly became known to both firemen and the public as the "Greenwich Street Volcano."

By 2 p.m. the fire had been raging for six hours, but to the firefighters it seemed hotter than ever. Smoky Joe Martin and his men had sustained considerable punishment.

The building's contents continued to flare up, showering the area with blossoms of super-heated sparks and flaming debris. Rumbles and explosions from deep within the structure finally caused Martin to rethink the dangerous position he and his men now occupied, so close to the building. Smoky Joe decided to change tactics.

The breastworks of wooden shields (the temporary use of doors etc.) were abandoned and Martin redirected his firefighting efforts to an aerial water assault from the roofs of the surrounding buildings. Additional alarms were sent, to bring fresh firemen to replace men suffering from exhaustion, smoke inhalation and wounds.

After several more firemen were injured while operating

from the rooftops, Martin pulled his men back further from the fire.

At 4 p.m. Martin was standing in the street, wondering what he could possibly do to put out the amazingly persistent fire, when he was joined by New York Mayor John Hylan. The mayor looked at the exhausted chief. Martin's face was burned; his eyes were bloodshot and almost closed by swelling. His breathing was labored; his shoulders and arms were limp from exertion.

The mayor asked, "How do you feel, chief?"

"I feel fine," Martin replied, then fainted dead away at the mayor's feet.

Martin was rushed to a first aid station. There, Doctor Harry Archer, Honorary Chief Medical Officer, worked on the injured fire chief. When Martin regained consciousness, Archer told him to go home. Martin flatly refused.

Dr. Archer knew that Martin had recently led an exhausting attack on a conflagration along the Rockaway peninsula. "Listen, Chief," said Dr. Archer, "you've been taking an awful beating. You're still weak from the Arvene fire, and you're past 60. You've got to go home."

Martin stood up and placed his dented leather fire helmet back on his head. "A man don't get his full strength till he's past 60," he told the doctor. "I got work to do!"

A compromise was reached. Archer allowed Martin to return to the fire under certain conditions. Smoky Joe was placed on a cot in a shop window near the fire and continued to direct his men's operations from that location.

After a few hours on the cot, Martin came up with another attack strategy. Instead of having his men aim hoses from rooftops, where they were vulnerable to showers of debris from explosions in the burning building, Martin decided to send his men to new positions inside the buildings surrounding the burning warehouse. At 8 p.m. Martin arose from the cot and returned to the streets to redirect the attack.

Hose after hose was repositioned under Martin's direction, until water poured from every window and fire escape overlooking the burning building. Eventually, 64 streams of water were directed into the fire from different vantage points. More than 216,000 tons of water were pumped into the burning warehouse—the largest volume of water directed at a single fire in the history of the New York City Fire Department. After a bulging wall fell on the Jane Street side of the building, water streams could more easily reach the seat of the fire.

By midnight the fire was clearly diminishing, although it continued to burn. At that point, over 200 firemen and police officers had been treated for smoke inhalation, and an additional 61 men had been hospitalized with burns, bruises, or lacerations. Two firemen had been killed: Lieutenant Schoppmeyer, killed by falling debris, and Fireman James H. Malone, who had fallen from a truck while relocating to another firehouse in Brooklyn.

The fire was declared under control 34 hours after it started. It continued to burn for a total of five days. Finally, one last eruption of the "Greenwich Street Volcano" occurred on the afternoon of July 23rd, sending walls crashing outward and destroying two houses. The fire was finally out.

Lt. Kilbride and his men were called out to another ammonia emergency on July 22, 1922, when ammonia fumes spread throughout a four-block radius following the blow out of a cylinder head in a condenser at the Shevers Ice Cream Company plant at 617 11th Avenue. Donning their gas masks, members of Rescue 1 went into the basement and shut off the escaping ammonia gas. The fumes penetrated the clothing of the rescue men and left them with burns.

L to R: Firemen Horacek, Dorritie, Fletcher, Tierney, Kistenberger, Clark, Joseph, Conners, Lt. Coffey and Fr. Varga. Lt. Kilbride can be seen behind the rig.

Afternoon diners in the Vesuvio Restaurant at 231 Mulberry Street, in the heart of Little Italy, noticed smoke seeping up through the floor. Moments later the owner appeared from the basement yelling "Fire!" This quickly emptied the restaurant.

It was August 3, 1922. First arriving companies rolled in and went to work battling the stubborn blaze. Assistant Chief Martin was passing by and saw the firemen at work and joined in. Watching as his brave men staggered from the cellar and fell unconscious on the street, Martin transmitted an additional alarm and requested Rescue 1. Members of Engine 20 and Hook & Ladder 9 entered the cellar and were soon fighting to stay conscious as a backdraft occurred.

To add to the complications, illuminating gas was leaking and mixing with the already thick noxious smoke. One by one, the firemen in the cellar fell unconscious including Lt. James Turbridy of Hook & Ladder 9 and Lt. Hugh Halligan of Engine 20 (later, the inventor of the famed forcible entry tool).

Rescue 1 arrived under the command of Acting Lt. John Milward. Donning smoke helmets and gas masks, they entered the cellar and carried out the 15 unconscious firemen and officers. Regrouping, Rescue 1 then took the attack line and began battling the cellar fire. After a long and difficult fight, the fire was extinguished.

A most unusual emergency faced Rescue 1 on August 18, 1922, when a flood of ammonia threatened the lives of all the aquatic mammals in the New York City Aquarium at Battery Park. The aquarium, located inside Castle Clinton (now a national landmark) had more than 100 tanks positioned around the circular design of the fort. Six large pools surrounded the seventh and largest pool in the very center of the structure. It was a very popular venue with tourists and locals alike. Noxious fumes were leaking into the exhibits from the engine room making the old castle structure uninhabitable. Rescue 1 was called to the scene.

Inside the aquarium, the fish contained in tanks faced no serious problem, but the sea lions, turtles, and the lone seal were having difficulty breathing. They huddled near the edges of their enclosure slapping their flippers against the walls and barking in alarm. Despite the fumes, the sea mammals resisted all efforts to drive them into the water, where it was thought they would be safer. The alligators however, appeared to be having no problems at all.

The rescue men pulled on their Draeger helmets and made their way to the second floor, where the leak was originating. This area housed a refrigeration plant that cooled the stored fish used to feed the mammals. As the leak was traced, Acting Lt.

Milward sent two smoke-helmeted rescue men back to the main hall to keep an eye on the animals and report back if conditions became worse. After a half hour the leak was located and repaired, and the main hall was vented, clearing the fumes. The company took up, happy knowing all the animals were okay.

Another building fire with leaking gas occurred in the early morning hours of October 4, 1922, inside the five-story building at 211 West 61st Street in Manhattan. As the first due units removed tenants over ladders, Rescue 1 was special-called. Firemen battling the smoky fire and began dropping unconscious from the gas-laced smoke. Rescue 1 arrived and was able to rescue a husband and wife from their second-floor rooms.

One of two searchlight units presented to the department by Hon Deputy Chief Edward Kenny in 1922

Two floors below, firemen were struggling to extinguish the smoky gas-laced cellar fire. After safely removing the unconscious couple, the helmeted rescue men joined the battle in the cellar. They were able to find and control the leak, then help extinguish the remaining fire. Firemen were working under the light being thrown by the new searchlight rig, recently presented to the fire department by Honorary Deputy Chief Edward Kenny. These two searchlight units were on Locomobile chassis and carried a variety of powerful lighting equipment.

Later that same day, Rescue 1 was special-called across the river to Brooklyn when ammonia fumes drove 100 persons from a three-story candy factory at 346 Cumberland Street. At 9:40 a.m. the factory workers began fleeing the building and were soon filling the sidewalks outside, driven out into the fresh air by the toxic fumes. A police officer saw their condition and called the FDNY. Meanwhile, a building engineer, Edward Herwig, donned a gas mask and went to the ammonia tank and searched for a leaking connection. As he tried to fix the problem the first fire companies arrived. Hook & Ladder 105 under the command of Capt. Michael Hartley arrived and sent in the call for Rescue 1.

Rescue 1 members with smoke helmets outside candy factory on October 4, 1922.

The Rescue arrived from Spring Street in only 10-minutes, with Lt. Kilbride in charge. He and his six men joined the engineer and found the condenser had blown off. They were able to isolate the problem and stop the leak. The entire building was searched and vented. After the fumes were safely cleared, everyone went back to work.

On November 1, 1922, Fireman Frank C. Clark, one of the original members of the company, was promoted to lieutenant. His new assignment was Engine Company 76 at 105 West 102nd Street (where he would work with my grandfather). Clark and his comrades helped establish the strategy and tactics now being employed by Rescue 1. They were blazing new trails that would eventually lead the fire service to both heavy and technical rescue specialties, as well as hazardous materials disciplines.

Six firemen from Hook & Ladder 9 narrowly escaped drowning on November 6, 1922, when they responded to a reported fire at 129 Crosby Street, a seven-story loft building. After the fire was knocked down by heavy outside streams, Hook & Ladder 9 went inside the water-filled building to check on the fire conditions. As they were chopping away near a bulging partition wall, a torrent of water was released, sweeping the fire crew from their feet. Firemen Wynn, Shoeck, and Miksovsky were dashed down the stairs, pinballing off the walls as they descended. Lt. Walter Lamb (a former member of Rescue 1) and Firemen Murphy and Murray were swept back into the second floor of the loft and were clinging to the only substantial object in sight, a stair railing.

Upon hearing the noise of the released water and believing it was the sounds of a collapse, Rescue 1 was sent inside and found the officer and his men in the water and hanging on for dear life. They were able to pull the men to safety and all returned to work.

Another elevator extrication call was received on November 11, 1922, from the American Novelty Company at 225 East 36th

Street in Manhattan. A 17-year-old boy was wedged between the floor of the freight elevator and the ceiling of the floor below. Rescue 1 and Hook & Ladder 7 worked together to free the young man, who lapsed into unconsciousness during the extrication. He was given the Last Rites by a local priest, as rescue men continued working around him. Once freed, the seriously injured youth was rushed to Bellevue Hospital.

The alarm box at the corner of Washington and Fulton streets was transmitted after the fourth floor of a six-story brick building at 195 Washington Street collapsed on November 14th. Six men were loading bags of onions when the floor beneath them gave way, plunging four of the men to the ground floor beneath a mass of tangled wreckage. The task of the rescue was further complicated by the clouds of onion dust hanging in the air.

Injured worker being removed from building collapse at 195 Washington Street.

Members of Rescue 1 tunneled through the debris to reach several of the injured men. All the trapped men were freed by rescue men, but one would later die from his injuries.

One worker killed in the collapse is carried away by firemen on November 14, 1922.

Scores of diners were driven from the restaurant at 423 Madison Avenue in Manhattan, on November 31, 1922, by ammonia fumes. A refrigeration pipe in the basement broke, filling the area with the toxic fumes. Rescue 1 arrived, donned their smoke helmets and descended into the vapor-filled basement. They were able to locate the leak, shut off the valve and repaired the damaged pipe. The fumes were vented, and the diners returned to their meals.

It was the afternoon of Christmas Eve 1922, when Rescue 1 responded to another ammonia leak, this time in the Italian

Hospital at 83rd Street at the East River. The gas had already permeated the cellar and was filling up the first floor where two young women were operating a switchboard. Both girls tied wet rags across their nose and mouth, and as the tears rolled down their faces they remained on duty and called for help.

Deputy Chief Thomas Dougherty arrived and special-called Rescue 1. The company arrived quickly and sent a team of men wearing masks into the fume-filled basement. As the rescue men worked stopping the leak in the basement, the girls made their way around the first-floor, opening windows and doors to relieve the pent-up gases.

At 10 a.m. New Year's Eve 1922, the workers in the chemical laboratory of the Defiance Manufacturing Company at 18 East 41st Street, a half block from the Public Library, began coughing and choking. The fire department arrived, and Rescue 1 was special-called. Lt. Coffey and Fireman Thomas Larkin entered the basement wearing smoke helmets and searched for the cause of the fumes.

Despite the protection of the smoke helmets, they were both overcome and had to be carried out by other members of Rescue 1. Returning to the street, Coffey and Larkin were revived. The rescue officer conferred with the chiefs and chemists from the chemical company. It was agreed that the gas was either chlorine, nitric acid, or hydrochloric. Boxes, jars and crocks filled with various dangerous chemicals were then carried out by rescue men.

Continuing his search, Lt. Coffey came upon an obscure compartment in the cellar and smashed it open with an axe. Inside he found a shell-shaped chlorine tank. With the help of Firemen Charles Kennedy and John Milward they dragged and carried the tank to the street. After five-hours of dangerous work, the situation was finally under control.

Fireman William Fletcher of Rescue 1 donning smoke helmet at East 41st Street chemical laboratory on December 31, 1922

Chapter 11: 1923

A new member was transferred into Rescue 1 on January 1, 1923, Fireman Matthew J. Crawley of Engine Company 72. Crawley, a veteran of the Great War, left the U.S. Army and joined the FDNY on January 6, 1920. He was assigned to Engine Company 72 on East 12th Street in Manhattan. A month after he joined the department, he was involved in a rescue that placed his name on the Roll of Merit with a Class II. He would also be awarded the Scott Medal for this rescue. The following year, his name appeared once again for a rescue made on February 8, 1921.

New Year's Day 1923 started off with a difficult and dangerous fire at 60 Wall Street. At 10:40 a.m. members of Engine 7 and Engine 4 followed Battalion Chief Joseph O'Hanlon to the 15th floor storeroom of a stockbroker firm. The door was forced open, and the firemen were immediately overwhelmed by a blast of carbon monoxide-laced super-heated smoke. The chief, two officers and a fireman all dropped to the floor unconscious. Other firemen, scrambled to drag and carry their comrades to safety. One fireman was rushed to the hospital as the others were revived.

Rescue 1 was special-called. As soon as they arrived, they donned their smoke helmets and entered the building. A team went to the 16th floor and bored holes through the floor directly above the fire. Water was then directed through the holes onto the fire below, a tactic often used at stubborn cellar fires.

With limited results from their indirect attack, Rescue 1 returned to the storeroom door and renewed their direct attack on the deep-seated fire. Conditions were so extreme, that even while protected by the smoke helmets, members could only operate for five minutes at a time. Eventually, after their determined attack, the flames were extinguished.

Chief officer and member of Rescue 1 observing ventilation holes on the floor above the fire.

Doctor Peenen of Beekman Hospital tending to Firemen Charles French of Engine 7 and William Gillan of Engine 6 after they were overcome on January 1, 1923.

On March 4, 1923, three alarms were required for a fire at 48 East 14th Street in Manhattan. This was an extremely tough job, with thick noxious smoke and a deep-seated fire in the rear of the 200-foot-deep penny arcade. Thirty firemen were overcome battling this blaze. Lt. Kilbride, and Firemen Milward, Fletcher, Kennedy, Larkin, Crawley, Varga, Kistenberger and Roggenkamp operated for more than two hours fighting the fire and carrying out their unconscious comrades.

March 30, 1923, would be a day the members of Rescue 1 would remember for quite a while. It began with a 5-alarm fire that started in the four-story building at 337 East 26th Street. The ground floor of this building housed the Madison Wet Wash Laundry. The upper floors held the Universal Box Company. The flames from this fire were noticed by a police officer who turned in the alarm. The flames raced through the paper box company, before extending into the L-shaped adjoining building that housed a printing company. This three-story building was filled with flammable materials. The rear wing ran behind the stone and brick structure, built originally as a branch of the city prison. It was in this 100-year-old building, now being used as an almshouse (a building to house the homeless,) that a huge back draft occurred.

The back draft toppled the stone and brick wall onto members of Engine 26 who were manning a hose line. With heavy fire now in three buildings, members hurried to the collapse area and began digging the trapped men out by hand. Two members of Engine 26, Firemen William Aiello and Julius Spanier were both crushed beneath the stones and were rushed to Bellevue Hospital. Sadly, both would die of their injuries.

After a grueling battle and as things were being brought under control, word came to the fire scene that another job had just come in. At 2 p.m. Chief Kenlon was informed of a major building collapse that had just occurred on Eldridge Street two miles south of the 5-alarm fire. Doctor Archer and Rescue 1 were released from the fire and soon were racing south toward the collapse.

The five-story building was under demolition when the collapse occurred. When a floor gave way, it carried with it the walls and floors of the building, as well as the top floor of the adjoining five-story building at 41 Eldridge Street, which was also being demolished. The trapped men were buried beneath scores of large beams and tons of bricks that had come to rest in a huge pile in the cellar. A large section of flooring lay cantilevered across the collapse pile.

Rescue 1 immediately moved into the collapse area through an opening made by the first due hook & ladder companies. They worked their way deeper into a void, cutting beams and supporting loose timbers as they went. They finally reached the men trapped beneath a huge lean-to collapse. One was dead, the other two in severe pain. As the area around them was shored, Doctor Archer was called for.

Archer removed his hat and coat and rolled up the sleeves of his white shirt. Clutching his medical bag, he carefully moved into the collapse pile, following the path cleared by Rescue 1. Doctor Archer examined the men before injecting them with morphine to ease their pain. A priest joined them briefly, administering the Last Rites to the pinned men. For an hour, rescue men carefully sawed under the watchful eye of Doctor Archer. Finally, the first man was freed. He was carefully carried out and placed on a stretcher. A few minutes later the second man was removed—alive.

As the rescuers began exiting, the collapse pile above them moved. The huge beams surrounding them groaned and shifted, dislodging smaller pieces that fell blocking their way out. For the next several minutes, the rescue men tunneled through the newly shifted debris. As they went to exit, it became apparent that Doctor Archer's foot was wedged fast. Archer was able to wiggle his foot free and rather than risk further cutting, his shoe was left in place.

Doctor Archer, his shirt filthy and in tatters and only wearing one shoe, joined the men from Rescue 1 who lined up to be congratulated by Mayor Hylan and Chief Kenlon. The impromptu ceremony was over quickly and minutes later the rescue men and other members of the department began the dangerous work of removing the body of the dead worker.

For his heroic work Doctor Archer was awarded the James Gordon Bennett Medal the following year. (According to the minutes of the Board of Merit dated November 23, 1923, a subcommittee was to be formed to consider the meritorious actions of the officer and eight men of Rescue 1, and the officers and members of Hook & Ladders 6, 9, & 18 for their heroic work at this collapse. There is no further mention of these reports in subsequent minutes or department orders. It appears no action was taken, and no formal recognition was given to these members.)

Members of Rescue 1 extricating trapped workers at Eldridge Street collapse. Rescue 1 men are wearing hats in the middle of the photo.

Injured worker is removed from the collapse by Rescue 1 members.

About a month later, on the afternoon of April 25, 1923, the company responded to a fire in a commercial building, where street cleaning machines were manufactured. Two alarms were transmitted for this very smoky East 18th Street fire. The fire apparently originated on the fourth floor where bamboo, rattan and hemp were stored. Fireman Charles Kennedy of Rescue 1 and other members were sent to the upper floors to remove some of the smoldering bales of bamboo.

Half smothered by carbon monoxide-laced smoke, Kennedy groped for a window. Dizzy from the toxic smoke he tumbled into an open elevator shaft and fell three stories to the ground floor. The dazed fireman was carried out and examined by Doctor Archer. Amazingly, Kennedy only suffered cuts and bruises and went home to rest for a short while before returning to duty.

On June 3rd 20 firemen were overcome at a 3-alarm fire that swept a six-story factory building at 182 Grand Street. Heavy smoke pumped from the building and drifted into the nearby tenements and the police headquarters building. Rescue 1 arrived, donned their masks and quickly began removing the unconscious firemen. They also set up an aid station and used the pulmotors to revive those knocked out by the smoke.

It was 8:25 p.m. on the night of June 7,1923, when an Amsterdam Avenue trolley car reached the top of the hill at 118th Street and lost its power. Suddenly, it began speeding down the eight-block-long grade. The plummeting trolley car was quickly out of control. The trolley operator leapt from his controls, as the trolley car jumped from its tracks. Two passengers also jumped. But three young women held on for dear life as the car reached 60 miles an hour before bouncing wildly across the curb and sidewalk and crashing into an occupied five-story apartment house.

The speeding trolley opened a huge gash in the apartment house from the basement to the ceiling of the third floor. The exterior walls crumbled and fell across the sidewalk and into the street covering the damaged trolley. Arriving fire companies called for Rescue 1 and the new searchlight rig as the evening darkened.

Rescue 1 arrived and helped shore up parts of the front of the building that were in danger of falling. Rescue men also entered the cellar and examined the structure for possible trapped victims. Sadly, one young girl was killed by the crash and two others seriously injured. All the injured were treated at the scene and then taken to St. Luke's Hospital.

Trolley car crash opens walls of La Salle Street apartment house.

The fumigation of a large milling company building, at Corlears and Water streets in Manhattan, cost the lives of three workers on July 22, 1923. That Saturday morning, the company foreman ordered all workers to leave the plant for the building's annual fumigation. Sadly, three men remained behind and were quickly overcome, as the fumigation company filled the space with deadly hydrocyanic acid gas. The introduction of the gas and the deadly consequences happened so quickly, the men never had a chance to make their presence known. The first idea there was a problem was when the family of one of the dead men inquired why he never returned home.

The man was located by workers wearing gas masks. His sister identified his body. A call went out for Rescue 1. They arrived quickly and donned their smoke helmets. They searched the entire building and found the two dead men. Working this dangerous job were Firemen Joseph Sullivan, John Conners, James Brown, Robert Tierney, William Hutcheon and Joseph Horacek.

Rescue men enter the deadly gas-filled building on July 22, 1923.

Rescue 1 responded to another elevator entrapment on July 26, 1923. A freight elevator operator was slowly being crushed between the freight lift and the wall of the elevator shaft, at 15 Catherine Slip. Deputy Chief Heffernan special-called Rescue 1 and they began working on the badly entangled man. As the rescue men worked, the trapped man lost consciousness. Rescue worked for an hour cutting away the iron bars of the elevator cage to release the man, but his injuries were too severe, and he died before he could be freed.

Later that same day, Rescue 1 was called to stop an ammonia leak at Max's Busy Bee Lunch & Bakery at 21 Ann Street. The newspapers reported that Lt. Walter Lamb, was in command. Lamb had served as a fireman in Rescue 1 from June 16, 1919, until his promotion on March 1, 1921, when he was assigned to Hook & Ladder 9. Walter Lamb's next promotion would be in a few months and would bring him back to Rescue 1. For the time being Lt. Lamb was detailed back to Rescue 1 as an officer.

Rescue 1 was back at the Knickerbocker Ice Company at 519 East 70th Street, on the late afternoon of July 27, 1923. A shattered cylinder head on a compressor allowed ammonia fumes to pour into the building, driving scores of workers and the tenants out of the adjoining buildings to the street.

Hook & Ladder 16 arrived first and under the command of Lt. John Tobin, evacuated the adjoining tenement. Rescue 1 arrived moments later, again under the command of Lt. Walter Lamb. They put on their masks and made a thorough search of the plant. They found one employee trapped and in distress on the second floor. He was removed from the gas-filled building via a ladder. The Rescue then moved to the compressor and shut off the flow of ammonia.

Daily News photo of Rescue 1 at an ammonia explosion in Ridgewood Queens Aug. 1, 1923.

On August 1, 1923, Fireman Peter F. Walsh from Engine 31 was transferred to Rescue 1. The former machinist joined the FDNY on July 1, 1913, and was assigned to Engine 118. He then transferred to H&L 127 in 1915 and to H&L 20 in 1918. Walsh also was assigned to Engine 57 a fireboat, and then to Engine 31.

On the same order, Fireman Paul Maron transferred from Rescue 1 to Hook & Ladder 107. Maron had been in Rescue 1 for three years and was placed on the Roll of Merit three times while a member of Rescue 1.

More than 50 firemen were overcome battling a fire in the five-story building of the Towers Warehouse Corporation at 281 West Street in Manhattan on August 26th, at 6:05 in the morning. The building, a former hotel, had heavy smoke and fire visible on arrival and additional alarms were transmitted. With so much heat and flame at the front entrance, it was decided to attack the flames by breeching the walls on various floors from the adjoining buildings.

One by one the firemen were overcome as the thick smoke began to take its toll. Members of Rescue 1 arrived, donned their smoke helmets and ventured into the thick smoke. Every few minutes they reappeared carrying out an unconscious fireman.

Extension ladders were used to gain access to the adjoining roofs. Lines were stretched and the flames were attacked from those vantage points. Conditions on the roof were slightly better than in the smoke-filled adjoining buildings, but even on the roof, firemen were still getting knocked out. The removal of unconscious firemen down long extension ladders proved a delicate job for the already exhausted firemen. The fire raged all day and required three alarms and additional men from Brooklyn and the Bronx.

A small boy fell into a sewer, 20-feet below the street, through the collapse of a manhole in Broome Street near Attorney Street at 5:30 p.m. September 26, 1923. The four-year-old was carried away by the water as his friends shouted for help. A huge crowd quickly developed and the FDNY was called.

Battalion Chief John McElligott arrived in command of Engines 15, 17 and 11, along with Hook & Ladders 6 and 18. Capt. Anthony Poggi of Engine 15 called for a scaling ladder.

"Don't go down there without rope around you, Tony!" shouted McElligott. A rope was tied around him before he disappeared into the sewer, the rope following him into the darkness. McElligott ordered every manhole cover opened and special-called Rescue 1.

Reaching Ridge Street in the tunnel below, Poggi shouted up the boy was not there. He returned to the original opening and climbed to the street. He then descended into another sewer on Cannon Street seven-blocks away. Meanwhile, McElligott ordered firemen into every manhole opening but after 15 minutes the search was still negative.

Poggi was driven from the sewer by pockets of gas and was ordered to rest as the search continued. Members of Hook & Ladders 18 and 6, and members of Rescue 1 entered the sewer and began searching. Fireman James Landres of Hook & Ladder 18 was moving through the sewer between Lewis and Goerck streets when the firemen in the street heard his shout, "Hold the ladder! I've got him!"

He climbed to the street with the little boy across his shoulders and gently placed the lad on the sidewalk. Both were soaking wet. Members of the Rescue closed in with a pulmotor and began resuscitation efforts. The machine ate up one tank of oxygen after another until four had been emptied.

Lt. Kilbride, however thought he still detected signs of life and ordered the boy placed in the rescue rig and resuscitation continued as they raced to the hospital. Sadly, the youngster died. Fireman Landres was also rushed to the hospital unconscious from the sewer gas.

For their heroic efforts at this emergency Capt. Poggi of Engine 15, and Firemen James Landers and Joseph Boyle of Hook & Ladder 18, and Firemen Thomas O'Toole and Joseph B. Martin Jr. (Smoky Joe's son) of Hook & Ladder 6 were placed on the Roll of Merit with Class III awards. Also receiving Class III awards for entering the sewer and searching for the boy were: Lt. Thomas Kilbride, Firemen Peter Walsh, Robert Tierney, William Fletcher and Joseph Sullivan of Rescue 1.

On October 18, 1923, Fireman Joseph Horacek transferred from Rescue 1 to Engine Company 274. Horacek had been a member of Rescue 1 for four years and was placed on the Roll of Merit five times during his time in Rescue 1.

Harry Wolff was an oiler at the Borden Farm Products Company building at 942 DeKalb Avenue in Brooklyn. On October 23rd while he was working in the building's engine room, the explosion of an ammonia tank threw him across the room and into a brick wall. He lay there unconscious, as around him the building filled with ammonia gas. Miss Edna Schmid, who also worked for the company, immediately wet a handkerchief and despite the choking fumes, warned 125 other workers who were able to escape the building clouds of ammonia vapor. She however, fell to the floor overcome by the fumes.

Arriving fire companies did what they could, until Rescue 1 arrived from Manhattan. Firemen William Hutcheon and William Fletcher donned smoke helmets, entered the deadly cloud and began their search. They located Miss Schmid and carried her to safety. They then returned for Wolff and carried him to safety, before they moved to the ammonia equipment and stopped the leak.

Firemen William Hutcheon and William Fletcher with smoke helmets outside Borden Farm Products Company, Brooklyn, on October 23, 1923.

Another elevator entrapment occurred on November 5, 1923, at 16 West Third Street in Manhattan. Rescue 1 and Hook & Ladder 20 arrived to find Nicholas Heimbauer, a 29-year-old man, caught between the wall and a heavy cased machine being delivered. The man remained conscious and was able to help direct the efforts of the rescue men. When the heavy box was finally moved, they found the man's right leg badly crushed. He was taken to St. Vincent's Hospital.

On December 1, 1923, Lt. John A. Coffey was promoted to Captain and placed in command of Engine Company 5. On that same day Lt. Walter L. Lamb, who had been detailed to Rescue

1 for a few months, was promoted to Captain and was officially assigned to Rescue 1. The company had been without a captain since McElligott was detailed to a fireboat after almost losing his life at the Park & Tilford fire on December 1, 1916.

A worker was killed in a most unusual accident at the Pennsylvania Railroad powerhouse in Long Island City. The 35-year-old worker, Fernando Mendes, was employed as a coal passer and somehow fell into the base of a flue within a 360-foot smokestack.

It was about 7 o'clock on Christmas Eve 1923, when Mendes' brother arrived at the powerhouse and reported his brother had never arrived home. The superintendent checked the time clock and saw Mendes had checked in, but never checked out of work. They decided he must still be on the grounds and a search was started, but the missing man was not found.

The next day, Christmas morning, the brother returned after Fernando failed to appear for a second night. Another search was started. Meanwhile, a water tender was inspecting the big boilers, when he noticed a small door leading to the flue was open. He reported this to the superintendent and after a few minutes it was decided the missing man must be in the flue. It was impossible to work near this door, the draft was so strong it would pull a man in. The heat in the flue was close to 1,000-degrees.

Orders were given to lower the fires, as a call went to the police and fire departments. Acting Chief Joseph Dewey of the 45th Battalion arrived and special-called Rescue 1 to the scene. The company arrived and broke out their special tools including smoke helmets, ropes and fire-proof clothing. They were taken to the area they believed the missing man to be and made examinations prior to entry.

Inside the small inspection door of the flue was a flange—like that of an old-fashioned stovepipe for shutting off the draft. Apparently, Mendes stepped on the flange, and it turned, dropping him into the bottom of the flue. Two members of Rescue 1 volunteered to make the descent using scaling ladders and ropes. They dressed in the fireproof clothing, donned their smoke helmets and climbed down into the base of the flue with ropes tied around them in case they had to be hauled back up. Streams of water were also played on them to protect them from the heat. The man's body was carefully lifted out of the flue, followed by the rescue men.

Chapter 12: 1924

The year 1924 started off a little differently for the members of Rescue 1. For the first time since 1916, the company had a captain in command. Walter Lamb, who'd spent two years as a fireman in Rescue 1 from June of 1919 until his promotion in March 1921, was back as the captain of the company. Lt. Thomas Kilbride was his second in command. The firemen assigned to Rescue 1 were: James Brown, John Conners, Matthew Crawley, William Dorritie, William Fletcher, William Hutcheon, Charles Kennedy, John Kistenberger, Thomas Larkin, John Mayr, John Milward, Charles Roggenkamp, John Ryan, Joseph Sullivan, Robert Tierney, Bela Varga and Peter Walsh.

The year 1924 was a leap year, and the evening of February 29th would prove to be very difficult and rather dangerous for Manhattan firemen. At 6:45 p.m. a cop walking his beat on Broadway noticed smoke drifting up through the sidewalk grate on Reade Street. He hurried to the spot and saw a fire in the cellar of 61 Reade Street. Dashing back to the corner he pulled the alarm box. Within minutes companies were rolling to a fire that would knock out 40 firemen including two battalion chiefs and Chief Kenlon himself.

The blaze started in the cellar of the five-story building and spread to a first-floor shoe and leather establishment. The billowing smoke, now filled with noxious fumes, knocked man after man to his knees, then rendered them unconscious. The men were falling so quickly, that Doctor Archer set up an emergency hospital in the store adjoining the fire building. Wave after wave of firemen pushed into thick walls of smoke only to be battered senseless.

Water accumulating in the cellar and subcellar were becoming dangerously high, adding the possibility of drowning to the growing list of dangers. After both battalion chiefs assigned to the fire had been dragged out unconscious, Chief Kenlon led a team into the subcellar to attack the fire. Several of the men around him dropped into the water, but quick work by other firemen saved them. Conditions were getting worse by the minute.

"This is one of the toughest cellar fires I've ever had to handle. . . . The fire itself is not hard to handle, but the smoke is certainly proving fearful to my men." Kenlon said.

Several firemen were in such bad condition that they had to be taken to the hospital. *The New York Times* reported:

> Among the firemen to go to the hospital was Captain Walter Lamb, commanding Rescue Squad No. 1. He carried out eight of his comrades and then pitched to the sidewalk unconscious. Physicians at Beekman Street Hospital reported his condition as more alarming than the others. (Lamb was one of nine hospitalized. Walter Lamb would soon be back fighting fires with Rescue 1. In fact, Walter worked almost 14 more years, with seven as a battalion chief.) The Reade Street fire required three alarms to extinguish.

Tuesday into Wednesday May 19-20, 1924, was an exhausting and dangerous night for New York City firemen. It all started just before 8 o'clock Tuesday evening, when Box 199 came in for a building fire at Broadway and Grand Street, the warehouse of Lord & Taylor (America's oldest-surviving department store operating since 1826). This fire would require 4-alarms and many hours to control. Thick clouds of smoke pumped from the building, dropping a dark shroud over the entire neighborhood. Visibility in the street outside the warehouse was zero. Firemen had to feel their way along parked apparatus, across the smoke-obscured street and sidewalks. Man after man dropped both inside and outside the building.

At one point, a deputy chief who'd twice ordered the deckpipe of Engine 30's hose wagon to be shut down and twice received no reply—sent his aide through the dense smoke, to find out why his order had not been carried out. The aide climbed carefully onto the hose wagon and inched toward the huge nozzle. There he found both firemen, slumped over the deckpipe, unconscious. The heavily stocked building, filled with dry goods, defied all attempts to extinguish it.

While this fire was at its height, another blaze broke out at the Battery, on the tip of Manhattan. This fire was in the Iron Steamship Company's base and would require 4-alarms to extinguish.

With little rest the exhausted men of Rescue 1 worked both fires, then responded to a special-call on Mercer Street. Thousands of workers were driven from their jobs by a cloud of white poison gas, when water splashed onto two large, leaky steel drums of muriatic acid in a subcellar at 137 Mercer Street. Lives were in danger and thousands of dollars' worth of fabrics and textiles were being ruined, as the emergency unfolded.

Rescue 1 arrived with Lt. Kilbride in command. The men donned smoke helmets and entered the deadly cloud. Conditions in the subcellar were extreme, as the rescue men examined the situation and developed a plan. The men were forced to move very slowly, as the acid ate into everything it touched. The men's boots were quickly destroyed while they wore them.

For two hours, they toiled trying to stop the leak and control the gas cloud.

Finally, the Rescue devised a plan and the leaking barrels were rolled into an elevator and raised to the street. Even in the clear air, the leaking drums proved difficult. One of the rescue men, procured a barrel of cement and attempted to construct a dam, to guide the leaking acid into the sewer. But the cement caused the acid to boil and sputter like molten lava and give off a suffocating cloud vapor. A hose stream was used to dissipate the vapors. The street was cleared of horses and people while the members of Rescue 1 plugged the leaking drums. The drums were taken to the city dock off Canal Street and dumped into the river.

Members of Rescue 1 with leaking barrels of muriatic acid at 217 Mercer Street on May 20, 1924.

The exhausted men of Rescue 1 finally found themselves back in quarters, reeking of smoke and acid fumes. They changed clothes, most of which had to be thrown away due to acid damage, and placed fresh smoke helmets on the rig as Lt. Kilbride tapped them back into service.

On May 24, 1924, a 15 X 30-foot concrete mixing platform, suspended above a 50-foot-deep building excavation collapsed, burying 14 workers. It was around 10 a.m. when the platform at the West 46th Street building site fell. One hundred workers were under, atop and around the platform when it dropped. Most men were strengthening the scaffold, weakened by dynamite blasts in the rock below. A huge concrete mixer was on top of the platform and shook and trembled when the blast was touched off. A half hour later, a truck loaded with rock was rumbling down the incline when the mass of timbers, rock, sand, mixer and all gave way and dropped into the abyss behind the truck.

In a doctor's office next to the excavation, Dolly Ben, a young nurse from Charing Cross Hospital in London, rushed to a window and saw immediately what had happened. A war nurse for five years, Dolly's instincts kicked in. Dashing from the office she turned in the fire alarm, then hurried into the collapse area where she began treating the injured workers. The fire alarm sent Deputy Chiefs Ross and Martin along with Chief Kenlon to the scene. Members of Rescue 1 and H&L 4 worked together, digging and cutting away timbers as the search began.

After four hours, the last body was found. In all, four workers were killed and 14 were seriously injured. Doctor Archer set up an aide station for the injured workers being taken from the collapse. Archer also climbed down into the collapse area, to treat some of the pinned workers while rescue men worked to free them.

Engines 65, 54, and 23 join with Hook & Ladders 2 and 4 and Rescue 1 at collapse site.

With the aid of H&L 4, Rescue 1 worked in wet cement and debris to free trapped workers.

Doctor Archer, in vest, treats an injured worker.

At 9:17 p.m. a distraught man jumped beneath the L train at the Grand Street station on June 2, 1924. Rescue 1 and the first due hook & ladder worked for 30 minutes to extricate the body.

On July 19, 1924, Rescue 1's third apparatus was placed in service. It was a Mack chain-driven AC-10 Bulldog that carried Mack registration number 736-866. This rig was slightly larger than the previous two rigs, reflecting the fact that more equipment was being assigned to the company. It was also a more heavy-duty design. This 1924 Mack remained in service with Rescue 1 until replaced in 1931.

New 1924 Mack with special tools. From left- rope rifle, saws and jacks, torch, pulmotor, rubber waders, smoke helmet with telephone and cable, and smoke helmets.

Firemen John Conners, Charles Kennedy, Robert Tierney and Charles Roggenkamp with smoke helmets and new rig.

Captain Lamb and his men responded to Brooklyn on September 2, 1924. It was shortly after 10 p.m. when ammonia fumes drove people from a restaurant at 1030 Gates Avenue. First due Engine 222, led by Capt. Harry Doherty, attempted to enter the three-story brick building, but were driven back by the ammonia cloud. Rescue 1 made a quick trip across the river and used their smoke helmets to enter the noxious cloud. After 20 minutes, they were able to stop the leak and begin clearing the air.

Rescue 1 was busy on September 6, 1924, when they responded to the Park & Tilford Building at 532 West 43rd Street. When the explosion in the engine room occurred, a nipple from the ammonia system blew off, striking one worker in the mouth and knocking out two of his teeth. Three men fell to the floor unconscious. Rescue 1 arrived and donned their smoke helmets. In the engine room they wrapped wet towels around the heads of the unconscious men and carried them to safety. Then Rescue returned and controlled the leak.

They had just finished clearing the fumes, when another alarm was received for an ammonia leak, in a chocolate factory downtown on West Broadway. Rescue 1 responded to that scene where 100 workers were driven from the building. The Rescue had this leak under control in a matter of minutes.

On September 13th Rescue 1 responded to 297 Cherry Street in Manhattan, a seven-story loft building. They were special-called to the scene by Battalion Chief John McElligott, who'd responded to a pulled alarm box, and found the leg of a 14-year-old boy, trapped between the elevator and the shaft wall at the third floor. Capt. Lamb directed the members of Rescue 1 as they cut through several feet of stone flooring and cut away iron grillwork with their torch. The youngster was freed and only had a broken ankle.

Rescue 1 worked another elevator extrication job on September 23rd at 79 East 139th Street. It took one hour to cut away enough metal and chip away brick work to free a crippled young man trapped between the elevator and the ceiling of the fifth floor. The lad was removed, but it was feared his already crippled leg might have to be amputated.

A very challenging fire was battled by the FDNY in Staten Island, on September 26, 1924. A fire, apparently incendiary in nature, was first seen burning the merry-go-round of the Midland Beach Resort. The flames were spreading quickly, as Deputy Chief William Beggins transmitted second and third alarms. The rollercoaster was soon in flames, and the strong northerly wind spread the flames to the Ferris wheel and across an open space, igniting the five-story wood-frame Richmond Hotel. It appeared that the entire resort would soon be ablaze.

A borough call was transmitted, and Manhattan dispatchers sent a second alarm assignment, normally assigned to a fire at the Battery, to the ferryboat landing. Eighteen pieces of fire apparatus, including Rescue 1's new rig, were placed on the ferryboat and taken to the fire scene.

With fire hydrants few and far between, long stretches of hose were needed to bring enough water to attack the growing fire front. Around 10 p.m. the wind died down, giving the firemen a slight advantage. Finally, the flames were subdued, but the cost of the fire was large. The resort was destroyed, along with four hotels and 15 private homes.

A sailor on leave and apparently trying to sneak into a dance hall on the third floor of a building at Columbus Avenue and West 66th Street, accidentally became wedged between the elevator car and the fourth floor on October 4, 1924. Building personnel attempted to free him, then called the police. They, too, tried to free him and called the fire department. Hook & Ladder 35 arrived and called for Rescue.

Working with Doctor Archer, the rescue men used prybars and their torch to lift the flooring and cut away steel work. Archer received a serious cut to his arm but was able to dress it himself, just before the rescue men freed the injured sailor, whom Archer treated briefly before sending him off to the hospital.

In October of 1924 Mayor Hylan met with the Budget Committee of the Board of Estimate, regarding the FDNY budget for 1925. Among the items agreed upon was $10,833 for a new Rescue Squad with apparatus, for Brooklyn and Queens. This included funds for a captain, lieutenant and 14 firemen for the new company. In addition, three new battalion chiefs, 43 captains, and 27 more lieutenants would be added to the department.

Chief Kenlon was quoted saying:

> It is high time that Brooklyn had its own Rescue Squad. There is only one such outfit in all Manhattan. It is therefore difficult, if not almost impossible, for this squad to reach any given Brooklyn point in time to affect any rescues.
>
> The Rescue Squad is planned to save lives. Every known scientific invention that will aid rescuers to enter places of danger to save human lives is made part of the squad's equipment.
>
> The increased use of ammonia in Brooklyn factories and office structures has presented a new problem. The ammonia fumes are deadly. When there is an explosion of fire the firemen are subjected to these fumes which may kill or make them unfit for duty.
>
> New York City secured its only Rescue Squad after a

> terrible lesson. During the fire which destroyed the Equitable Building a man was caught under heavy steel beams. The fire raged around him.
>
> The firemen could see the man in torture, but could not enter the inferno, as they did not have any equipment that would keep them alive long enough to rescue the man. Many vain attempts were made.
>
> Now the Rescue Squad can go anyplace. It has acetylene torches that can cut through any metal and masks that permit the Rescue Squad to remain in places that ordinarily would mean certain death.

Rescue 1 responded to a ship fire on October 10th at Pier 6, the foot of 42nd Street. The Dollar Lines passenger ship the *President Polk*, was moored when a fire was discovered around noon. Rescue 1 used their smoke helmets, as they attacked the fire with a hose line. The bulk of the fire was in the cargo of syrups, spices and nuts, but spread to ship's other contents and fittings. Rescue 1 also located a missing stevedore, who was found in a stateroom, dead from smoke inhalation.

Despite the fact there were around 200 people onboard at the time of the fire, only one person was killed. Many of the ship's crew were Chinese "coolies" who had been sleeping in a hold when the flames broke out. In their excitement, many jumped overboard and were promptly rescued.

For their heroic efforts Lt. Kilbride, and Firemen Dorritie, Milward, Roggenkamp, Kistenberger, Fletcher and Kennedy were placed on the Roll of Merit.

On November 14, 1924, a major fire burned through a two-square block area of Jersey City's waterfront. Started by an explosion in the subcellar of a saltpeter plant, the flames were soon roaring and driven by strong winds into the exposures. The entire Jersey City Fire Department was on scene, battling the flames for hours, bolstered by mutual aid from Bayonne, Hoboken and Newark, who manned the empty firehouses. The FDNY sent their fireboats the *John Purroy Mitchel* and the *New Yorker* to the scene to help.

At 2 p.m. FDNY Commissioner Joseph Drennan received a phone call requesting additional help be sent to Jersey City. Drennan, accompanied by Chief Kenlon, drove to Washington and Cortland streets, where they transmitted alarms that brought 20 engines, 6 hook and ladders, Rescue 1, and the Department ambulance. Three ferryboats were arranged and the apparatus was loaded and brought across the river.

Then Commissioner Drennan and Chief Kenlon drove to New Jersey to confer with Jersey City Chief Boyle. Approaching the busy Chief, Commissioner Drennan announced, "We've rolled over, Chief, and are ready to help."

Chief Boyle's astonishment was so apparent, that Drennan asked whether or not he'd called for help.

"I did not. Nor did I authorize it," he replied.

After a brief conference between the New Yorkers and Chief Boyle it was decided to head back to Manhattan, as they didn't need any help.

It was never learned who placed the call.

Chapter 13:
1925

A major construction accident occurred on January 10, 1925, at 310 West 30th Street, when a one-ton section of recently poured concrete crashed from the eighth floor through to the basement. The 10 X 10-foot section had been removed on all the floors, to allow the construction of a staircase. As two workers with wheelbarrows filled with sand and cement stepped onto the "green" flooring, it gave way, dropping them and their load to the floor below. Each of the sections then failed floor by floor, until the workers, their loads and the green concrete had all collapsed into the basement, burying the two workers under broken concrete, sand and scaffolding.

The fire department responded, and Rescue 1 was assigned to the alarm. The first two workers were obviously dead when Rescue 1 reached them, but another worker was also trapped and seriously injured. The Rescue was able to use jacks and hand tools to lift large concrete pieces to free the injured man. Rescue 1 provided first aid, before carrying him to the street, where ambulance surgeons took over.

On January 26, 1925, Fireman Peter Walsh was promoted to Lieutenant and remained in Rescue 1. This day would prove to be a long and difficult one for the FDNY. It started at 10 a.m. with a fire in the cellar of a tenement at 15 Stanton Street. As the first due companies moved into the building, they were met by a wall of smoke laced with carbon monoxide. One by one the firemen dropped to the floor unconscious. Other firemen outside rush to aid their comrades but were themselves overcome.

Rescue 1 was called and helped remove the overcome firemen and set up an aid station where 25 unconscious firemen were treated with pulmotors. Neighbors brought bedding outside to help comfort the downed firemen.

All but five firemen were revived and returned to work. Lt. George Morris, Fireman Joseph Brady, Thomas Brenan of Engine 17, Firemen James Maher of Engine 33, and Victor Dignes of H&L 9, were taken to the hospital.

Lt. Peter Walsh pointing out where to shoot the line gun.

Then, in the snow and wind, firemen fought for four hours, to subdue a 4-alarm fire in a six-story loft building at 83 Canal Street. This fire was in the heart of one of the most congested tenement districts in the city. Six families were driven to the street as the firefighting commenced. Firemen were able to keep the flames from extending to the adjoining buildings, and things seemed to be calming down when an oil tank exploded on the fifth floor.

Battalion Chief John Callahan and the engine company he was directing, were all blown down a flight of stairs without serious injury. The explosion set the flames to extending again. The building was an "L" shaped structure, with entrances on both Canal and Eldridge streets. The Eldridge Street entrance was only a few doors down from the quarters of Hook & Ladder 6. The company was already out extinguishing a small rubbish fire in a store at 85 Eldridge Street, a block and a half away.

A person passing by saw the smoke from this new fire and hurried to the firemen already working the rubbish fire and reported the blaze. By the time Battalion Chief Helm and the remainder of the first alarm assignment arrived, the fire had such a good head start that a second alarm was transmitted. Fanned by strong winds the flames extended rapidly from the second floor up and through the roof. Smoky Joe Martin arrived and transmitted a third alarm.

Heavy smoke spread through the adjoining building at 81 Canal and firemen were forced to evacuate that building, directing the six families to shelter in the firehouse. Two of the women driven from their homes by the fire set up a temporary restaurant in the quarters of Hook & Ladder 6. They made coffee for the other displaced tenants and for the firemen.

On February 3, 1925, the FDNY received alarm Box 857, for a fire in the Dobbs Hat Company at 618 Fifth Avenue, a five-story building just across from St. Patrick's Cathedral. The smoky basement fire imperiled 100 women working inside the building and another 200 in the adjoining structures. First arriving companies raised ladders and plucked six women from smoke-filled windows as hose lines were pulled into position. While moving through the heavy smoke, Fireman James Reilly of Hook & Ladder 4 fell through a trap door on the fourth floor. He was rushed to Bellevue Hospital with a possible fractured spine.

The second alarm brought Rescue 1 to the scene, under the command of Acting Lieutenant William Fletcher. With the rear fire escapes filled with trapped women, Rescue 1 split into teams and began search and rescue. To compound the dangers, the buildings at 616, 618, and 620 Fifth Avenues were all interconnected by fire doors. Smoke spread quickly up the elevator shafts and through heating flues, filling the buildings with thick noxious smoke.

The sounds of the arriving multiple alarm companies drowned out some of the cries for help within the fire building. At one point, a piece of paper floated down from a smoke-filled window and landed at the feet of a police officer. He opened the note, which read: "It is getting terrible up here, Send help."

Running to the firemen, the cop handed them the letter and pointed to the fifth-floor window. In an instant, a portable ladder was raised, and seven women were quickly removed. The ladder was then moved, and several men were pulled to safety.

Acting Lieutenant Fletcher, the husky Missourian, was a 38-year-old former ironworker and elevator constructor, and was said to have had a grip like a vise. Fletcher, the father of three, rescued a photographer trapped on the top floor. Then he led a team into the smoke-filled cellar to extinguish the fire. Several Rescue 1 members, including Fletcher and Fireman John Conners were overcome and were carried by their comrades to the street where Doctor Archer set up an aid station at 628 Fifth Avenue.

As the firefighting continued, Doctor Archer was very busy reviving the overcome firemen. Fletcher regained consciousness and pleaded with Archer to return to his company. "I'm alright doctor," he said. But Archer could tell he had taken a very dangerous amount of smoke and had him rushed to Bellevue Hospital. An hour later William Fletcher passed away. The cause of death was listed as smoke narcosis.

Fletcher was the first member of Rescue 1 to die in the line of duty. He'd joined the FDNY in June of 1914 and worked in Hook & Ladder 2 before joining Rescue 1. His name appeared on the Roll of Merit four times. Honorary Deputy Chief Robert Mainzer, a personal friend of Fletcher, sent $1,000 to the widow. He also wrote a letter that accompanied the money that read:

> Your husband met with a most heroic death trying to save the lives of others. He was true to the tradition of the New York City Fire Department. Our hearts go out to you in deep sympathy for your great bereavement, and I want to assure you that no one in this city can feel any worse about your husband's noble death than I. I fully understand that neither checks nor any financial aid will ever take the place of your dead husband, but none the less it must be a comfort to you to know that we are thinking of you at your hour of trouble.

Fireman William Fletcher is helped to a waiting ambulance by Fireman William Dorritie (right) and another Rescue 1 member.

Fireman William R.P. Fletcher
5555—February 3, 1925

On February 7, 1925, Fireman Frederick Kaiser from Hook & Ladder 9 transferred to Rescue 1.

The following month, on March 1, 1925, Rescue Company 2 was organized and placed in service with Captain Walter A.

O'Leary in command. O'Leary had been an original member of Rescue 1. Appointed in 1909, he worked in Hook & Ladder 104, before transferring to Manhattan. He worked in Engine 21 and 33 before joining the new Rescue Company. He was promoted to lieutenant in 1918 and worked in Engine 14. He was promoted to captain in 1922 and was given command of Hook & Ladder 6, until the formation of Rescue 2 in 1925.

O'Leary's lieutenant was Peter F. Walsh of Rescue 1. The members of the new rescue company were, Firemen William A. Gillan of Engine 6, Francis A. Anderson of Engine 210, Earl H. Cain of Engine 215, Henry Robin of Engine 283, James J. Boyland of H&L 102, Dennis J. Walsh of Engine 10, James J. Cummings of Engine 201, Anthony S. Zummo of Engine 237, John J. Hederman of Engine 237, William J. Barry of H&L 102, Raymond J. Fleming of H&L 110, George F. Lohr of H&L 112, John G. Zablotny of H&L 118, and John Kistenberger of Rescue 1.

Then on March 8, 1925, Rescue 1 held a quiet celebration in company quarters to mark their 10th anniversary. The aroma of corned beef and cabbage filled the Spring Street firehouse as the members of Engine 30 and Rescue 1 sat down with several invited guests including Chief John Kenlon. A few of the original members joined the 15 current members for the meal. The only member from the original group still in the company was Lt. Thomas Kilbride.

On April 16, 1925, Fireman Cornell M. Garety transferred from Hook & Ladder 26 to Rescue 1. Garety, a former laborer, was born in Hoboken, New Jersey, on July 30, 1891. The World War I veteran was a private in Company B, 14th infantry. He joined the FDNY on June 16, 1916, and was assigned to Hook & Ladder 115 in Brooklyn. In March of 1917 he transferred to Hook & Ladder 24 and remained there until 1924, when he transferred to Hook & Ladder 26. He was already on the Roll of Merit twice before joining Rescue 1 in 1925. (Garety would serve as a fireman in Rescue 1 until his promotion to Lieutenant in 1926. Four years later, he would return to Rescue 1 as Captain. He would eventually be awarded the James Gordon Bennett medal for his rescue of trapped firemen in May of 1932. Garety was later promoted to Battalion Chief and served in the ninth battalion until his retirement in 1942.)

More than 100 persons were injured in a panic that followed a short-circuit of a subway car at about 9 a.m. on May 19, 1925. The problem occurred in a Lexington Avenue subway, a train car's-length south of Grand Central Station. The train had been experiencing electrical issues since its start at 59th Street. Lights were flickering as the motorman drove toward Grand Central. Just short of the station there was a flash, and the train jerked to a halt. A second bright flash was followed by a sizzling and crackling sound. Suddenly, thick clouds of black, suffocating smoke rolled up from beneath the fifth car, then billowed inside through the open windows.

Scores of screaming women began pushing their way back and forth in the cars. Another bright flash and loud report heightened the frenzy. The motorman was struggling to keep the passengers calm, while he moved from his box to shut off the current in the third rail. The panic only worsened, and the rushing passengers pinned him against the door. He was able to free himself, opened the front door and dropped down to the tracks. He ran back to where a purple light signified a shut-off box. He threw the switch deenergizing the third rail. This however, also plunged the train into darkness, further stoking the panic.

Women began smashing windows and trying to jump through the jagged frames of glass. The conductor and train guards finally gave up trying to calm the passengers and opened the train doors. The frantic passengers stumbled and fell onto the tracks. The track area was now filled with smoke, panicked passengers and darkness.

Above on the sidewalk, pedestrians noticed smoke coming up through the sidewalk grates and pulled the fire alarm box. The FDNY responded quickly along with ambulances and surgeons from several hospitals. Chief Smoky Joe Martin arrived and began to assemble his forces, as the passengers below were just reaching the station platform. Fire companies, including Rescue 1, moved into the subway and began the evacuation of the train and the surrounding track areas. It was at this point firemen noticed the third rail had been re-energized.

The fire proved to be minor in nature, the smoke however was debilitating and only worsened the panic as people struggled to breathe. The trains and the tracks were cleared, and the injured were treated. More than 100 people were injured with 11 requiring hospitalizations.

A fire in the afterhold of the U.S. Navy destroyer USS *Coghlan*, was spreading faster than the crew could control and help from the FDNY was requested. It was the night of May 30, 1925, when Manhattan fire companies responded to the ship's location in the North River at 18th Street. An ensign was missing below decks, and members of Rescue 1 donned smoke helmets and searched below for the missing man. Thick smoke was being produced by burning ropes, brushes and cleaning fluids and the flames were inching closer to stored torpedoes, as the rescue men searched nearby. Five hose lines were stretched from shore-based hydrants and the battle began. Rescue 1 was able to locate the unconscious sailor and carry him to the main deck, where he was revived. The fire was extinguished, and the weary firemen took up.

A man cleaning the College of the City of New York's chemical vault, sprinkled water on the stone floor, as he had done every day for years, when suddenly flames sprang up around him and danced across the 50-foot long and 20-foot-wide vault. As he ran from the vault, he saw the fire closing in on more than 5,000 jars, tubes and bottles containing several hundred varieties of chemicals. College chemists believe a leaking crock of sodium covered with kerosene, spread a puddle across the floor that evaporated. The addition of water on the unprotected pure sodium ignited the flames around 11 a.m. August 4, 1925.

The first fire companies to arrive could do little, faced with the roaring furnace of chemicals. Deputy Chief Thomas Dougherty special-called Rescue 1 to the location on Amsterdam Avenue at 138th Street. Rescue 1 arrived under the command of Lt. Thomas Kilbride and conferred with the chemistry staff. The true danger quickly became apparent: besides the numerous chemicals, many of which were water reactive, a large amount of ammonium nitrate was also stored inside. This highly explosive chemical compound was being threatened by the increasing temperatures around it.

Donning gas masks the rescue men moved toward the blazing vault. They tried applying several different fire extinguishing agents with no results. It was decided that water was the only remaining option. With the help of the units on scene, hoses were stretched to the vault area and masked rescue men directed streams from the vault doorway. At first, the only effect seemed to be to lift the fire off the floor and make it burn on the surface of the rising water.

As the pool of water deepened the chemicals were still erupting, and Lt. Kilbride decided that it was time to vent the vault. A team of firemen with mauls was sent to the sidewalk above the vault. They quickly pounded a hole through the concrete opening the vault to daylight. Inside the blazing chamber, the lighter chemicals were burning out and the heavier were under the artificial lake formed by the hose stream run-off.

Despite receiving painful chemical burns where the rising water got above the tops of their boots, the rescue men held their position working the hose streams into the super-heated vault. After two hours of dangerous work the fire was brought under control. Among the injured were Lt. Kilbride and the crew of Rescue 1: William Hutcheon, William Dorritie, James Brown, Joseph Sullivan, John Milward and John Kaiser.

Fireman John Milward posses for newspaper photo at college chemical fire.

Different types of fires, present different types of challenges. Ventilation is often difficult to accomplish, especially in large fire-proof buildings with cellars and subcellars. Ship fires pose similar problems, with available ventilation and limited access to locations within the ship.

One specific type of fire—an under-pier fire had all these dangers and difficulties mixed together. The piers were built upon a latticework of creosoted pilings that supported, quite often, a concrete deck with multi-storied structures built on top. These fires were, and still are, very difficult to extinguish.

It was 5:21 on the afternoon of August 31, 1925, when Manhattan Fire Alarm Box 901 was transmitted for a fire at Pier 95 at the foot of West 55th Street on the North River. An employee of the Furness Bermuda Steamboat Line noticed a fire, in the sub-flooring underneath the concrete. He attempted to extinguish the fire himself and burned his hands. He then notified workers on a coal barge moored nearby and they also tried to extinguish the fire with no success. The FDNY was called.

Four fireboats and numerous land-based fire companies descended on the pier. With the tide rising, it was becoming more and more difficult to hit the body of fire underneath the blazing pier. A group of firemen climbed down onto floating wooden rafts. Laying flat, they tried to direct their streams upwards, as a strange greenish yellow smoke chugged from the creosoted pine timbers of the sub-flooring. Fireman after fireman fell to the toxic smoke.

Smoky Joe Martin requested help from the Consolidated Gas Company who sent their emergency crew. They teamed up with Rescue 1 and using a large drill, numerous holes were cut through the pier's flooring and cellar pipes were lowered into the 12-inch space below. Four alarms were transmitted, and 75 firemen were knocked out battling this fire.

Flames broke out within a five-story tenement at 256 West 39th Street, between Seventh and Eighth avenues on the afternoon of August 27, 1925. The old building was slated for demolition in several days. The fire spread quickly to the adjoining buildings and two alarms were transmitted sending nine engines, three hook & ladders, a water tower and Rescue 1.

Quick action prevented the flames from reaching the nearby Plymouth Hotel. Lines were stretched into the hotel and used to stop the extending flames in the rear of the adjoining structures.

A crew of men was in the process of renovating an old four-story dwelling at 26 West 47th Street and converting the structure to offices on December 11, 1925. It was late afternoon and large sections of plaster and lathing were being removed and the resulting debris shoveled outside, when a major collapse occurred. The two upper floors and attic dropped in a mass of timber, bricks, and plaster dust. As the dust cloud cleared, the crew realized workers were pinned beneath tons of beams and debris.

The first arriving units removed several lightly trapped workers to safety. Rescue 1 arrived and began to tunnel into the area where two men were trapped. For several hours Captain Walter Lamb, Fireman Bela Varga and Fireman Cornell Garety carefully worked their way to the pinned men. They cleared away enough debris to allow a priest quick access to administer the Last Rites should things go badly. Doctor Archer joined them providing medical help and then fed liquids to the trapped men to keep up their strength.

As the sky darkened to evening, an electrical engineer from a nearby building rigged up a mast with lighting, to make the rescue work safer within the tottering structure. As the last beams were moved away and the crushing weight was cleared, the men were gently pulled free and quickly placed on oxygen and carried to a waiting ambulance.

For their life-saving efforts under very dangerous conditions the three rescue men were placed on the Roll of Merit with Class II awards.

Firemen Roggenkamp, Dorritie, Tierney, Larkin, Fullam, Tischler, Conners, and Capt. Lamb.

Chapter 14: Ten Years of Service

The first ten years of service by Rescue Company 1 were unique in many ways. The idea to "save" the Rescue for big fires, was quickly changed by adding additional initial alarm assignments starting in 1916. No firemen want to stand idle while fires are being fought nearby. As the company gained experience and added tools and techniques to their repertoire, they served more and more often.

While there may have been some resentment of the new company when they first started, their continuing effectiveness in the most difficult situations had proven to the average fireman, there were now smoke-helmeted brothers that had their backs. Because of Rescue 1, most firemen now breathed less ammonia, illuminating gas, and other toxic mixtures. Every member of the FDNY however, still faced thick smoke without breathing protection every day. Even the members of Rescue 1 worked most fires without using the smoke helmets. This, and the beatings they took— even with the smoke helmets, took its toll on the rescue men.

Of the ten men chosen to staff the company back in 1915, only one man, Thomas Kilbride was still working in the company ten years later.

John McElligott, the first captain, who was almost killed at the Park & Tilford fire in December of 1916, was officially transferred to Engine Co. 78, the fireboat *George B. McClellan,* on October 9, 1917. He was promoted to Battalion Chief on April 16, 1922, and assigned to the 4th Battalion. He became a Deputy Chief in 1925. He later became both Chief of Department in 1932 and Fire Commissioner from 1934 until 1941. He was cited for bravery five times in his career.

Edwin Hotchkiss, the first Lieutenant, was promoted to Captain on November 11, 1916, and remained in Rescue 1 until

December 24, 1916, when he was given command of Hook & Ladder 12. He retired in June of 1920 as the Captain of Hook & Ladder 20 (and Acting Chief of the Fifth Battalion). He was cited for bravery three times in his career.

Thomas Kilbride remained in Rescue 1 until May of 1933, a total of 18 years. He was promoted to Lieutenant on August 1, 1919, and remained in Rescue 1. Kilbride would act as Company Commander after the death of Frank Blessing and continued until Walter Lamb was assigned as captain in 1925. Kilbride was cited for bravery 11 times during his career and spent his last year working in the Bronx before retiring in September 1934.

John Ryan worked in Rescue 1 until he was detailed as aide to Chief Kenlon. Cited for bravery eight times in his career, he was detailed as an aide to Chief and Commissioner John McElligott in 1938 before retiring in 1940.

Frank Clark had been a member of Rescue 1 for seven and a half years when he was promoted to Lieutenant on November 1, 1922. He was assigned to Engine Co. 76 and worked there for the next five years. Cited for bravery seven times in his career, he retired in 1928.

Alfred Kinsella had worked almost five and a half years at Rescue 1 when was promoted to lieutenant on September 1, 1920, and returned to Engine 74. He was promoted to captain on February 1, 1927, and given command of Engine Company 26. Kinsella, cited for bravery six times in his career, retired on March 13, 1927. After retiring Kinsella worked for the Mine Safety Appliance Co. (MSA) and wrote technical articles about rescue work that appeared in National Safety News and other publications.

Alfred Henretty transferred back to Hook & Ladder 15 on January 1, 1917. He had worked in Rescue 1 for almost two years. Henretty continued working in H&L 15 and was cited for bravery two more times until he retired in 1926.

Walter O'Leary was promoted to Lieutenant on May 1, 1918, and assigned to Engine 14. On June 3, 1922, he was promoted to Captain and given command of Hook & Ladder 6. Then in 1925 when Rescue Company 2 was organized O'Leary was placed in command and continued until he was promoted to Battalion Chief in 1930. O'Leary then became Chief McElligott's aide in 1938. He was cited for bravery eight times during his career, before retiring in 1940.

John Mooney transferred to Hook & Ladder 137 in June of 1916. On February 6, 1917, he retired after only 13 years on the job. The official medical report stated that Mooney was totally and permanently physically disabled with chronic bronchitis, emphysema and asthma—not in the line of duty. So, after passing special physical and medical exams just a few years earlier to join Rescue 1, Mooney was no longer fit for fire duty. Despite being on the Roll of Merit seven times, with the Bennett, Wertheim and two Department Medals, John Mooney retired with an annual pension of only $725 a year.

James Shaw left Rescue 1 in 1916 when he was promoted to Engineer of Steamer. He was later promoted to Lieutenant and Captain. While in command of Engine Company 159 on

Staten Island, Shaw responded to a fire involving Midland Beach Colony bungalows on March 12, 1924. It was 2:40 in the morning and companies were battling a fire that had spread to two cottages under construction. After an hour's battle the fire was brought under control. Captain Shaw was wading in hip deep water pulling hose some thousand feet from his rig, when he slipped and fell into a creek.

He was helped by members of his company and continued working. He again fell into the icy water and this time also suffered some internal injuries. After returning to quarters, he said he wasn't feeling well, and an ambulance was called. Captain James Shaw was taken to Staten Island Hospital, where he died eight days later. Despite the fact he was injured at a fire, his death was not listed as line-of-duty.

Francis Blessing was detailed to Rescue 1 from the start and was promoted to Lieutenant in 1917. He returned to command the company and sadly died from pneumonia on March 15, 1920. The 35-year-old firefighter was cited for heroism seven times during his 13-year career.

William Dorritie joined Rescue 1 in July of 1915, and worked in the company until July of 1937 for a total of 22 years. Dorritie took part in a special event during his first several months of service when he was part of the FDNY contingent at a large military athletic tournament held in Madison Square Garden. He was one of 25 hand-picked members of the department's demonstration team. They scaled the façade of a "four-story house" (specially constructed for this drill) using scaling ladders, slid down ropes, lowered people by rope and jumped into life nets. These same skills were again utilized in the Midnight Alarm fundraisers at Madison Square Garden in 1937. He'd spend the next several years working in headquarters or teaching at the school of instruction. Dorritie was cited for bravery 14 times during his career. He died in 1941 while still on the job.

Rescue 1 was so unique when they first started in 1915, they not only captured the imagination of the nation's firefighters, but also proved to be good press for many newspapers and magazines and were used often in various advertisements.

The NEW YORK FIRE DEPARTMENT HAS PUT IN PULMOTORS and smoke helmets to protect the lives of their men.

This has been done on account of the wonderful work of these machines at the New York Subway accident. The above shows this Helmet squad training with the Draeger helmets.

EFFICIENCY IS EXPECTED OF YOUR FIREMEN THEN GIVE THEM SMOKE HELMETS AND PULMOTORS TO WORK WITH.

Let us tell you about scores of other FIRE DEPARTMENTS BESIDES NEW YORK.

Our literature is interesting and instructive

THE DRAEGER OXYGEN APPARATUS CO.

408 First Ave., Pittsburgh, Pa.

Special Pittsburgh Agents, for our New York Representatives

The WOLF SAFETY LAMP CO. OF AMERICA, Inc.

All in their Day's Work

CLATTERING hoofs—clanging bells—sibilant shrieks of sirens. Down the avenue roared the apparatus of a great metropolitan fire department to where thick, black billows of smoke belched from a cellar-way.

Another call for daring, accepted without question. Firemen, swelling their lungs with air, rushed into the engulfing smoke, into the cellar inferno. The crowd closed in to watch—heard a muffled explosion—then fell back coughing and gasping.

A chemical blaze! And ten men below!

Chiefs gathered and consulted—then one ran one way, one another.

A foreboding hush fell. Men looked into other men's eyes, and dumbly looked away. Finally someone whispered, "Why don't they come up?"

Another roar of sirens. Then a shout of relief. The Rescue Squad, with Draeger Smoke Helmets and Pulmotors, had come. And then came ambulances, each with its Pulmotor ready for use.

A quick donning of Draeger Helmets, a last look around—and the Rescue Squad rushed down into the smoke of the cellar.

There was hope now, and men smiled anxiously. Hours seemed to pass. Then, one by one, the rescuers came back, each carrying to the waiting Pulmotors a limp, lifeless hero overcome in his duty.

The blaze was forgotten now. The crowd had eyes only for the Pulmotors as they alternately expanded and contracted the lungs of the insensible firemen, filling them with oxygen-enriched air, clearing them of the deadly smoke and chemical fumes, nursing and fanning back to full vigor the dying spark of life.

One by one the men rose; some to be helped into an ambulance; some to go home to rest.

Again the fire became the centre of interest. But it was a different smoke that now whisked through the grating—thin streaks that foretold the end. Up the ladder came the Rescue Squad, doffing their helmets and eyeing the crowd with a self-possessed air that seemed to say, "Well, what's the excitement?"

(Continued on next page)

(Continued from previous page)

LEE Puncture-proof CORD TIRES

For SAFETY—SERVICE—SAVING

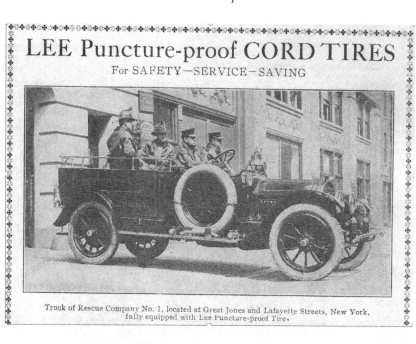

Truck of Rescue Company No. 1, located at Great Jones and Lafayette Streets, New York, fully equipped with Lee Puncture-proof Tires

Glossary

Alarm Signals—the primary communications system employed by the FDNY during the early 1900's was the telegraph. A system of wires, gongs, bells, telegraph keys, and street alarm boxes were all tied together at the Fire Alarm Headquarters. Alarm boxes sent an automatic identifying signal to the dispatcher. This was then manually sent out to the appropriate companies over the bell circuit. Upon their return to quarters after the alarm, companies would use a telegraph key to advise the dispatcher they were back in quarters available for fire duty. If the company was out-of-service for any reason the dispatcher was notified the same way. Additional alarms, special calls and other appropriate coded signals could be transmitted by officers using the telegraph key inside the street alarm box.

Backdraft—an explosion of the gaseous byproducts of incomplete combustion caused by the sudden introduction of oxygen.

Borough Call—signal transmitted after a 5th alarm to bring additional apparatus and manpower from one borough of the city to another.

Cockloft—the area above the ceiling on the top floor and the underside of the roof. Usually an open space that runs the entire length and width of the building.

Exposure—a place considered to be threatened by flames. This could be the building next door, to the rear, or even areas of the building already on fire. The FDNY numerically designates exposures in a clockwise fashion. #1 is to the front of the building on fire (usually the street). #2 is the building to the left. #3 is the building to the rear. #4 is the building to the right. The term "auto-exposure" is when fire travels within the same building. For example: flames from a lower floor window lapping up and igniting the floor above. Or fire burning through from floor to floor.

Department Orders—directives sent from headquarters to all companies. They cover everything from transfers, alarm assignments, retirements, promotions, appointments, announcements of death, the decisions of the commissioner as it relates to charges against members, the Roll of Merit and medal recipients, and any other department business.

Engine—apparatus for pumping water through hoses; early models were pulled by hand and then pumped by hand by teams of men, next came steam powered engines pulled by horses, until modern diesel and gasoline powered engines replaced the horse. Engine is also the generic name for the company of men assigned to such a unit. High Pressure Engine Companies were not equipped with regular engines, but rather with hose wagons. They operated with excellent success in areas of the city served by the high pressure hydrant system. They could stretch and operate several hoses from a single high pressure hydrant.

Engineer of Steamer—a rank above fireman but below a company officer. This firefighter operated the steam engine while pumping at fires.

Hose line—a series of connected sections of hose used to deliver water at fire operations. Also called "handlines." These hoses were "stretched" to the point of operations. ("Stretched" originally meant to pull tight to avoid kinks that restrict water flow.) "Take Up" is an order originally given to take the hose up out of the street; it now refers to any company's finishing their work, securing their equipment and leaving the scene.

Ladder Company—a company of men assigned to hook & ladder. Their basic assignment is to ladder the building, force entry and search for trapped occupants. Also called a "Truck Company."

Loft—a building with high ceilings originally used as a commercial structure, manufacturing and storage.

Medal Day—the day set aside for the annual presentation of FDNY medals for valor. In early years, with only one medal to award, it was often held held every two years. The ceremony was held at various locations in past years; City Hall is now the preferred location weather permitting.

Nozzle—the business end of a hose line. On handlines it allows the control of water flow by opening and closing a built-in valve. Nozzles on large caliber streams shape the flow of water for better reach.

Rescue Company—a company of specially trained firefighters that are assigned a special apparatus that carries tools for major emergencies, building collapses, accident extrications, underwater search and rescue, etc.

Scaling ladder—a ladder built with a single beam in the middle. The ladder's steps were fastened to the beam. Very easily handled by one man, they were an effective but dangerous method of continuing beyond the reach of conventional ladders.

Tapped in—Before telephones and computers, fire companies used a telegraph key and tapped signals to the dispatcher. This sparked a variety of related terms: When a fireman was injured and was no longer able to work he was said to have "tapped out," referring to the dispatcher's code for "Out-Of-Service."

Took up, Take up—originally referred to taking hose up from the street, but quickly broadened to all fire companies or units. The chief was telling the company they should gather and stow their equipment and return to the firehouse.

Water Tower—apparatus used to deliver large caliber streams of water to upper stories. A piped waterway delivered water up a raised mast. They ranged in size from the original 1879 50-foot version with one nozzle, to the 60-foot versions with two nozzles. The last water tower was purchased in 1930. They were placed out of service in 1957.

Acknowledgments

The stories contained in this book are taken from documented sources including New York City Fire Department Medal Day Books, Minutes of the Board of Merit meetings, Department Orders, and other FDNY publications, as well as the many newspapers and magazines in print at the time. The Library of Congress online newspaper archives have opened the nation's reported history to anyone willing to dig through the years of information. Several books were also very useful for this and other projects: *Wheels of the Bravest* by John A. Calderone and Jack Lerch published by *Fire Apparatus Journal* in 1984, and *The Last Alarm* by Michael Boucher, Gary Urbanowicz, and Fred Melahn, 2006.

Special thanks to Deputy Assistant Chief John W. Norman III, my former captain and Captain John Cerillo, the current captain of Rescue 1, for their friendship and critical eyes and great suggestions for this book.

I'd like to thank those who have helped me with my research:

First and foremost is the staff at the FDNY Mand Library. The late Honorary Chief of Department Jack Lerch. Jack was always a friend and a trusted resource. His knowledge and enthusiasm will be greatly missed.

Also from the library crew, Dan Maye, Fred Melahn and John Paulson have been very generous with their time, help and enthusiasm.

Working on various projects over the years, has helped

me build an impressive personal fire library of reports, stories, scrapbooks, books and photos. Those that have contributed information include, Herb Eysser FDNY Dispatcher 124 (retired), Battalion Chief Jack Calderone (a true wealth of historical information and a guy who's been there, done that!), Bill Noonan, Gary Urbanowicz, Paul Wormsley, Paul Geidel, Ray Pfeifer, Dennis Whittan, Frank Sutphin, Tom Donnelly, David Handschuh, Bill Bennett, Fred Kopf, Danny Alfonso, Ed Pospisil, Ed Sere, Vincent Dunn and Peter Micheels.

The photos in this book are from various collections including Herb Eysser, Jack Calderone, Gary Urbanowicz, Rescue Company 1, the FDNY Library, the FDNY photo unit, and my personal collection.

About the Author

Paul Hashagen began fighting fires in 1976. In 2003, he retired from the FDNY after 25 years of service, with 20 of those years in Rescue Company 1. He is a former Chief of the Freeport Fire Department and is still a member of Excelsior Hook & Ladder Company No. 1. Paul was a contributing editor for *Firehouse Magazine* for more than 20 years, writing numerous feature articles and the monthly historical column *Rekindles*. Paul was also a contributing author at *FireRescue* magazine. He has written several books and numerous stories on the history of the fire service, including *The Bravest 1865-2002,* the official history of the FDNY.

Paul has appeared several times as a fire historian on the History Channel and the A&E Network. He was a lead instructor at the FDNY Special Operations Command Technical Rescue School for ten years and taught at the FDNY Probationary Firefighters School. Paul has lectured across the country on firefighter rescue, and historical topics.

Paul was inducted into the *Firehouse Magazine* Hall of Fame, Class of 2017.

Visit his website at www.paulhashagen.com or on Facebook at Paul Hashagen-author.

Paul and his wife Joanne, live in Massapequa, New York.

Made in the USA
Las Vegas, NV
22 November 2024